THE MEDIA GAME

AMERICAN POLITICS IN THE TELEVISION AGE

STEPHEN ANSOLABEHERE
University of California at Los Angeles

ROY BEHR
Office of the Lieutenant Governor of California

SHANTO IYENGAR
University of California at Los Angeles

MACMILLAN PUBLISHING COMPANY
New York

MAXWELL MACMILLAN CANADA
Toronto

Editor: *Bruce Nichols*
Managing Editor: *John Sollami*
Production Manager: *Roger Vergnes*
Cover Designer: *Sheree Goodman*
Illustrations: Publication Services, Inc.

This book was set in 10/12 Janson by Publication Services, Inc. and was printed and bound by R. R. Donnelley & Sons. The cover was printed by Phillips Offset.

Macmillan Publishing Company
866 Third Avenue, New York, New York 10022

Macmillan Publishing Company is part of
the Maxwell Communication Group of Companies.

Maxwell Macmillan Canada, Inc.
1200 Eglinton Avenue East
Suite 200
Don Mills, Ontario M3C 3N1

LIBRARY OF CONGRESS CATALOGING-IN-PUBLICATION DATA

Ansolabehere, Stephen
  The media game : American politics in the television age / Stephen Ansolabehere, Roy Behr, and Shanto Iyengar.
    p.   cm. — (New topics in politics)
  Includes index.
  ISBN 0-02-359965-0 (pbk.)
  1. Television broadcasting of news — Political aspects — United States.   2. Television and politics — United States.   3. Public opinion — United States.   I. Behr, Roy L., 1958– .   II. Iyengar, Shanto.   III. Title.   IV. Series.
  PN4888.T4A57   1993
  302.23'45 — dc20   92-21876
                              CIP

Printing: 3 4 5 6 7   Year: 6 7 8 9

ACKNOWLEDGMENTS

This book was made possible through the encouragement and help of several institutions and individuals. The John and Mary R. Markle Foundation and the University of California provided the essential financial support. We were fortunate to have had the assistance of two unusually gifted UCLA students: Terri Hall devoted the summer of 1991 to tracking down a host of relevant statistics and documents, and Sharmaine Vidanage (now a graduate student in political science at UCLA) provided continuous, all-around research support and advice. Useful readers' suggestions were provided by Timothy Cook, Williams College; Herbert Jacob, Northwestern University; Kathleen Knight, University of Houston; Martin Wattenberg, University of California, Irvine; and Christine Williams, Bentley College. Finally, we thank Bruce Nichols—our editor at Macmillan—for his guidance and patience.

Contents

v

CHAPTER 7

THE MULTIPLE EFFECTS OF TELEVISION ON PUBLIC OPINION 139

CHAPTER 8

THE CONSEQUENCES OF POLITICAL CAMPAIGNS 157

CHAPTER 9

PUBLIC OPINION AND THE POWER TO GOVERN 189

C H A P T E R   1

AMERICAN POLITICS IN THE AGE OF TELEVISION

Once upon a time politicians communicated directly with their constituents. They gave speeches—directly to those they governed. They delivered their messages personally, through newspapers controlled by their political parties, or leaflets passed out by their supporters. They met and spoke directly with the citizens they represented. Because they controlled the primary means of communication, politicians and their parties were assured that the people would hear exactly what they wished them to hear.

That day no longer exists. Politicians still give speeches, but few Americans listen to them. Members of Congress still send out vast amounts of information and newsletters (at the taxpayers' expense), but few constituents bother to read them. Elected officials still tour their districts, but few citizens meet them in person. And, for a variety of reasons, political parties have much less control over what elected officials say and what the mass media report than ever before.

Today, political leaders communicate with the public primarily through news media that *they do not control*. The news media now stand between politicans and their constituents. Politicians speak to the media; the media then speak to the voters. The media can filter, alter, distort or ignore altogether what politicans have to say.

The emergence of this two-step flow of communication has radically altered the behavior of politicians, and it has also dramatically affected the relation of individual citizens to the political process. The purpose of this book is to explore these changes and their implications.

How do politicians use the media to get their messages across to voters? Do elected officials give certain issues undue attention because the news media have a particular interest in them? Are other issues (which may be more important) ignored simply because they are less likely to be conveyed by the media? How do political leaders, confronted with shrinking resources and ever-growing demands for government services and benefits, use the media to mobilize public support for their policies?

What about the voters? How do poorly informed citizens, confronted with complex issues and events that have little direct impact on their everyday existence, develop an understanding of public affairs? How do citizens get to "know" their elected officials? Do citizens' opinions and preferences form the basis for public policy?

These questions are fundamental to democratic theory and practice. This book suggests that they can be answered in part by an understanding of the powerful effects of the news media in general and television news in particular on the behavior of both politicians and voters.

Television as the Window on the World

The great majority of citizens encounter the outside world and the course of public affairs through their television sets. Although newspapers, radio, and interpersonal conversations still play important roles in the dissemination of information, television news now plays the dominant role in bringing public events to the attention of the masses.

The invention of television has fundamentally altered the lives of individuals. Few innovations have had so great an impact on people's allocation of their time. Few, if any, new technologies have changed so dramatically the ways in which—and extent to which—people experience events and their culture. Today, Americans spend more time interacting with their television sets than with other people. According to recent surveys, the typical American household watches television for more than six hours every day. The number of dwellings with television sets exceeds the number with flush toilets.

In short, television has emerged as a crucial intermediary between the individual and society. Television news provides much of the intelligence on which voters' political judgments and choices rest. "Making the news" can therefore prove to be either a critical asset or a major liability for public officials and politicians. Those who succeed in shaping the content of television news also succeed in influencing how Americans think about politics.

The increasing importance of television has many significant implications for the political process. As we have seen, politicians can no longer communicate directly with citizens, and the media now act as a filter. But surprisingly, as independent news organizations have become the principal channels of political communication, the electoral accountability of political officials has actually *decreased*.

How is that possible?

Politics is Darwinism in action. Those who best adapt to new surroundings survive; those who cannot, become extinct. Before the advent of the modern media age, political debate and communication were the province of political parties, and politicians were required to conform to the views expressed by party leaders. Today, however, the influence of party leaders has been reduced, and the mass media cover politicians as individuals, not as party members. Candidates must thus fend for themselves, and the survivors are those who can most effectively carve out their own identities in the media jungle.

Television has forced successful politicians (incumbents and non-incumbents alike) to adopt new styles of political rhetoric and leadership. Media management, image building, credit taking, blame avoidance, and public relations, along with related interpersonal skills, have become more important to electoral success than policy expertise, problem-solving skills, or the ability to forge coalitions and enact legislation. Appearance and imagery have become paramount considerations. Officeholders can be thrown out simply because they project (or fail to project) particular personality traits.

The breakdown in party-based coalitions and the rise in importance of individual reputations have made politicians less motivated to address "difficult" problems. Because voters are more likely to relate to congressional representatives and senators as individuals (rather than as Democrats or Republicans), elected officials have to keep their distance from unpopular decisions or policies (such as increased taxes). By promoting electoral individualism and the cultivation of personal reputations, television has eliminated the incentives for politicians to engage in coalition formation and brokering—the necessary ingredients of successful problem solving in a pluralistic society.

On the face of it, the increased distance between candidates and their parties should not, by itself, make politicians less accountable. Because virtually all Americans are in a position to catch at least a glimpse of their elected officials in action, the public should be able to vote on the basis of their performance. If the country is experiencing prosperity, voters should reward incumbents at the polls; if a congressional representative voted to weaken regulation of savings and loan institutions, constituents could vote him or her out; and so on. Increased access to information on public affairs should make it easier for people to vote on the basis of incumbents' past performance.

The increased importance of television, however, has had precisely the opposite effect on public opinion. Because television news coverage of major issues tends to be fragmented and devoid of much thematic or substantive content, it tends to limit the extent to which voters hold politicians or governmental institutions responsible for national problems. Confronted with a parade of news stories describing particular instances or illustrations of national issues—a homeless person, an unemployed worker, a congressional representative who bounces checks, a terrorist bombing, a victim of violent crime, and so on—Americans reason about these issues in terms of individual and private motives rather than historical, social, or political forces.

A further obstacle to strict electoral accountability is the fact that political leaders have become increasingly adept at manipulating the media for their own political gain. The news invariably emanates from official sources, and incumbent politicians, of course, have every reason to avoid taking responsibility for controversial issues. An incumbent president is not likely, for instance, to issue a press release suggesting that his administration is more interested in foreign policy than domestic economic problems. Because they are granted privileged status as sources of information, incumbent politicians may enjoy just as much influence over what citizens hear today as they did during the era of direct communication.

Overall, therefore, the new system of political communication has weakened citizens' control over their representatives. Faced with such striking changes, we have set out to examine the extent and details of the effects of the modern media on politics. How do the media operate? What factors determine the selection of news stories? How do candidates and elected officials exploit the media to futher their own political objectives? How have the media affected voters, elections, and the caliber of political leadership?

Overview

This book is organized into four broad sections. The first section (Chapters 2 and 3) describes the institutional framework of contemporary media politics. Chapter 2 traces the evolution and structure of broadcasting from the early days of radio to the present, summarizing the major technological developments leading to the formation of the television networks, identifying the various economic factors that constrain the content and form of television programming, and discussing the regulatory environment of broadcasting.

Chapter 3 describes the everyday flow of news and the forces that affect its content. Americans live in an incredibly media-rich society, in which television is the dominant medium. People have become heavily dependent upon television for news about the world, nation, state, and local community. Within the television industry, however, there is considerable competition for viewers. The three major networks no longer enjoy predominance, and new sources such as CNN have made their presence felt. Chapter 3 also surveys the forces that influence the production of news. In particular, this chapter shows how the professional culture of journalists and the routines and incentives of news organizations affect the content of reporting. In the case of television news, for example, the need for "good pictures" significantly inhibits the medium's ability to provide in-depth, analytic reporting of public affairs issues.

The second section (Chapters 4 and 5) turns to a discussion of how politicians attempt to exploit the media. Chapter 4 outlines the various changes in campaign rules and procedures adopted since the 1960s and documents how these changes have simultaneously made the media a vital accessory to campaigns and relegated party leaders to the role of mere observers. It addresses the relative importance of paid media (political advertising) and "free" media (news coverage) in campaigns and describes the strategies that candidates use to exploit both to their maximum advantage. The prevailing themes in campaign news are described in terms of the structural tension between reporters' efforts to maintain objectivity and candidates' efforts to determine the content of the news.

In Chapter 5 we move from the subject of election campaigns to the general relationship between television news and government. How has television affected the way presidents and other leaders conduct themselves in office? We describe the strategy of "going public" (using public opinion to influence rival elites) and the premium this strategy has placed on rhetorical leadership. This new style of government, which emphasizes direct exposure of government officials to the approval or disapproval of the public, has also led to the proliferation of public relations specialists of all kinds. In addition, the ever-present concern for public image has made it increasingly difficult for elected leaders to take a clear stand on troublesome problems.

In the third section of the book (Chapters 6 through 9) we take up the impact of television on ordinary citizens. First we describe the history of political communication research—from the 1950s, when the media were thought to have minimal consequences, to today's media-dominated campaigns. We then detail the multiple effects of media presentations on public opinion, including learning effects (such as information gain and opinionation), salience effects (including agenda setting and priming), and persuasion. In Chapter 7, we summarize the multitude of studies that have examined these effects in the context of television news coverage. In Chapter 8 we sharpen the focus to show how these effects manifest themselves during election campaigns. Campaign advertisements and televised debates, for example, both exert agenda-setting effects: The issues emphasized in the ads and discussed in the debates become more salient to voters. Overall, the evidence presented in Chapters 7 and 8 suggests that television is a crucial force in American politics and that the politician or candidate who can obtain access to television enjoys huge political advantages.

The final chapter in the "effects" section (Chapter 9) illustrates the various effects of public opinion on the ability of leaders to govern. In it, we show how fluctuations in the popularity of national and state chief executives (the president and governor, respectively) affect their power to lead. Politicians' popularity provides a fascinating focal point for many of the questions raised by this book. According to one view, popularity is determined primarily by the course of events (and the resulting pattern of news coverage), and political leaders are, for all practical purposes, captives of history. Thus, a governor who inherits a huge budget deficit and is forced to respond by raising taxes may risk alienating key supporters and thus weaken his ability to negotiate with state legislators. We describe how this particular scenario weakened state administrations in California, Connecticut, and New Jersey.

An alternative view of popularity, however, is that elected leaders have considerable ability to manage the news. Thus, a president who has polished rhetorical skills and is adept at distancing himself from and evading responsibility for negative outcomes may be able to create an illusion of effective leadership regardless of the course of events. For example, Ronald Reagan maintained his "teflon" reputation even in the face of serious policy failures such as the killing of more than 200 American marines by terrorist bombs in Beirut.

In the book's final section we consider the important question of whether today's system of media politics in fact strengthens the practice of democracy by informing the public and invigorating the "marketplace of ideas." We identify several standards for evaluating the performance of the media in regard to its two major obligations—educating the public and monitoring the behavior of public officials. Chapter 10 takes up the media's role as educator and examines the quality of news presentations in terms of their ability to mirror or distort reality, their ideological neutrality, and their substantive content. Chapter 11 considers the monitoring role of the media. It describes how reporters and editors have increasingly abandoned the adversarial posture toward politicians in favor of a deferential model of journalism. In other words, because reporters rely heavily on official sources, they do not generally investigate or attempt to substantiate the statements of public officials.

Finally, in our closing chapter, we show that the relationships among the players in the media game are continually evolving. After all, the game is really the game of politics and at least three sets of players—politicians, voters, and the media—are involved. Both the politicians and the media use increasingly sophisticated techniques to manipulate or monitor one another, while voters pay only casual attention to the proceedings except on election day. In the final analysis, therefore, improving the results of the media game will require all three participants to place the pressing problems facing this society ahead of their own selfish interests.

THE NEWS MEDIA

Until 1950, news came to most Americans through the newspaper or by word of mouth. In the 1990s, though a smaller number of newspapers still flourish, the vast majority of Americans get their news from television.

The development of commercial broadcasting (described in Chapter 2) has fundamentally altered the flow of information in American society. Universal access to television makes it possible for the entire nation to observe events as they occur. Never before have politicians been able to command such a vast audience. As Supreme Court Justice William Brennan observed in 1973, television is "potentially the most effective marketplace of ideas ever devised."[1]

Of course, Americans do not rely exclusively on television. As residents of the most information-rich country on earth, people have daily opportunities to read, listen to the radio, and converse with friends, associates, and talk-show hosts. As consumers of information, Americans have a huge array of options (which we describe in Chapter 3). Increasingly, however, television is the source of choice.

In this section we begin by describing the complex network of relationships between local stations, television networks, government

---

[1] *Columbia Broadcasting System v. Democratic National Committee*, 412 U.S. (1972) 94, p. 195.

regulatory agencies, and advertisers that makes up the broadcasting industry. Next, we outline the major sources of public affairs information, distinguishing between print and broadcast media, and national and local outlets. Finally, we discuss the essential features of news and identify the factors that determine its production.

C H A P T E R   2

THE RISE OF BROADCASTING

American politics has not been the same since radio station KDKA, Pittsburgh, signed off on November 2, 1920. By today's standards that election night program wasn't much of a broadcast. The weak, 100-watt transmission consisted of a saxophone solo and the results of the presidential race between Warren Harding and James Cox. Nor was it the only broadcast that evening, since station WWJ in Detroit also provided election night coverage.

KDKA's broadcast that night differed from other radio transmissions in that it had a sponsor, Westinghouse Electric. Westinghouse purchased time with the hope of creating demand for its new product—Westinghouse radio sets. The strategy worked; Westinghouse created a mass market for radio and paved the way for television.[1]

KDKA's election night coverage in 1920 signaled the birth of commercial radio. In 1920, KDKA was the only radio station licensed to provide regular broadcasting services.[2] Broadcasting has since grown into a multibillion-dollar industry that reaches almost every household in the United States. Today, there are more than 9,000 radio and 1,400 television stations, and of the 92 million households in the United States 98.6 percent have at least one television set.[3]

[1]E. Barnouw, *A Tower in Babel: A History of Broadcasting in the United States—to 1933* (New York: Oxford University Press, 1966).

[2]Barnouw, 1966, p. 4.

[3]Department of Commerce, *Historical Statistics of the United States, Colonial Times to 1970*, series R93-105, (Washington, D.C.: U.S. Government Printing Office, 1975), p. 796; Department of Commerce, *Statistical Abstract of the United States, 1990*, 110th ed., table no. 914 (Washington, D.C.: U.S. Government Printing Office, 1975), p. 550.

It is the public's near-universal access to television that makes the broadcasting industry work. Although much has changed in the technology of broadcasting, the basic idea behind Westinghouse's sponsorship of news coverage by KDKA remains the driving force in the industry. Television's enormous viewership represents millions of consumers who can be wooed through advertising. The broadcasters — the local stations, networks, and cable companies — are in a sense intermediaries. They develop, distribute, and broadcast programming designed to attract as large an audience as possible, and then sell access to that audience to advertisers.

In this chapter we describe the main components of the modern broadcasting industry. First, we look at the audience. Who watches television, and what do they watch? Next we turn to the broadcasters — the local stations, networks, and cable companies that, under general guidelines laid down by the federal government, develop, produce, market, and distribute the "product," that is, the programs. Finally, we examine advertising, the financial wellspring of the industry.

Audiences

Television is truly a mass medium. Unlike newspapers, television has no literacy barrier. Access simply requires ownership of a television set, which nearly 99 out of 100 American households have achieved.

At times virtually the entire national audience can be captivated by specific events. On November 24, 1963, 96 percent of the American public tuned in to television following the assassination of President Kennedy. On July 20, 1969, 720 million people, one-fifth of the world's population, watched a live broadcast of American astronaut Neil Armstrong setting foot on the moon. In 1981, 740 million people around the world watched the wedding of the Prince of Wales. Over the weekend of October 10–12, 1991, 90 percent of the households in the United States tuned in to some part of the Senate hearings on the charges of sexual harassment leveled against then–Supreme Court nominee Clarence Thomas.

Under normal circumstances, however, there is no single vast viewing audience, but many audiences. Typically, stations compete fiercely to attract large audiences and also particular categories of viewers that the program's sponsors would like to reach—yuppies, baby boomers, teenagers, children, ethnic groups, and so on. The aim of most television programming is to appeal to the interests of particular groups within the general population. In this sense, television operates in both broad and narrow markets. Competition within the television marketplace is governed by what David Poltrack, senior vice president for research at CBS, has aptly called the "rating game"—the never-ending quest for larger audiences.[4] Two ratings services—A. C. Nielsen and Arbitron—provide independent estimates of the number of households tuned in to the various channels at any given time. Both companies base their estimates on data generated by random samples of American households. Nielsen monitors viewership in 1,700 households (which volunteer their participation) by installing a small device that records when the television is turned on and what channel it is tuned to. Arbitron uses a more personal approach: It sends logbooks to 2,400 households, whose members then record what they watch. Both companies record the age, income, gender, and consumer behavior of their respondents. These data, as we shall see later, play a vital role in determining the revenues of TV stations and networks.

Although Nielsen's and Arbitron's techniques for estimating viewership differ, their profiles of the TV audience reveal that the medium has indeed become the great American pastime. The typical American works seven hours per day, five days a week. This leaves roughly six to seven hours for leisure on weekdays. Most of this time is spent watching TV. According to both Nielsen and Arbitron, the average American watches TV for four hours every day, and a typical household has the TV on for more than seven hours on an average day.[5]

A closer look at the ratings confirms that the TV audience is differentiated according to gender, age, income, and other social characteristics and that each group has identifiable viewing patterns. With the exception of sports programs, more women watch television than men. The average audience (per minute) during prime-

[4]David Poltrack, *Television Marketing: Network, Local, and Cable* (New York: McGraw-Hill, 1983), ch. 2.

[5]A. C. Nielsen Co., *The Nielsen Report on Television* (Northbrook, Ill.: A. C. Nielsen Co., 1990).

time network broadcasts consists of 9.8 million women and 7.4 million men.

The extent of TV viewership varies with age. Children under 5 watch almost 26 hours of TV a week; those between 6 and 11 watch 23 hours a week; and teenagers watch 22 hours a week. Viewership jumps to 26.5 hours a week among the 18–34 age group, increases again to 30 hours a week for the 35–54 age group, and reaches an impressive 39 hours per week among people over 55 years of age.

While TV viewership increases steadily with age among adults, it is also affected by household income. Households with an annual income below $30,000 watch almost 53 hours of TV per week; households with more than $60,000 of annual income tune in for just under 48 hours per week.

Demographic groups differ not only in their relative addiction to TV but also in the types of programs they watch. The Nielsen and Arbitron data map the composition of each program's audience with considerable precision, a fact that makes these data especially valuable to advertisers. Women are especially attracted to situation comedies and general dramas. Males are drawn to sports and feature films. In 1990 the top three shows among adult women were the "Bill Cosby Show," "Golden Girls," and "A Different World." The highest rated shows for adult men, by contrast, were CBS's "60 Minutes," ABC's "NFL Monday Night Football," and CBS's Sunday coverage of the NFL. Children and teenagers tuned in to the "Bill Cosby Show," "A Different World," and the "Hogan Family" most often.

Although there are robust differences across demographic groups, the daily viewing patterns of particular groups have traditionally been quite stable. Broadcasters divide the television day into three segments—morning, daytime, and prime time. The morning segment—between 6:30 and 10:00 A.M.—has the lightest viewing. Daytime is the period between 10:00 A.M. and 4:00 P.M.), and prime time, of course, is the period of highest viewership—programming between the hours of 8:00 and 11:00 P.M. on both the coasts, and between 7:00 and 10:00 P.M. in the central time zone.

Many types of programs are broadcast during several time periods. For example, children's shows are broadcast chiefly on Saturday mornings, but have begun to penetrate prime time. Sports, specials, and news programs are sprinkled throughout the broadcast day, but regular newscasts are presented between 5:00 P.M. and 7:00 P.M. and at 10:00 or 11:00 P.M.

Broadcasters

Just as audiences are differentiated along various demographic factors, the broadcasting industry consists of very diverse entities including manufacturers of television sets and broadcasting equipment, producers of programs, networks, local stations (which are often affiliates of networks), advertisers, and others. Hundreds of corporations are involved in the creation, production, and distribution of television programs and advertisements. And 1,500 local stations transmit these messages over the airwaves.

Local Stations

The local station is the building block of the industry. Decisions about what programs are aired and, ultimately, responsibility for what is transmitted over the airwaves rests with the management of local stations. Understanding local stations, however, requires more than just looking at their operations. Broadcasting traditionally has not reflected the classic marketplace envisioned in economic texts in which the "invisible hand" of competition rules. The airwaves are themselves a public good subject to significant governmental regulation limiting the use of each broadcast frequency to a single broadcaster. The regulation of frequencies dates back to the early days of radio when it was recognized that unrestricted use would make the airwaves too congested. As we shall see, legal restrictions on who may broadcast can lead to significant distortions in the marketplace of ideas.

Government Regulation: Origins of the FCC
The justification for government regulation of the airwaves is that access cannot be made readily available to all comers. The operation of a newspaper printing press does not exclude or interfere with the activity of some other press. The reception of radio and television broadcasts, by contrast, requires signals that are free from interference. To eliminate interference among the signals, the frequencies have to be sufficiently separated. Until the early 1960s,

for example, television sets had only 13 channels designated for the reception of VHF (very high frequency) signals. Although technological improvements have made it possible for many more stations to broadcast, the airwaves are finite— "one person's transmission is another's interference."[6]

During the early days of radio, broadcasting was essentially unregulated. The secretary of commerce issued licenses to stations but had no control over the activities of broadcasters. This presented little difficulty because demand for airtime was light. Only a handful of companies produced radio receivers, catering to a small number of amateur operators. Most cities had only one transmitter station. In cities where demand for airtime was high, the broadcasters worked out voluntary time-sharing arrangements.

Sudden growth in the broadcast industry during the mid-1920s led to intense competition for listeners. The resulting congestion of the airwaves in the late 1920s led to a system of regulation that has shaped the growth of the industry ever since. Stations increased the power of their transmitters, allowing them to reach audiences beyond their immediate locales. Broadcasts from Pittsburgh reached Detroit; Chicago stations interfered with those in Denver. Some broadcasters abandoned their designated frequencies in search of open airwaves. Larger companies, who were in the broadcasting business to stimulate demand for receivers, expressed concern about the chaos on the airwaves.[7] They feared that unregulated broadcasting would decrease the public's demand for radio sets.

Eventually, Congress intervened. A new agency, the Federal Communications Commission (FCC), was created to replace the Federal Radio Commission and regulate all interstate broadcast and wire communication. As an independent regulatory commission, the members of the FCC are appointed by the president (with the consent of the Senate). The agency was to grant licenses free of charge on either a one-year provisional basis or for a three-year term.[8] At the end of the term the station could apply for renewal.

[6]Erwin Krasnow, Lawrence Longley, and Herbert Terry, *The Politics of Broadcast Regulation* (New York: St. Martin's Press, 1982), p. 22.

[7]Gleason Archer, *The History of Radio to 1926* (New York: The American Historical Society, 1938), p. 249.

[8]This has since been extended to a five-year term for television licenses and a seven-year term for radio. 49 C.F.R. Section 1020 (1991).

The FCC could deny or modify a license if it determined that the station had failed to live up to the commission's standards. Congress originally created the FCC to serve a traffic cop role. Radio broadcasting had been characterized for the preceding decade as a hodgepodge of local stations doing more or less as they pleased and interfering with each others' transmissions. The FCC was to ensure that transmissions were properly routed by specifying the channel, the power, and the hours of operation for each station. In other words, the FCC was to regulate the airwaves by guaranteeing particular stations protected access to designated local media markets.

Refinements in television technology in the 1940s forced the FCC to take a more active role in the oversight of the industry. Between 1939, when the National Broadcast Company successfully transmitted experimental television signals from its New York City station, and 1948, the number of licensed television stations grew to 108. The FCC wished to avoid much of the clutter that it was still trying to sweep out of radio. The agency voted in 1948 to freeze the licensing of new stations until it had worked out a method by which television stations could be fairly assigned. After 73 days of hearings and three years of deliberations, the commission established the Table of Assignments.

The Table of Assignments defined the way in which television stations were to be allocated to cities. Broadly speaking, the number of stations assigned to a city depended on the size of the city. In 1952 the criteria were defined as follows: Cities of 1 million or more in population were eligible for between six and ten stations; cities with populations of between 250,000 and 1 million residents qualified for four to six stations; communities of 50,000 to 250,000 would be assigned two to four stations; and areas with fewer than 50,000 residents would be eligible for one or two stations. Most major communities were initially given a limited number of stations. With the exception of New York City and Los Angeles, each of which began with seven stations, no city was assigned more than four VHF (Channels 2 through 13) licenses. Each community with a radio station generally received a television station. As a result of these rules, many communities have at least one television station, but very few cities are served by more than three broadcasters.

The First Amendment and Broadcasting
The solution to the problem of congested airwaves— governmental
restrictions on access to the airwaves—laid the foundation for another problem. The usually small number of broadcasters in each
locale did not ensure a competitive setting in which public affairs and
politics could be discussed from a variety of perspectives. Through
its licensing authority, the FCC had essentially granted local broadcasters a monopoly over the airwaves. Those who owned these
licenses could essentially control what was broadcast into the marketplace of ideas.

Congress had anticipated this difficulty. The Communications
Act of 1934 treated broadcasters as trustees for the benefit of the
public. Licensees were granted free and exclusive use of a scarce
public resource (the airwaves) as long as they acted as agents for the
"public interest, convenience, and necessity." The Communications
Act itself said little about what the public interest entailed and what
the government could do to keep broadcasters from violating the
public trust. Over the years, however, through the administrative
actions of the FCC, legislation enacted by Congress, and the decisions of the federal judiciary, broadcasters have been subject to a
variety of government rules and regulations.

The most important restrictions are the equal time rule (part of
the 1934 Communications Act) and the fairness doctrine (introduced
by the FCC in 1949 and suspended in 1987). The equal time rule
was designed to promote equal access to the airwaves. Under the
rule a broadcaster that sold time to a legally qualified candidate for
any public office was required to provide the same opportunity to
any other similarly qualified candidates. The concept of equal time
was expanded in the 1960s to include nationally broadcast speeches
by the president, such as the State of the Union address. Under the
equal time rule the opposing political party is entitled to the same
amount of time, free of charge. Over the past 50 years, the FCC has
created only limited exceptions to the equal time rule. Equal time
need not be provided to balance coverage in regularly scheduled
newscasts, news interviews, documentaries, and news coverage of
"live" events.[9]

---

[9]Fred Friendly, *The Good Guys, the Bad Guys, and the First Amendment: Free Speech vs.
Fairness in Broadcasting* (New York: Random House, 1977), p. 214.

In addition to providing ground rules that ensure political candidates equal access, the FCC has also sought to encourage broadcasters to provide free and open discussion of public issues. In 1949 the FCC implemented the fairness doctrine, which requires that stations (1) provide a reasonable amount of air time to coverage of controversial issues of public importance, and (2) accord a reasonable opportunity for the voicing of contrasting viewpoints concerning these issues.[10] The fairness doctrine was enforced through the license renewal process in which the stations were required to document their compliance.

The FCC gradually extended the rules of the fairness doctrine to apply to statements about individuals rather than just abstract issues. Thus, when a broadcast included a personal attack on a public figure, the station that aired the attack was required to notify the person who was attacked and offer him or her a reasonable opportunity to respond.[11]

The consequence of the equal time rule, fairness doctrine, and related rulings by the FCC was the creation of a double standard with respect to the rights enjoyed by the media under the First Amendment. While the print media enjoyed complete First Amendment freedoms from government interference, broadcasters were subject to significant regulation. In the words of one former chairman of the FCC, "Limitations on broadcast content that would be unconstitutional if applied to the print press have been routinely upheld when applied to broadcasting. Although broadcasters have First Amendment rights, they are subordinate to the rights of the viewing public."[12]

A pair of United States Supreme Court cases illustrate this double standard. The first case, *Red Lion Broadcasting v. FCC*, involved a radio broadcast. Timothy Cook, a liberal political analyst and author, was the subject of a commentary by the Reverend Billy James Hargis. Cook heard the broadcast on station WGCB, owned by Red Lion Broadcasting Company. He requested free time to reply,

---

[10] FCC, *Report on Editorializing by Broadcast Licensees*, 13 F.C.C. 1246 (Washington, D.C.: U.S. Government Printing Office, 1949).

[11] *Red Lion Broadcasting v. FCC*, 395 U.S. 367, 386 (1969).

[12] Charles Ferris and Terrence Leahy, "Red Lions, Tigers and Bears: Broadcast Content Regulation and the First Amendment," *Catholic University Law Review* 38 (1990), p. 309.

but Red Lion refused. Cook complained to the FCC. Responding to Cook's complaint, the FCC declared that Hargis's broadcast constituted a personal attack and that by denying Cook an opportunity to respond, WGCB had violated the fairness requirements. The commission suspended WGCB's license. Red Lion challenged the FCC's decision and the constitutionality of the fairness doctrine as a violation of the broadcaster's freedom of speech. After a two-year court battle, the Supreme Court upheld the FCC's action, stating that "because of the scarcity of frequencies, the Government is permitted to put restraints on licensees in favor of others whose views should be expressed on this unique medium."[13]

Six years later, the Court decided a case involving similar facts, except that the attack was made in a newspaper editorial. The *Miami Herald* published two editorials criticizing Mr. Pat Tornillo, a candidate for the Florida House of Representatives. (Tornillo had been the executive director of the Florida Classroom Association, which had participated in an illegal teacher strike in 1968.) Under a Florida statute newspapers that "assailed" a candidate's character or official record were required to provide the right of reply. The paper denied Tornillo's request to respond. The case eventually reached the U.S. Supreme Court. In stark contrast to the outcome in *Red Lion*, the Court struck down the governmental regulation (in this case, the Florida statute) as unconstitutional. In a unanimous opinion the justices reasoned that

> the choice of material to go into a newspaper, and the decisions made as to limitations on the size and content of the paper, and treatment of public issues and public officials—whether fair or unfair—constitute the exercise of editorial control and judgment. It has yet to be demonstrated how government regulation of this crucial process can be exercised consistent with First Amendment guarantees of a free press.... [14]

Despite the potential for significant regulation of broadcast programs, the FCC has rarely used a broadcaster's compliance with the equal time rule and fairness doctrine as a basis for denial of a license. Over the last 40 years, the FCC has received close to 2,600 requests for new commercial television licenses and has denied or revoked

---

[13] *Red Lion Broadcasting v. FCC*, p. 390.
[14] *Miami Herald Publishing Co. v. Tornillo*, 418 U.S. 241 (1974).

only 595. Most of the denials were, however, based on scarcity of frequencies in cities that already had ample numbers of broadcasters. Since 1976 the FCC has refused only about one application per year on grounds related to the fairness doctrine.

In the 1980s the Reagan administration appointed several new members to the FCC, all of whom were strongly committed to a "free market" approach to broadcasting. The FCC conducted studies that purported to show that the fairness doctrine exerted a "chilling effect" on broadcast programming. In addition, the FCC reasoned that the original rationale underlying the fairness doctrine—the difficulty of obtaining access to the airwaves at a time when broadcast frequencies were essentially a scarce resource—was no longer applicable because advances in technology had made it possible to accommodate many stations in any given locale.[15] Therefore, in 1987 the FCC decided to repeal the fairness doctrine. Congress attempted to overrule the FCC by passing a bill that would have codified the provisions of the fairness doctrine, but it was vetoed by President Reagan.

In short, although the equal time rule remains in effect, broadcasting has been significantly deregulated in the past decade. The FCC has acknowledged that the airwaves no longer represent a scarce public good, but are instead an open marketplace governed by laws of supply and demand. Access to the airwaves is now determined largely by financial and technical ability.

Networks

TV is big business. In large markets like Los Angeles and New York the annual operating budget for a typical TV station exceeds $20,000,000. The most significant expense is programming—which constitutes nearly 40 percent of a typical station's annual budget.[16] Local stations have long dealt with the high cost of programming by depending on a common supplier of programs. Companies such as RCA and Columbia Phonograph had developed transmitters capa-

[15]"FCC kills 'Fairness Doctrine,' but Congress Will Renew Fight," *Congressional Quarterly Weekly Report*, August 8, 1987, p. 1796.
[16]Barry L. Sherman, *Telecommunications Management* (New York: McGraw-Hill, 1987), pp. 113–14.

ble of simultaneously sending the same programs to different communities. These developments led to the creation of the national networks that would dominate the broadcasting industry.

On November 15, 1926, the National Broadcasting Company (NBC)—then a joint venture of RCA, Westinghouse, and General Electric—started the first truly national radio network, with 25 stations serving 21 cities. A year later Columbia Phonograph formed the Columbia Broadcasting System (CBS). Along with several local networks, such as the one created by TV station WEAF in the New York City area, NBC and CBS had become the dominant force in broadcasting by the end of 1934. Of 650 commercial radio stations operating in the United States in 1934, half were associated with networks and one-fifth were exclusive affiliates of NBC.

The same corporations that created radio networks were in the forefront of efforts to structure the television industry. Once again NBC took the lead. The company rented space in the Empire State Building to operate an experimental TV station in 1931. On April 30, 1939, NBC broadcast the opening of the World's Fair, and the first TV station was on the air. Two years later the FCC granted the corporation a license for regular television broadcasting. CBS soon started building a network to compete with its rival NBC. NBC, in turn, had become so large that it split its network into two—the blue and the red. In 1943 the company sold its blue network to Edward Noble, and the American Broadcasting Company (ABC) was born. Today each of the networks has over 200 affiliates, constituting the heart of television broadcasting.

In many respects, networks appear to be mysterious artifices. The actual organization consists of little more than a bundle of contracts by which a group of stations link their operations. What networks do provide is programming. They offer member stations a full slate of shows in exchange for a fraction of the advertising revenues raised during the programs. Typically, the network offers affiliates more than 90 hours of programming a week. The offerings include news programs, prime-time dramas and situation comedies, and daytime shows like soap operas and talk shows. The local broadcaster decides what mix of network and local programs to air, and the network pays the affiliate for each hour of its material that is used. The actual amount that the network pays depends on the size of the local market. In New York City the networks pay the local licensee an average of $10,000 per hour of air time. Reimbursements in the smallest communities are as low as $100 per hour. In exchange for the network payments local stations provide advertising time to the networks. In a given time slot one-half to three-quarters of the advertising time is controlled by the networks. The exchange has proven lucrative for both participants. In 1980 network payments to affiliates totaled $350 million. This arrangement enables approximately 90 percent of the stations affiliated with a network to make a profit, compared to only 65 percent of the independent stations.[17] The networks themselves took in $5.1 billion from advertising sold through their nets.[18]

Early in the 1940s the FCC recognized the effect that networks were having on the broadcast industry. Network broadcasting had expanded the scope and scale of the mass media dramatically. In the commission's words,

> Chain broadcasting makes possible a wider reception for expensive entertainment and cultural programs and also for programs of national or regional significance which would otherwise have coverage only in the locality of origin. Furthermore, the access to greatly enlarged audiences made possible by chain broadcasting has been a strong incentive to advertisers to finance the production of expensive programs.[19]

The networks also posed a threat. Like chain stores, ABC, CBS, and NBC could operate their stations at such low cost as to prevent other stations from opening. The FCC foresaw that rather than allow too many broadcasters to serve a locale, the creation of networks could lead to too little competition. Independent stations might have difficulty competing against more profitable network affiliates. In 1941, to break the hold of the networks, the agency imposed the chain broadcasting rules on the industry.

The chain broadcasting rules reaffirmed the central tenet of the Communications Act—that broadcasting is, or at least should be, a local affair. The rules have three prongs. First, the agency allowed

[17] Bruce Owen, *Economics and Freedom of Expression: Media Structure and the First Amendment* (Cambridge, Mass.: Ballinger, 1975).

[18] Department of Commerce, *Statistical Abstract of the United States*, 110th ed., (Washington, D.C.: U.S. Government Printing Office, 1990).

[19] FCC, *The Report on Chain Broadcasting* (Washington, D.C.: U.S. Government Printing Office, 1941), p. 4.

local licensees to set the terms of contracts with networks. In the 1920s and 1930s the networks forced local stations into exclusive contracts, with long terms of affiliation. The FCC stipulated that stations could affiliate with any network they chose to, even several, and that contracts of affiliation could run no longer than three years. Second, the commission ruled that no network could own more than five VHF stations and one UHF station. In 1941 NBC and CBS owned the prime stations in the 10 largest cities in the United States. The commission held that this "bottling-up" of the best markets discouraged other networks from forming. Third, the FCC granted licensees discretion over programming and advertising. Previously, the networks forced local broadcasters to carry the full slate of network material, preventing stations from developing their own programs. Moreover, the networks set the rates that local stations could charge for advertising, reducing the station's financial independence. The FCC ruled that local broadcasters have the right to reject any network program and that local stations can sell advertising at any rate they choose.[20]

Even under these strictures, the networks have thrived. In the early 1980s CBS, NBC, and ABC owned five stations apiece. Although this is a small number of stations, each network reached slightly more than 20 percent of the national television audience through licenses it held. Since then, the FCC has further relaxed the limits on network ownership, allowing the networks to own up to 12 commercial television stations, but the combined audience in these stations cannot reach more than 25 percent of the national total.

Networks remain the predominant source of programming. Most local affiliates do not have the capability to produce shows beyond the local news and talk shows. Compensation provided by the networks provides an additional incentive not to acquire shows independently. Network material consequently takes up most of the time in an affiliate's day. The actual mix of local and network programming depends on the nature of the contract between a licensee and the network. A typical daily schedule is shown in Figure 2.1. On a typical 18-hour broadcast day—between 6:30 A.M. and 12:00 midnight—local programming accounts for only five and a

---

[20]These regulations are spelled out in the FCC's *Chain Broadcasting Report*. A good summary is contained in the majority opinion in *NBC v. U.S.* 319 U.S. 190.

Monday–Friday		Saturday		Sunday	
6:30 A.M.–7:00 A.M.	Local	6:30 A.M.–8:00 A.M.	Local	6:30 A.M.–8:00 A.M.	Local
7:00 A.M.–9:00 A.M.	Network news	8:00 A.M.–2:00 P.M.	Network children's	8:00 A.M.–12:00 P.M.	Network miscellaneous
9:00 A.M.–10:00 A.M.	Local				
10:00 A.M.–4:30 P.M.	Network daytime	2:00 P.M.–6:00 P.M.	Network sports and local	12:00 P.M.–6:00 P.M.	Network sports and local
4:30 P.M.–7:00 P.M.	Local	6:00 P.M.–6:30 P.M.	Network news	6:00 P.M.–6:30 P.M.	Local
7:00 P.M.–7:30 P.M.	Network news	6:30 P.M.–8:00 P.M.	Local	6:30 P.M.–7:00 P.M.	Network news
7:30 P.M.–8:00 P.M.	Local prime time	8:00 P.M.–11:00 P.M.	Network prime time	7:00 P.M.–11:00 P.M.	Network prime time
8:00 P.M.–11:00 P.M.	Network	11:00 P.M.–sign-off	Local	11:00 P.M.–sign-off	Local
11:00 P.M.–11:30 P.M.	Local news				
1:30 A.M.–sign-off	Local				

Figure 2.1 Daily Program Schedule for a Typical Television Station.
Source: David Poltrack, Television Marketing: Network, Local, and Cable (New York: McGraw-Hill, 1983).

25

half hours. The remaining twelve and a half hours are provided by the network.

Even though the three major networks remain the predominant actors in the broadcasting industry (collectively the big three brought in $10 billion dollars in 1990), all is not well in networkdom. All three networks have been acquired by conglomerates (General Electric in the case of NBC, Capital Cities Communication in the case of ABC, and Sony in the case of CBS). These mergers have resulted in significant managerial changes. The networks' news divisions, in particular, have come in for harsh treatment. Their budgets have been slashed, large numbers of bureaus have been closed, and reporters have been laid off.

The biggest problem facing the networks is the shrinking audience. Ratings for the networks' prime-time programming have dropped markedly since 1990, with obvious consequences for the bottom line. In the 1990–1991 season, the aggregate audience for ABC, CBS, and NBC dropped to 62.4 percent, down from 66 percent in the previous season and 85 percent in 1980. NBC alone lost 1.7 million viewers each weeknight from 1989 to 1991. Because of declining revenues, all three networks have lowered their compensation to affiliates. In 1991, for example, CBS decided to stop reimbursing locals for carrying its sports programming.

The troubles in the world of network television can be summarized in two words: cable television. The emergence of cable and other competitors (such as the Fox network) has freed viewers from their long dependence on the big three. Symptomatic of the networks' eroding power is the decision by Bill Cosby, America's most-watched TV personality, to syndicate his new comedy show ("You Bet Your Life") directly to local stations, bypassing ABC, CBS, or NBC.

The Rise of Cable Television
Community Antenna Television, or cable TV, has changed the very foundation of the medium by changing its technology. Traditionally, television signals have been broadcast through the air to individual homes. Cable systems, by contrast, broadcast signals to a community antenna. The signals are then sent by wire to individual homes, dramatically reducing the amount of interference among television signals. Viewers get clearer reception, and broadcasters gain access to many more frequencies.

Commercial cable systems have been in use in the United States since 1948. In 1952, 70 cable systems connected 14,000 households. Until the 1970s the cable audience grew much more slowly than the audience for broadcast television. Two obstacles—one technological, the other legal—were removed in the 1970s.

Technologically, early cable systems were limited by the reach of their signals. Before 1975 broadcast signals were received as easily by each household as they were by a community antenna. In 1975 RCA launched Satcom 1, a satellite with transmitters powerful enough to send signals long distances but requiring special receiving antennae on earth. Cable services could now offer clearer pictures than could ordinary broadcasts. The strength of the satellite transmissions also permitted the cable systems to offer more channels to viewers.

FCC regulations in the 1960s and early 1970s raised barriers to the spread of cable. Specifically, the agency limited the number of channels to 20, including the networks. In addition, cable companies were precluded from carrying distant stations presenting the same network programming as local stations. Over the course of the 1970s the courts struck down limits on the number of channels, rules granting local network affiliates exclusive rights to cable access, and regulations on the content of cable programs. By 1981 the cable industry was essentially deregulated.

Deregulation brought cable to greater numbers of people and a greater variety of programs to viewers. Only a tenth of the United States was served by cable in 1980. By 1990, 55 percent of U. S. households were connected to cable systems. While cable companies are still required to carry the local network affiliates, they offer a great variety of channels from distant cities, ones that provide highly specialized programming, like C-SPAN and Home Shopper's Network, and even new networks, such as the Cable News Network and Turner Broadcasting. The expansion of cable has simply meant a greater variety of channels available to Americans. In 1985 only 19 percent of all households received 30 or more channels. By 1989, that figure grew to 45 percent, and 54 percent of the households in the United States received more than 20 channels.

Cable's growth has come at the networks' expense. Prime-time network shows have lost fully a quarter of their audience in less than a decade. As cable television reaches new cities, the networks' immediate fortunes are likely to continue their recent decline. The most notable effect of cable television, however, was a major impetus to the deregulation of broadcasting. As we noted previously, the Federal Communication Commission's reason for repealing the Table of Assignments and other regulations on broadcasting was that the development of cable television systems had effectively ended the scarcity of available channels. The technology of broadcasting was no longer a barrier to free and open communication of ideas.[21]

The effects of cable on the future development of the broadcast industry will be significant. Satellite technology has created a worldwide audience for a wide-ranging menu of television programs (see insert). CNN, for example, is now using two satellite feeds to reach 75 million households worldwide, including 17 million outside the United States. The British Broadcasting Corporation, in collaboration with a Hong Kong–based satellite network, has announced plans to air newscasts and documentaries worldwide. Japanese and European broadcasters are also planning global networks. Marshall McCluhan's notion of the "global village" is about to become operational.

Advertisers

The wealth of the television industry is impressive by any standard. In 1990 net revenues at CBS amounted to $3,261,200,000. Yet TV programs themselves generate no money. Newspapers and magazines can raise cash through circulation; broadcasts, however, are public property, making it impossible for television and radio stations to charge subscription or user fees.[22] The massive revenue needed to run stations and networks therefore comes almost wholly from advertising. Broadcasters "sell" viewers to their advertisers.

In August of 1922 the Queensboro Corporation, a real estate developer in Jackson Heights, Long Island, contacted the station manager at radio station WEAF, New York, about advertising cooperatively owned apartments over the air. The station shied away from advertising as such, but sold the owner of the Hawthorne Court

---

[21]Note that there is considerable controversy over the issue of scarcity and over the validity of the FCC's claims concerning the elimination of scarcity.
[22]The exception, of course, is cable TV.

Co-op 10 minutes of air time for $50 to deliver a speech about the joys of living in Jackson Heights.[23] Tidewater Oil, American Express, Gilette, and others soon took to the New York airwaves. By the time the FCC licensed the first commercial television station, advertising had already become the staple of the broadcasting industry. Even with the recent rise of cable (pay) television, commercial advertising remains the industry's backbone. In 1990 television grossed over $26 billion from commercials.[24]

Buying and Selling Advertisements
The market for commercial television time is divided into two tiers: network and spot markets. Agreements between networks and local stations grant the networks the lion's share of advertising time. These arrangements vary considerably from station to station and from time period to time period. The typical split gives the network nine minutes and the local station three minutes of commercial time per hour.[25] Time purchased directly from ABC, CBS, or NBC for national ads constitutes the network advertising market. Time purchased from the local stations is called spot advertising. In 1990 networks raised slightly more than $9 billion from their time. Local stations brought in approximately $14.5 billion from spot ads. (The larger revenue from local advertising is explained by the sheer number of local stations.)

The sale of advertisements closely resembles the sale of other commodities, like winter wheat or airline tickets. Advertisers buy a particular time slot, usually between 10 and 60 seconds long, on a given day during a specific show. For example, one may buy 30 seconds of air time during the first commercial break of the CBS "Evening News" on April 2, 1992. Once that moment is past, however, the time is worth nothing. Advertising slots sometimes go unsold. As with other commodities, the seller (i.e., the station)

[23] Friendly, 1977, p.22.
[24] Newspapers have not escaped the transformation of commercialism and mass consumption. The newspaper industry receives slightly more than three-quarters of its revenue from advertising and only one-quarter from circulation. See Owen, 1975, chap. 2.
[25] David F. Poltrack, *Television Marketing: Network, Local, and Cable* (New York: McGraw-Hill, 1983), p. 135.

prefers to let the commodity perish rather than sell it for a very low price.

Advertising also has the flavor of an auction in which the time ultimately goes to the highest bidder. A station manager may have promised air time to an advertiser. If another advertiser offers to pay a higher price, the station may break its original agreement and sell the new firm the time slot. The old advertiser is bumped to another day or time. Many advertisers find this undesirable, for they want to be certain that their ads reach a specific audience on a specific day. Stations have tailored their advertising sales to the different types of advertisers by selling two rates: preemptible and nonpreemptible (also known as fixed-rate) time. A firm that does not wish to be bumped pays a premium price, while a firm that does not care about being bumped or is willing to risk preemption, pays a lower rate.

Traditionally, the price of a commercial time was set by the station. The local station or network would set the prices for each time slot in advance and publish those prices on a *rate card*. An advertiser would determine what sort of audience it would like to reach and which time slots it would like to purchase. Depending on the size of the audience, the advertiser would contact either the local station or the network. If the advertiser wanted to reach a particular geographic market, it would buy time from local stations. To reach a national audience with a single message, an advertiser would buy time from the network. Over the last decade, buying and selling television advertisements has become considerably more complicated. Now prices for air time are set by negotiation. An advertiser first determines what sort of audience it would like to reach and then sends a proposal to the station manager or network advertising representative. The station manager or network advertising representative makes a counter offer. Negotiations continue until the parties agree on a price and time. The price that an advertiser pays, however, may change even after a deal is struck with the broadcaster. Another advertiser may offer a higher price for the time. Just as often, the show may not do as well as expected, and the advertiser becomes dissatisfied with the original deal. The station and the advertiser then agree to an alternative spot, either to replace one that was bumped by another advertiser or to make up for the poor ratings of a show.

Increasingly, advertisers and stations agree not on time slots but on rating points. For example, rather than purchase a 30-second spot on the "Rug Rats" episode that will air on January 10, 1993, the advertiser may purchase 10 rating points on a children's show on Nickelodeon during the month of January. It is left up to the network to determine the particular date and sometimes even the show on which the ad will air.

This system of pricing has strongly influenced the campaign decisions of political candidates (as described in Chapter 4). The size of the television audience makes paid advertising a desirable outlet for political campaigns. The least expensive (preemptible) time is typically priced about 50 percent below the fixed (nonpreemptible) rate.[26] If a candidate buys preemptible time, however, his or her campaign ads may be bumped from the queue. Unlike product advertising, political advertising depends on timing for its effectiveness. Candidates are thus under pressure to buy the more expensive, nonpreemptible time. As media consultant Frank Greer exclaimed, "I don't know of a campaign in their [sic] right mind that doesn't buy fixed time. You're crazy, in the pressure of a campaign, if you don't."[27]

The higher price of fixed time forces candidates either to raise large campaign chests or to use other, less efficient media such as direct mail. In addition, campaign organizations often lack the expertise of the media buyers who work for corporations. Although the number of media-savvy political consultants is increasing, most are not experienced at negotiating prices with television producers. As a result, politicians can often end up with the most expensive rate charged by a station.

In theory, candidates are not supposed to be subjected to this sort of treatment. The Federal Elections Campaign Act of 1971 established the "lowest unit rate" rule, which stipulates that during the 60 days prior to an election (45 days for a primary), local broadcasters are required to charge candidates the lowest rate charged to any other advertiser for comparable time. A candidate is thus entitled

---

[26] Paul Hoff, *Beyond the Thirty-Second Spot* (Washington, D.C.: Center for Responsive Politics, 1988), p. 72.

[27] Quoted in Hoff, 1988, p. 73.

to the same price as an advertiser who gets a volume discount for purchasing, say, 200 spots.

In practice, however, the stations ignore the lowest unit rule. In 1990 the Federal Communications Commission carried out spot audits of 20 television stations in five cities during the summer primaries. Four of every five stations charged political candidates more than they did other advertisers. In one city, candidates paid an average of $6,000 for a 30-second spot, while the average price charged to other advertisers for similar time was only $2,713.[28]

In 1991 California Governor Pete Wilson (a Republican) and Lt. Governor Leo McCarthy (a Democrat)—who had run against each other in a 1988 Senate race—sued 22 California TV stations for overcharging their campaigns during the 1988 campaign. The suit alleged that the stations did not adhere to the lowest unit rate rule. As of early 1992 the suit was still tied up in court.

Media Markets

Prices for advertising vary not only by time of day and by the preferences of the advertiser, but also by market. The *area of dominant influence* (ADI) is the geographic boundary of a media market. ADI is a measure of common audience developed by Arbitron, but it has become the standard measure of the media markets in the television industry.[29] Arbitron defines an ADI as the county or counties in which the broadcasters from a certain city enjoy the greatest share of the audience. For example, the Los Angeles ADI covers Los Angeles, Ventura, Orange, San Bernardino, and Inyo counties. The majority of households in each of these five counties are served by a common set of broadcasters in the vicinity of the city of Los Angeles.

Figure 2.2 shows the 15 ADIs that serve the state of California. There is tremendous variability in the land mass covered by these districts, ranging from the enormous Los Angeles ADI to the tiny Palm Springs ADI. None of the areas overlap, even though the reach of their broadcasts does. San Francisco stations are readily

[28]Thomas B. Rosenstiel, "Candidates' Ad Rates Too High, FCC Says," *Los Angeles Times*, September 8, 1990.
[29]The facts in the following discussion are taken from the *Television and Cable Factbook*, vol. 59 (Washington, D.C.: TV Digest, Inc., 1991).

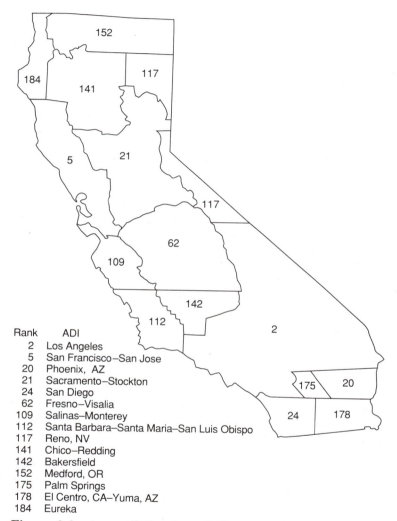

Rank   ADI
  2   Los Angeles
  5   San Francisco–San Jose
 20   Phoenix, AZ
 21   Sacramento–Stockton
 24   San Diego
 62   Fresno–Visalia
109   Salinas–Monterey
112   Santa Barbara–Santa Maria–San Luis Obispo
117   Reno, NV
141   Chico–Redding
142   Bakersfield
152   Medford, OR
175   Palm Springs
178   El Centro, CA–Yuma, AZ
184   Eureka

Figure 2.2   Areas of Dominant Influence (ADIs) in California, 1990 (Numbers refer to national rank of ADI).

Source: Reconstructed by authors using the definitions of ADIs in the *Television & Cable Factbook*, No. 59, Washington, DC: Television Digest, 1991, and a county map of California.

received in the Sacramento and Salinas areas. Los Angeles stations easily reach the Bakersfield, Las Vegas, Palm Springs, San Diego, and San Luis Obispo ADIs. The spread of cable has greatly increased the overlap.

The ADI provides a rough picture of the potential market that an advertiser can reach. There are 212 ADIs in the United States. The largest is New York City. Covering just under 7 million households, it is able to support 15 commercial television stations. Second is Los Angeles, where 17 commercial stations serve 4.8 million households. The smallest is Glendive, Montana, with one station reaching just 5,000 households.

The price that advertisers pay is closely tied to the size of the ADI. Discrepancies in price among the various markets can be enormous. In the largest ADI, New York City, the average price of a 30-second spot ad is roughly $14,000. This works out to $1415 to reach one rating point of the New York market. In Glendive, Montana, the average 30-second spot costs only $16 per rating point.

The geography of television markets affects campaign decisions in two ways. First, since advertising prices are closely related to area, advertising in some states and legislative districts is very costly and in others is quite inexpensive. A gubernatorial candidate in Montana can reach 500 rating points with her commercials for less than what a New York candidate will have to spend to reach 10 ratings points. This forces politicians in states like California and New York to rely on free media and news coverage rather than advertising.

Second, politicians will use commercial television to the extent that the borders of their political constituencies overlap with the geography of media markets. As a general rule, the greater the congruence between a media market and a political district, the greater the return from paid political advertisements. If the district is much smaller than the media market, as is the case for representatives from New York City or Los Angeles, campaign advertisements will reach a much larger audience than they need. Politicians, in this case, will reach too many people. If the district is serviced by many media markets, politicians need to advertise in many markets to reach a large share of the voters. Any one ad will reach too few voters in a given district. The state of New Jersey, for example, is covered primarily by ADIs centered in Philadelphia and New York City. The bulk of the viewers in these ADIs are outside the state of New Jersey.

These simple economic considerations significantly constrain the media campaigns of politicians. Many candidates for the U. S. House of Representatives and most candidates for local offices find TV too expensive and too inefficient for their purposes. For national and statewide offices, though, television is usually the best outlet for paid campaign messages. Most presidential, senatorial, and gubernatorial candidates use paid television advertising as a key component of their political campaigns.

Summary

Television is not a monolithic medium, although the media are frequently treated as single entity. There are moments when television attracts a truly national, even worldwide, audience, but the medium is in fact composed of thousands of companies—local stations and networks. Even though there is a tendency toward concentration in this industry, most of these companies are not national. They reside in specific geographic areas, and within these areas they reach multiple and segmented audiences.

Like it or not, access to these audiences depends ultimately on the economic resources. To obtain a license, a broadcaster need only demonstrate that it has the money to run a profitable station. Advertisers, including politicians, buy access to the airwaves and thus access to potential consumers. Most importantly, financial considerations shape the programming offered by broadcasters. Only wealthy stations in large media markets can afford extensive news programming and teams of reporters.

The health of the television industry, however, has implications that extend beyond economic concerns. Television is America's primary source of public affairs and political information. Economic pressures on the industry may diminish the public's ability to stay informed about current events. The availability and flow of public affairs information is the subject of the next chapter.

Suggested Readings

Gleason Archer. 1938. *History of Radio to 1926*. New York: American Historical Society.

Eric Barnouw. 1966. *A Tower in Babel: a History of Broadcasting in the U.S.—to 1933*, vol. 1. New York: Oxford University Press.

———. 1981. *Tube of Plenty: The Evolution of American Television*. New York: Oxford University Press.

———. 1978. *The Sponsor: Notes on a Modern Potentate*. New York: Oxford University Press.

Stanley Besen et al. 1984. *Misregulating Television: Network Dominance and the FCC*. Chicago: University of Chicago Press.

Alex Block. 1990. *Outfoxed: Marvin Davis, Barry Diller, Rupert Murdoch, Joan Rivers, and the Inside Story of America's Fourth Television Network*. New York: St. Martin's.

Peter Boyer. 1988. *Who Killed CBS?* New York: Random House.

Robert Bower. 1985. *The Changing TV Audience in America*. New York: Columbia University Press.

Daniel Dayan and Elihu Katz. 1992. *Media Events: The Live Broadcasting of History*. Cambridge, Mass.: Harvard University Press.

Fred Friendly. 1977. *The Good Guys, the Bad Guys, and the First Amendment: Free Speech vs. Fairness in Broadcasting*. New York: Random House.

Paul Hoff. 1988. *Beyond the Thirty-Second Spot*. Washington, D.C.: Center for Responsive Politics.

Phyllis Kanss. 1991. *Making Local News*. Chicago: University of Chicago Press.

Erwin Krasnow, Lawrence Longley, and Herbert Terry. 1982. *The Politics of Broadcast Regulation*. New York: St. Martin's Press.

Judith Lichtenberg (ed.). 1990. *Democracy and the Mass Media*. New York: Cambridge University Press.

Fred McDonald. 1990. *One Nation under TV: The Rise and Decline of Network TV*. New York: Pantheon.

Bruce Owen. 1975. *Economics and Freedom of Expression: Media Structure and the First Amendment.* Cambridge, Mass.: Ballinger.

Bruce Owen and Steven Wildman. 1992. *Video Economics.* Cambridge: Harvard University Press.

David Poltrack. 1983. *Television Marketing: Network, Local, and Cable.* New York: McGraw-Hill.

Barry Sherman. 1987. *Telecommunications Management.* New York: McGraw-Hill, 1987.

GETTING THE NEWS

The United States is a media-rich society with news outlets for every taste and inclination. There are 17,000 daily newspapers, at least 11,000 magazines, 10,000 radio stations, more than 2,500 book publishers, and 1,500 television stations. All these sources transmit huge quantities of information about virtually every aspect of American life.

In tracing the flow of information in contemporary American politics, we will distinguish between print and broadcast sources. In addition to differences in the number of people they reach, these sources differ in their technologies of communication, the amount and type of information they provide, and the makeup of their audiences.

Print Sources

More than 100 million Americans (80 percent of the adult population) read a daily newspaper on a regular basis. On Sundays the figure rises to 120 million.[1] Unlike network newscasts, newspapers are multifaceted and can provide readers with much more than news. Editorials, entertainment, TV and movie listings, sports, comics, and classified advertisements all compete with political events for the reader's attention. More than 40 percent of newspaper readers

---

[1]*Advertising Age*, May 20, 1991.

say that they usually read only certain pages or sections of their paper.

While the typical American newspaper is published locally, several papers are distributed nationally.[2] *USA Today* is available everywhere. The *New York Times*, publishes not only metropolitan and suburban editions, but also Midwestern and West Coast editions (printed in Chicago and California, respectively). Similarly, the *Wall Street Journal*, with its specialized coverage of financial and corporate news, enjoys a national audience.

Typically, the major national papers maintain a large contingent of reporters in Washington as well as other reporters scattered across the globe in key locations. Smaller papers cannot afford to maintain reporters in Washington or overseas. These papers provide coverage of national and international events by relying on the wire services. The two major American wire services are the Associated Press and United Press International. Reuters and Agence France Presse are the major international services. By subscribing to a wire service, a small paper in Iowa can publish a Washington correspondent's eyewitness account of a presidential news conference on its front page.

Only a few American newspapers have vast audiences. The typical newspaper enjoys a circulation of approximately 25,000. Table 3.1 shows the circulation figures for the 20 largest newspapers. Compared to the number of viewers who watch television news, the readership of major newspapers is small. *USA Today* has a paid circulation of 1.5 million (and total readership of nearly 5 million). The combined daily circulation of the *New York Times*, *Los Angeles Times*, and *Washington Post* is only 3 million. The typical audience for a single network newscast, however, is nearly 20 million viewers.

Americans also keep abreast of public affairs by reading magazines (see Table 3.2). The three major news magazines—*Time*, *Newsweek*, and *U.S. News and World Report*—enjoy a combined circulation of 10 million. These magazines focus on the major events of the week and tend to resemble one another closely in content and format.

---

[2] Ownership, however, is usually not local. Most American papers are part of "chains" owned by companies such as Knight-Ridder and Gannett.

Table 3.1 Twenty Newspapers with the Largest Circulations, 1990

Rank	Newspaper	Circulation
1	Wall Street Journal	1,795,448
2	USA Today	1,491,844
3	Los Angeles Times	1,177,253
4	New York Times	1,114,830
5	Washington Post	791,289
6	Newsday	763,972
7	New York Daily News	762,078
8	Chicago Tribune	723,178
9	Detroit Free Press	598,418
10	San Francisco Chronicle	553,433
11	New York Post	552,227
12	Chicago Sun-Times	531,462
13	Boston Globe	504,675
14	Philadelphia Inquirer	503,603
15	Newark Star-Ledger	470,672
16	Detroit News	446,831
17	Cleveland Plain Dealer	413,678
18	Minneapolis-St. Paul Star Tribune	408,365
19	Dallas Morning News	406,768
20	Miami Herald	396,067

Source: Ira Teinowitz, "Circulation Reparation," *Advertising Age* (November 4, 1991), p. 35.

Table 3.2 Average Monthly Circulation of the Three Major News Magazines, 1990

Magazine	Total Number of Copies Sold	Change from 1989
Time	4,339,029	−5.6%
Newsweek	3,180,011	+1.0
U.S. News & World Report	2,209,996	+4.6
Total	9,729,036	−1.3%

Source: Audit Bureau of Circulations, *FAS-FAX: United States and Canadian Periodicals* (January 1991), pp. 21, 31, 33.

Broadcast Sources

✗ Television news comes from either the networks or local stations.

Network News

At the national level, the three television networks are the primary carriers of news. The networks' regularly scheduled public affairs programming is limited to daily evening newscasts (such as the "NBC Nightly News"), and weekly prime-time news programs (such as CBS's "Sixty Minutes"). Originally, the networks' newscasts were only 15 minutes long. CBS and NBC adopted the current 30-minute format on Labor Day, 1963. ABC followed suit five years later.

The networks also air sporadic special reports that focus on major events such as international crises, wars, presidential elections, and other such breaking stories. In addition, all three networks provide prime-time public affairs programming such as "20/20," "48 Hours," and "Sixty Minutes," and interview programs such as "Nightline."

The content of network news, which is nearly uniform across the three networks, consists of a summary of the day's major events in Washington, the nation's major cities, and foreign capitals. In Washington the federal government, and especially the presidency, is the major focus of the cameras. The president and the executive branch are covered regularly; there is generally at least one story each evening from the White House correspondent. Stories focusing on the Pentagon and Department of State are also prominent. The other branches of government are much less newsworthy. As one scholar has described the networks' preoccupation with the White House, "435 members of the House and 100 members of the Senate compete for the crumbs of network time left after the president has gotten his share."[3]

On a typical weekday the combined audience for the ABC, CBS, and NBC nightly newscasts is some 50 million Americans. This may

---

[3] Kathleen Jamieson, *Eloquence in an Electronic Age* (New York: Oxford University Press, 1988), p. 14.

seem like a small daily audience, considering that nearly 80 percent of the adult population reports that television news is their primary source of political information. However, no other medium reaches an audience of this magnitude.

Since 1950 television news programs have gradually supplanted newspapers and other print media as the major source of information. Figure 3.1 shows the percentages of the American public who reported that they relied on television news, newspapers, or a combination to keep up with public affairs during the period 1959–1991. Since 1967, when 73 percent of the adult population read a newspaper every day, readership has declined by approximately 1 percent

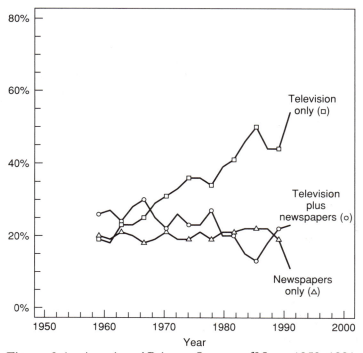

Figure 3.1 Americans' Primary Sources of News, 1959–1991.
Source: Roper Organization, *America's Watching: Public Attitudes Toward Television, 1991* (New York: Author, 1991).

each year to 51 percent in 1990.[4] Television overtook newspapers as
the public's preferred source in 1960 and has continued to increase
its dominance ever since. Between 1980 and 1990 the percentage of
Americans reporting that they rely solely on television has increased
from 39 percent to 58 percent. In contrast, the percentage relying
solely on newspapers has remained stable at approximately 20 percent. Currently, television news enjoys a wide margin as Americans'
preferred method for keeping up with the world.

Television news is also the most believed source of public affairs
information. If exposed to conflicting reports from different media
sources, 55 percent of the public indicated that they would believe
television, while only 21 percent would give greater credence to
newspapers.[5] As Figure 3.2 reveals, Americans rate television news
much more favorably than newspapers, magazines, or radio broadcasts on various indicators of source credibility. Americans increasingly consider television news to be less biased and more accurate
than news from print or radio sources.

Although so-called "self-reports" of media exposure may be un-
reliable as evidence,[6] the amount of advertising expenditures allocated to the various media sources suggests that the American
public is watching television increasingly. Television's share of the
advertising dollar has climbed inexorably. In 1950, 36 percent of
all advertising expenditures were spent on newspaper advertising,
11 percent on radio, 14 percent on direct mail, and only 3 percent
on television. By 1970, newpapers' share of the advertising dollar
had dropped to 29 percent, radio's share to 7 percent, direct mail's
had remained at 14 percent, and televisions's had skyrocketed to 18
percent. In 1990, newspapers' share of advertising expenditures had
shrunk to 25 percent and television had climbed to 23 percent.[7]

[4]*New York Times*, December 30, 1991, C6.
[5]*America's Watching*, New York: Television Information Office, 1987.
[6]People might say that they rely primarily on television, but this might not be an
accurate representation of their actual behavior. Because they watch so much television, perhaps people exaggerate the extent to which they rely on television news for
public affairs information. Moreover, the fact that people report watching so much
television ignores huge differences in viewer attention. While the typical person's
television set may be on for six hours a day, for a good share of that period no one
might be watching.
[7]*Statistical Abstract of the United States*, 1991

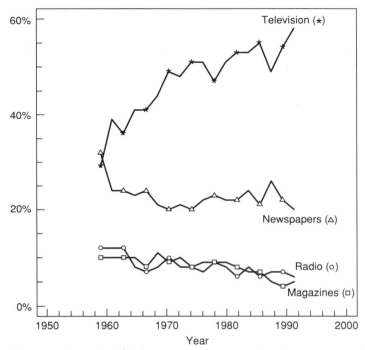

Figure 3.2 Which Source Do Americans Find Most Credible? (1959–1991).
Source: Roper Organization, *America's Watching: Public Attitudes Toward Television, 1991* (New York: Author, 1991).

The competition among the networks for viewers of news programming is intense. The networks evenly split the 50 million person audience that watches nightly news. During 1989, for example, CBS and ABC battled for the title of "most watched newscast." ABC won the ratings war by .05 rating points—less than 50,000 people in a nation of 253 million.[8] ABC's "World News Tonight" won 10.14 rating points, 20 percent of the viewership in its time period. The "CBS Evening News" won 10.09 rating points, also 20

---

[8] One rating point translated into 921,000 viewers.

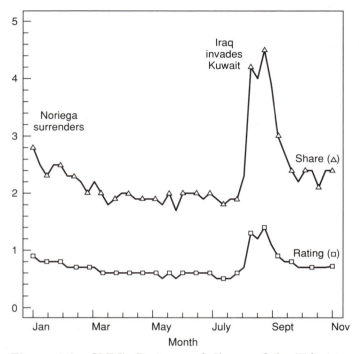

Figure 3.3   CNN's Ratings and Shares of the Television Audience, January 1, 1990, to November 4, 1990. (Shares are measured as percentages of the total viewing audience.)
Source: Constructed by authors from figures provided by Turner Broadcasting Research.

percent of the viewership. And the "NBC Nightly News" was close behind, receiving 9.44 rating points, or 19 percent of the viewers.[9]

A good share of the audience for the nightly news, however, probably consists of "inadvertent" viewers who have their television sets tuned to a network news broadcast only because they are

[9]Robert Goldberg, *Anchors: Brokaw, Jennings, Rather and the Evening News.* Secaucus, NJ: Carol Publishing Group, 1990, p. 372.

awaiting a local newscast or a syndicated rerun that follows the national news. In other words, not everyone who watches the national news is particularly interested in public affairs; for many people, watching the news may be an exercise in killing time until "Wheel of Fortune" comes on.

On occasion, the quest for higher ratings has cost anchorpersons their jobs. "NBC News," for example, dismantled the highly regarded team of Roger Mudd and John Chancellor in the early 1980s in response to weak ratings and installed Tom Brokaw as sole anchor in 1982. Chancellor stayed with the network as a commentator, and Mudd moved to the Public Broadcast Service's "McNeil/Lehrer Newshour." With the exception of the "CBS News," the network evening programs have experienced considerable turnover among anchorpersons over the past two decades.

In addition to the three networks, the increasing role of cable television in the 1980s has made CNN (Cable News Network), on occasion, a major source of news. A majority of American homes are now wired for cable. As Figure 3.3 reveals, during periods of major "breaking" events (for example, the war in the Persian Gulf, the Senate Judiciary Committee's hearings on the confirmation of Judge Clarence Thomas, and the failed military coup in the Soviet Union), CNN made significant inroads into the networks' viewing audience. During the U.S. bombing of Baghdad, for instance, Peter Arnett and his crew—the only Western TV team permitted to stay in Iraq—captivated audiences all over the world. For the first time in CNN's history, it won over 10 percent of the TV audience.[10] During more tranquil times, however, CNN's audience is far smaller.

The Public Broadcasting Service, which was originally funded entirely by the federal government but is now funded mainly by private contributions, also produces a regular newscast—"The Mac-Neil/Lehrer Newshour." Co-anchored by Robert MacNeil and Jim Lehrer, the one-hour length of this program allows in-depth reporting and lengthy interviews with a variety of experts. However, the "Newshour" attracts only a tiny audience of mostly very educated people who have a strong interest in political matters.

[10] Peter Arnett's reporting from Iraq also earned him the condemnation of Senator Alan Simpson (Republican of Wyoming), who characterized him as a "traitor."

Local News

As the term implies, local news is news that is close to home. While network news is a compilation of reports from Washington, New York, Chicago, London, Moscow, and Tel Aviv, local news is filled with reports .rom state, county, and municipal venues. Unlike network newscasts, which tend to feature government officials, local news is much more attuned to the "man in the street"—the victim of a mugging, the winner of a lottery, and eyewitnesses to local events.

Although the audience for network newscasts is huge, even more people watch the local news. In the first place, there are many more opportunities to watch local news—programs run in the morning, evening, and late-night time slots. Moreover, many local newscasts run for 60 or 90 minutes. The audience ratings for local news programs typically exceed those for network newscasts. One study compared the audience for local and network news in eight media markets. For 18 of the 22 stations that were studied, the local news programs had more viewers, and on average the difference was four ratings points.[11]

The greater interest in local news is understandable. It is, after all, news about one's own community. The locals also offer "sexier" news, usable information, such as the weather forecast, and information with significant entertainment value (sports results and movie reviews, for instance). And on many occasions (particularly during the "sweeps" weeks when ratings points are updated), local newscasts focus on subjects designed to catch the viewer's eye (such as the latest trends in swimsuits). The high ratings for local news combined with the relatively low production costs for local news programs have made local news programming highly profitable for station owners.

The growing revenues from local news programs (in some cases, profit margins for local newscasts have reached 50 percent) has encouraged both the "affiliates" (television stations affiliated with one of the networks) and independent stations to broaden and expand

---

[11] Stephen Hess, *Live from Capital Hill: Studies of Congress and the Media*, (Washington, D.C.: Brookings Institution, 1991), p. 37.

their local news coverage.[12] Channel 9 (KCAL) in the Los Angeles area, for example, now broadcasts a three-hour (8 P.M.–11 P.M.) prime-time newscast Monday through Friday. To fill the expanded air time for local news, more and more stations supplement the usual fare of community news with news stories from correspondents in Washington, London, Moscow, or Cairo. Local stations in large cities have established news bureaus in Washington. The growth of satellite technology and the formation of "video wire-services" such as CONUS (an acronym for Continental U.S.) and Potomac News Service has made it possible for local stations to acquire "customized" Washington stories (at low cost), thus providing their viewers with live coverage of breaking national and international events.

In the case of election campaigns, local news is usually where the action is. Local stations have more time to cover campaigns, and in many instances campaigns are exclusively local affairs. Given the relatively large amounts of air time devoted to local news programming, the typical viewer obtains more information about almost *all* political campaigns from local news outlets. (The only possible exception is the presidential race during the closing stages of the campaign when the candidates concentrate their efforts in the most populated areas.) Given the prominence of local television news in the information flow, it is surprising that there is virtually no research concerning the content of this medium and its effects on viewers. As we shall see in Part III, most studies of the impact of television news on public opinion have focused on national as opposed to local sources.

To summarize, information about public affairs is increasingly delivered by television. Television news enjoys significant advantages over the print media as a source of information—a bigger audience, the power to cover events "live" without significant delay, and the ability to provide the "sound and light" to grip the audience's attention. Because of these objective advantages, television news also enjoys a favorable reputation and a high degree of credibility with its viewers.

[12] *New York Times*, July 1, 1985, D1.

The Nature of News

Reporters, editors, and others in journalism like to claim that news is a reflection of reality, a mirror image of events and issues. As Walter Cronkite signed off each evening during his long tenure as anchor at "CBS News", "And that's the way it is. . . . "

The theory that the news mirrors reality is largely wishful thinking. The facts demonstrate that the news is far from an undistorted reflection. (A more detailed critique of mirror-image theory is provided in Chapter 10.) Consider the following example. In early 1984 millions of Ethiopians were threatened by severe food shortages and famine. The death toll was already in the thousands when ABC correspondent Bill Blakemore sensed that this was an important story for the evening news. He requested permission to fly to Ethiopia to cover the story. His superiors, however, instructed him to assemble film footage and file a second-hand report from Rome (where he was based). He did so, but the report was never aired. As Blakemore later described his thoughts, "There are people dying, but they're only black."[13]

Six months later, all three networks broadcast daily reports on the same subject after the British Broadcasting Corporation (BBC) aired a lengthy report featuring close-up pictures of infants and children who were obviously on the verge of death by starvation. "NBC News" borrowed this report in early October, and the African famine then became the most covered event of late 1984. Why was the famine such a hot story in October and November, but not worthy of attention and development in February? The answer lies in the incentives facing reporters and editors.

The Ethiopian famine clearly illustrates that the same event can receive either saturation coverage or none at all. As this episode demonstrates, the news does not closely mirror reality; rather, the news is simply what gets reported. The process of reporting—the incentives and professional values of journalists and their daily routines are crucial to understanding the end product. This view is sometimes referred to as the *organizational model* of news, meaning

---

[13] Quoted in Peter Boyer, "Famine in Africa: The TV Accident That Exploded," in Michael Emery and Ted Smythe (eds.), *Readings in Mass Communication* (Dubuque, Iowa, William C. Brown, 1986), p. 293.

that the standard operating procedures of news organizations determine which stories and issues will receive coverage and which will be ignored.

What Gets Reported

For the individual reporter or editor, the key requirements of newsworthiness are *accessibility* and *appropriateness.* Accessibility refers to the feasibility and cost of covering particular events or issues. For national reporters based in Washington, agencies of the federal government are convenient and inexpensive subjects of news coverage. Sending Bill Blakemore to Ethiopia with a film crew, on the other hand, would have entailed significant organizational and financial costs for ABC. For the political correspondent covering a presidential campaign, the most accessible source is the campaign organization itself. For the local television correspondent interested in crime, the police department and the county courthouse are particularly accessible sources.

Appropriateness concerns the suitability or "fit" between events and the particular needs of the reporter's medium or audience. In general, there are important differences between what constitutes a suitable story in television news and in print sources. A story that includes considerable movement and color is more interesting to a correspondent for "CBS News" than to a correspondent for the *Wall Street Journal.* Local and national outlets also differ in their approaches to news. Weather conditions are reported regularly by local newscasts but are ignored by network newscasts unless some part of the country experiences particularly bad weather.

How News Is Reported

Television news is essentially a headline service operating under powerful commercial dictates. The constraints of time, advertisers, and the need to achieve high ratings explains why most television news reports focus on concrete acts and breaking events. Television news is thus primarily episodic, taking the form of an event-oriented report that depicts public issues in terms of concrete instances (for example, the plight of a homeless person or a teenage drug user, the bombing of an airliner, an attempted murder, or a politician's press conference). Episodic stories present on-the-scene coverage of "hard" news in a fast-paced and visually compelling manner. The opposite of the episodic report is the *backgrounder*—a story that provides related background material and in-depth, interpretive analysis. Examples of background or *thematic* coverage include reports on changes in government welfare expenditures or policy programs, the social or political grievances of groups undertaking protest activity, and the backlog in the criminal justice process. Whereas the episodic story depicts concrete events that illustrate issues, the backgrounder presents abstract or general information. Visually, episodic reports feature "good pictures," while backgrounders feature "talking heads"—experts or participants talking to the cameras. The MacNeil/Lehrer Newshour, unlike most network-originating news programs, consists primarily of background stories. The networks simply don't have air time available to present thematic background on all newsworthy issues. (Nor, in most cases, are such stories deemed capable of capturing and holding the average viewer's attention.) The only opportunity for thematic reporting on network news is provided by the "special assignment" segment of the newscast such as CBS's "Eye on America" or ABC's "American Agenda."[14]

The dominance of the episodic "frame" in television news has been established in a number of studies. For example, television news coverage of mass protest movements focuses more closely on specific acts of protest than on the issues that gave rise to the protests. This pattern characterized network coverage of the protests against the Vietnam War and the development of nuclear energy.[15] The identical pattern is observed in television news coverage of labor-management disputes, where scenes of picketing workers get more air time than discussions of the economic and political grievances at stake.[16] Event-oriented stories also account for most

---

[14]Backgrounders also take longer to prepare, and because they include interpretation and commentary, they are more susceptible to charges of journalistic bias.

[15]Todd Gitlin, *The Whole World Is Watching: Mass Media in the Making and Unmaking of the New Left* (Berkeley: University of California Press, 1980); William Gamson and Andre Modigliani, "Media Discourse and Public Opinion on Nuclear Power," *American Journal of Sociology* 95 (1989): 1–37.

[16]Glasgow University Media Group, *Bad News* (London: Routledge & Kegan Paul, 1976).

news coverage of international terrorism; information about specific terrorist acts is not accompanied by information about related historical, economic, or social antecedents.[17]

Organizational Routines

Bureaucratic requirements of news organizations also affect the selection of events to cover and the nature of the coverage.

Beats

Editors typically assign reporters to "beats." In the case of American news organizations, beats are generally locations where news is expected to occur. The most common type of beat is a particular government agency or office. For national reporters, the White House, the Department of State, and the Pentagon are among the most desirable and prestigious beats. The White House correspondent, for instance, is virtually guaranteed a front-page or lead story on a regular basis. The White House beat is therefore a sure catapult to journalistic stardom. As Martin Tolchin, White House correspondent for the *New York Times*, explains, "I have had stories on p. 1 just because the president burped."[18] Subject matter or topical beats (such as education, science and technology, or the economy) are less attractive because they are not such good "news cows." Correspondents assigned to these beats have to do more homework and cannot count on getting their stories into the news on a regular basis.

A striking example of the importance of beats in determining the production of news is television's coverage of the 1991 war in the Persian Gulf. More than 50 percent of the lead stories on the evening newscasts came from just three beats—the "Golden Triangle," consisting of the White House, Pentagon, and State De-

---

[17] David Altheide, "Format and Symbol in Television Coverage of Terrorism in the United States and Great Britain," *International Studies Quarterly* 31 (1987): 161–76; Shanto Iyengar, *Is Anyone Responsible? How Television Frames Political Issues* (University of Chicago Press, 1991).

[18] Quoted in Michael Grossman and Martha Kumar, *Portraying the President* (Baltimore: Johns Hopkins University Press, 1981), p. 61.

partment.[19] Despite the fact that the major events of the day were often taking place in Baghdad, Geneva, Kuwait, Riyadh, Moscow, or other overseas locations, the majority of television coverage originated from Washington.

The system of assigning reporters to cover beats known to be newsworthy places a high premium on government organizations and spokespersons as sources of news. The substantial dependence of reporters on official sources has been well established. In Leon Sigal's classic (1973) study of the sources used by *New York Times* and *Washington Post* reporters, over three-fourths of all news stories were based on government sources.[20] This pattern still holds. As one writer describes it,

> For reporters, the most credible information or the hardest data are accounts which come from the "most competent" news sources, who, in turn, are bureaucrats and officials recognized as having jurisdiction over the events in question.[21]

For the contemporary journalist, official announcements, news releases, and government press briefings are the essential ingredients of the "news net." The prominence of official voices in the news has obvious implications for what gets reported. Stories that ignore official sources or run counter to the mainstream ideological consensus (e.g., stories questioning the virtues of free enterprise) are less likely to surface. While there should be no objection to having reporters tell us what government is doing, the objection is that reporters don't dig any deeper. We examine the workings of this system of "deferential journalism" more closely in Chapter 10.

Pack Journalism

Because most reporters depend heavily on the same official sources, they end up reporting the same news. In addition, there is a well-

[19]Timothy Cook, "Domesticating a Crisis: Washington Newsbeats, Human Interest Stories and International News in the Persian Gulf War," presented at the Science Research Council, Seattle, Wash., September, 1991.
[20]Leon Sigal, *Reporters and Officials* (New York: D.C. Heath, 1973).
[21]Mark Fishman, *Manufacturing the News* (Austin: University of Texas Press, 1980), pp. 93–94.

defined pecking order in the journalism profession by which reporters for the most prestigious papers (most notably the *New York Times* and *Washington Post*) act as "leading indicators" of the news. Stories printed in these trend-setting papers often reappear in the network evening newscasts and are circulated by the wire services across the country. This pattern, which is sometimes referred to as "pack journalism," ensures that the media will tend to focus their attention on the same subjects. On the morning of February 10, 1992, for example, the *New York Times* ran a front-page story on the televised advertisements being aired by the presidential candidates in New Hampshire. That evening, Debbie Derzel, the news director of Station KPIX in San Francisco, who had read the *New York Times* story, decided to do a special segment on the local 10 o'clock news dealing with political advertising in the presidential campaign.[22]

Just as pack journalism leads newspapers and television stations to cover the same stories, it also means that they miss the same issues and stories. Although the Pentagon's illegal sales of arms to Iran had been continuing for months, the story was never broken by an American outlet. Rather, American reporters learned of the scandal only after a tiny Lebanese news magazine, *Al Shiraa*, published an exposé.

Audience Considerations

In addition to searching continually for authoritative news, reporters must also design a story that will attract and keep the attention of the audience. For most Americans, politics and government are not high-priority matters. Therefore, reporters must be able to simplify complex events or issues into understandable "stories." They accomplish this by several means—focusing on events that have strong dramatic elements including conflict, suspense, sex, and violence; emphasizing happenings that are out of the ordinary, injecting coherence and structure into events; and covering issues that have some degree of personal relevance and can be made to feature individual participants. Standard "plots" and "scripts" include that of the individual pitted against the bureaucracy, inefficient and wasteful government, and the perils of urban life.

[22] Personal communication with Ms. Debbie Derzel.

The 1991 Senate Judiciary Committee hearings concerning the confirmation of Judge Clarence Thomas for the U.S. Supreme Court epitomized the ingredients of a compelling news story. Professor Anita Hill (a Yale-educated black woman) alleged that Judge Thomas (a Yale-educated black male) had subjected her to sexual harassment at work. The charges involved sexually explicit language; featured a dramatic confrontation between two articulate and credible individuals, both of whom had followed a "rags to riches" life path; and focused on an issue that was personally relevant to many working women (and men). Moreover, the testimony presented in the hearings had the potential to defeat Judge Thomas's confirmation by the Senate. Given these dramatic qualities, it is not surprising that on the first day of the hearings (Friday, October 11) some 30 million households tuned in. On Saturday and Sunday the three major networks were unable to cover the hearings continuously due to the usual weekend fare of sporting events. However, the drawing power of the Hill-Thomas hearings was such that the Public Broadcasting Service (which was the only broadcast outlet to carry every minute of the hearings) was able to attract as many viewers as each of the three commercial networks. Nationwide, the hearings drew a bigger viewing audience than college football, the baseball playoffs, or the National Football League. On Saturday NBC and ABC carried the hearings and received ratings of 26.5, compared to a rating of 9 for CBS, which broadcast the fifth game of the Atlanta-Pittsburgh baseball playoffs.[23]

Fairness and Objectivity

The final consideration in the production of news is a basic professional norm—fairness and objectivity. Ever since the demise of party-controlled newspapers, the news media in America are expected to be nonpartisan. While newspapers and magazines do publish editorials in which particular views or causes can be championed or condemned, news coverage and editorials are considered entirely separate functions, and editorials are segregated in a special section. Reporters are trained to describe events factually and objectively. As

[23]"Hearings Capture Big Audience," *New York Times*, October 13, 1991, A20.

we will see later, there is considerable controversy over the extent to which the news media actually live up to this ideal.

In practice, the norm of objectivity produces what is called "point-counterpoint" reporting. If there are two sides to an issue, the reporter will present both. A news story on extending unemployment benefits for an additional period will include both a discussion of the millions of people whose benefits have expired and who therefore stand to benefit from the extension (the Democratic perspective) as well as a discussion of the cost of the extension (the Republican perspective). If the news report is a backgrounder and includes interpretation and analysis, the individuals interviewed will typically represent both political parties.

To summarize, both the print and electronic media tend to harvest news primarily from official sources. The nature of news tends to differ depending upon the particular medium. Television news is generally packaged in an episodic form designed to maximize audience appeal. Both print and broadcast outlets subscribe to the norms of nonpartisan and ideologically neutral presentation of the news.

Campaign Coverage

In the rest of this chapter we apply these generalizations concerning the production of news to news coverage of election campaigns. Here we show that the "horse race" and "character" are the two most newsworthy aspects of political campaigns and that political reporting closely adheres to the norms of objectivity and fairness.

& CONFLICT

Horse Race Coverage

Parades, balloons, rallies, and candidates mingling with crowds have always been the stuff of campaign news. With the advent of television, these visually absorbing images have become the staples of news coverage. Countless studies of campaign journalism (both print and broadcast) have shown that the news invariably focuses on the campaign as a contest or race. News reports on the candidates' standing in public opinion polls, their advertising strategies, the size of the crowds at their appearances, their fund-raising efforts, and their electoral prospects far surpass coverage detailing their issue positions, ideology, prior experience, or decision-making style. Instead of educating the public on the serious matters of the candidates' qualifications, aspirations, and platforms, the networks "devote most of their election coverage to the trivia of political campaigning. . . . What the viewer watches—the campaign trivia the networks so prominently display—is precisely how the viewer describes and defines the election world he cannot see with his own eyes."[24] While some recent analyses have shown that media critics have exaggerated the dominance of horse race coverage,[25] there can be no doubt that it accounts for a large share of campaign news. As Robinson and Sheehan put it, "Horse race coverage permeates almost everything the press does in covering elections and candidates."[26]

One of the reasons for the prominence of the horse race in the news is that it is relatively easy to cover—or generate. Most of the major news organizations have themselves become public opinion pollsters. This type of information is therefore readily accessible to reporters (in many instances, at the touch of a computer key).

From the perspective of television reporters and editors, horse race coverage is desirable not only because it has "good pictures" and is easy to write, but also because the analysis is relatively concrete. The candidates' electoral prospects—their standings in the opinion polls, fund-raising efforts, delegate counts, and other indicators are objective, unbiased information about the state of the election contest. The horse race is thus one aspect of the campaign that lends itself to objective reporting. However, in recent years television coverage of the horse race has become increasingly interpretive; today news reports frequently include interviews with campaign consultants who explain and often debunk the candidates' image-making activities. Whereas the networks aired 37 such interviews in 1988,

---

[24]Thomas Patterson and Robert McClure, *The Unseeing Eye: the Myth of Television Power in National Elections* (New York: Putnam, 1976).

[25]See, for example, Henry Brady and Richard Johnston, "What's the Primary Message?," in Garry Orren and Nelson Polsby (eds.), *Media and Momentum: The New Hampshire Primary and Nomination Politics* (Chatham, N.J.: Chatham House Publishers, 1987), pp. 127–186.

[26]Michael Robinson and Margaret Sheehan, *Over the Wire and on TV: CBS and UPI in Campaign '80* (New York: Russell Sage Foundation, 1980), p. 148.

not once was a campaign consultant or analyst interviewed on network news during the 1972 campaign.[27]

As news coverage of the horse race aspect of campaigns has become ever more refined, the amount of coverage devoted to the candidates' messages has continued to dwindle. In general, the fast-paced nature of television news means that candidates must be able to condense their rhetoric and speeches into "sound bites"—brief segments of news reports that show the candidates speaking. Candidates strive to come up with attention-getting phrases and catchy punch lines that symbolize their campaign. Candidates who fail to insert "telegenic" material into their speeches simply get less coverage. In recent years, the list of notable sound bites has included "Where's the beef?" (Vice President Walter Mondale criticizing Senator Gary Hart for not being substantive enough during the 1984 Democratic primary); "You're no Jack Kennedy" (Senator Lloyd Bentsen's 1988 put-down of Senator Dan Quayle during the vice-presidential debate), and "Read my lips, no new taxes" (President George Bush's pledge in 1988).

The trend in television news coverage of campaigns has been toward ever shorter and shorter sound bites. In the 1968 campaign the average length of the sound bite was sixty seconds; by 1988 it had shrunk to nine seconds![28] Before we condemn broadcast journalists for failing to present the candidate in his or her own words, it should be noted that newspapers also fail to quote politicians extensively. In a recent *Washington Post* story on the reactions of President Bush and Congressional leaders to the 1990 election, the average quotation consisted of fewer than 10 words.[29]

The continual emphasis on the strategic side of the campaign has crucial consequences for candidates. In presidential campaigns the media seize upon the initial contests, most notably the Iowa caucuses and the New Hampshire primary, as critical early indicators of the eventual outcome. In fact, the volume of news reports devoted to the Iowa and New Hampshire contests is far out of proportion to the

[27] Daniel Hallin, "Sound Bite News: Television Coverage of Elections," *Journal of Communication* (Spring, 1992), forthcoming.
[28] See Hallin, 1992.
[29] G. R. Boynton, "The Disappearing Sound-Bite," *Political Communication Report* (Moorehead, Minn.: Moorehead State University, 1991).

number of delegates at stake in these states. In 1984, for example, the New Hampshire primary received more news coverage than *all* the primaries in the Southern and border states. With less than 3 percent of the national population, New Hampshire and Iowa together accounted for 32 percent of the news coverage accorded the 1984 presidential nomination campaign.[30]

Candidates who fare well in these early contests, because of the large number of news stories they attract, benefit from "momentum"—their campaigns attract large numbers of volunteers and large cash contributions, and their poll ratings shoot up, providing their campaign with significant impetus. Conversely, the press label as "hopeless" those candidates who do poorly in these early primaries, thereby sounding the death knell to their efforts. In between these two extremes are the "plausible" contenders—candidates who have yet to demonstrate that they can win, but who manage second- and third-place finishes (such as Jerry Brown in the 1992 Democratic primaries).

The most important element of horse race coverage during the early phases of the campaign concerns the ability of candidates to surpass journalists' expectations or "seedings" of the contestants' chances. If a candidate who was previously considered merely plausible succeeds in winning a primary, his or her success is even more newsworthy simply because it exceeded expectations. In 1980 Ronald Reagan was the Republican front runner, and George Bush was not given much of a chance for the nomination. However, Bush defeated Reagan in the Iowa caucuses. Immediately, news coverage of the Bush campaign more than quadrupled.[31] The same outcome occurred on the Democratic side in 1984. By placing second in the Iowa caucuses, Gary Hart was suddenly labeled a serious threat to Walter Mondale. Interestingly, Hart, had received only 2,000 votes more than George McGovern (who placed third). But since McGovern had long been dismissed as not being a serious candidate (after his disastrous showing in the 1972 presidential election), McGovern's campaign received virtually no additional coverage. Thus, even though Hart and McGovern received essentially the same level

[30] William Adams, "As New Hampshire Goes...," in Orren and Polsby, 1987, pp. 42–59.
[31] Michael Robinson and Margaret Sheehan, 1980.

of support, Hart became the talk of the nation's reporters while McGovern quickly disappeared from the scene.

The Character Issue

During John Kennedy's brief tenure as president, the American public had no inkling of his numerous extramarital activities. Although Kennedy's appetite for extramarital sex was well known to most members of the Washington press corps, they chose not to report it. (Indeed, many reporters had personally witnessed JFK's encounters with other women.) It was only several years after the assassination of President Kennedy that these facts began to be aired in the national media.

The traditional unwillingness of the press to inquire into the intimate activities of national figures, including presidents, changed dramatically during the 1980s. Because of his near-upset of Walter Mondale in 1984, former Senator Gary Hart was considered the major contender for the 1988 Democratic presidential nomination. However, Senator Hart had a well-known reputation for womanizing, which proved to be his undoing. In response to the various allegations, Hart issued a challenge to the press. "Follow me around. I don't care...about the womanizing question. I'm serious. If anybody wants to put a tail on me, go ahead. They'd be very bored."[32]

The very same day (May 3) that Hart's comments appeared, the *Miami Herald* reported that Hart had spent the previous night in his Washington condo with a young woman from Miami. Reporters from the paper had "staked out" Hart's residence and filmed ex-model Donna Rice entering at night and leaving the next day. The Hart-Rice incident was front-page news for several days thereafter. Later, Hart was asked on national television whether he had "ever committed adultery." (He evaded the issue by responding, "I don't have to answer that question.") From that point, his campaign was history. He withdrew on May 7, 1987, when a reporter from the prestigious *Washington Post* notified his campaign that the paper was about to run a story on his long-standing relationship with a woman in Washington.

---

[32] E. J. Dionne, Jr., "Gary Hart: The Elusive Front Runner," *New York Times*, May 3, 1987, p. A38.

More recently, Arkansas governor Bill Clinton's campaign for the 1992 presidential nomination was dogged by allegations of marital infidelity. Gennifer Flowers, a former state employee in Arkansas, claimed that she had carried on a 12-year affair with the governor. He denied the charge. Ms. Flowers's story initially appeared in a tabloid, but the charges were immediately picked up and repeated in the "respectable" press and all broadcast outlets.

Obviously, the news value of politicians' private lives has become magnified over the past 30 years. Today, the habits, tastes, and other personal traits of public officials are considered fair game for reporters. In recent years, there have been several instances in which the character issue has been injected into presidential campaigns. On the Democratic side, Thomas Eagleton, Geraldine Ferraro, Joseph Biden, Gary Hart, Michael Dukakis, and Bill Clinton have all suffered at the polls because the spotlight was turned on some aspect of their private lives. Republicans have also suffered, as a result of their own or their spouses' transgressions, as indicated by the cases of Richard Nixon, Gerald Ford, Pat Robertson, and Dan Quayle.

Why have the media suddenly become preoccupied with the character issue? In the first place, the norms of campaign journalism have very clearly shifted. In the 1950s and 1960s an incident concerning a candidates's private life was considered irrelevant "unless it seriously impinged on his or her public performance."[33] The reluctance to probe into the closets and bedrooms of politicians was also due to the all-male composition of the national press corps and the resulting locker room view of male behavior. Beginning in the 1970s, more women became journalists, and more correspondents were assigned to cover political campaigns. Moreover, the events of the 1970s, including Watergate and several instances of congressional representatives and senators engaging in particularly bizarre and inappropriate behavior, suggested that personal weaknesses could have political relevance. The intense competition for readers and viewers also created pressure for more revealing and

---

[33]Larry Sabato, *Feeding Frenzy: How Attack Journalism Has Transformed American Politics* (New York: Free Press, 1991), p. 30.

"juicy" news stories.[34] Today, therefore, the candidates' love lives (Gary Hart, Ted Kennedy, Bill Clinton), control over their emotions (Ed Muskie and Pat Schroeder), language (Jesse Jackson, Bob Kerrey), law school records (Joe Biden), avoidance of military service (Dan Quayle and Bill Clinton), and even food tastes (George Bush and broccoli) have all been deemed newsworthy. As the veteran political correspondent Robert Novak has described the prevailing journalistic view, "Private conduct is a road map to public action."[35]

While most of the news about character in recent campaigns has addressed episodes in which candidates appear weak, dishonest, or immoral, reporters also focus (in many cases with the active encouragement of the candidates) on positive traits. At the outset of the 1988 presidential campaign, for example, the Bush campaign was preoccupied with overcoming the candidate's widespread image as weak, subservient, and indecisive—what the press unkindly referred to as the "wimp factor." The nationally televised "encounter" with CBS anchorman Dan Rather on January 25, 1988, an event that many believe had been planned by the Bush campaign, provided Bush with a convenient opportunity to demonstrate that he could not be pushed around.

The day after the nine-minute confrontation, Bush declared that the incident had not been planned in advance and that he was "very happy" with his performance.[36]

Fairness and Objectivity

Campaign news, like all other news, is expected to be nonpartisan and neutral. Almost every candidate, however, complains that he or she is not given as much attention as his or her competitors, that

---

[34]A telling case of the competitive pressures facing reporters is described by Sabato. "*Express-News* columnist Paul Thompson broke a front-page story about Mayor Henry Cisneros' extramarital affair in October 1988. Cisneros had told Thompson of the romance on condition of confidentiality, but Thompson unilaterally violated the ground rule because he feared his rival newspaper was about to publish the story. 'I wasn't going to be shut out on some ethical punctilio,' noted Thompson." (Sabato, 1991, pp. 57–58)

[35]Quoted in Sabato, 1991, p. 83.

[36]*Facts on File*, vol. 48, no. 2462 (January 29, 1988), p. 50. Immediately following the exchange, Bush commented, "The bastard didn't lay a glove on me."

coverage is too negative, and that reporting is distorted, biased, and designed to damage.

Research on campaign reporting has found that the press is, on the whole, neutral toward the candidates.[37] The most systematic study of the content of campaign reporting was carried out by Michael Robinson and Margaret Sheehan during the presidential campaign of 1980. Robinson and Sheehan examined all campaign stories broadcast by "CBS News" and filed by United Press International over the course of the entire campaign. Their findings indicate that news coverage of campaigns is scrupulously objective in the sense that the news conveys information about specific events, occurrences, or statements as opposed to inferences and analyses of these events, occurrences, or statements. Campaign news reports contain little editorial flavor. Robinson and Sheehan also demonstrated that the evaluative tone of campaign reporting (whether the news presented was relatively "good" or "bad") was invariably neutral. Eighty percent of the news reports were neutral.[38]

Robinson and Sheehan's study thus illustrates that the values and norms of public affairs journalism carry over to campaign journalism. Reporters strive to convey hard factual information rather than interpretation and commentary. Of course, as we will see in the next chapter, reporters have considerable discretion in choosing which particular events, occurrences, or statements to cover, and these choices can have profound consequences for candidates. Campaign reporting may be objective, but the consequences of campaign reporting for the candidates is far from neutral.

To conclude, the news is the product of a well-developed system of reporting. This system places a premium on stories that are easy to obtain from sources considered authoritative. Because the news is a product that must attract an audience in order to generate revenue from advertisers, reporters must use presentations that are likely to prove interesting to the audience. Simplicity, clarity, color, and clear story lines are the hallmarks of news reports. These same qualities, of course, are generally absent from the fuzzy and ambiguous world

---

[37] According to a study of the 1972 presidential campaign, "most news stories cannot be coded as favorable or unfavorable to a candidate, a political issue or party." Richard Hofstetter, *Bias in the News* (Ohio State University Press, 1976), p. 50.

[38] Robinson and Sheehan, 1980, chap. 5.

of politics and public affairs. All told, therefore, the news is much more than a simple reflection of the day's main events. It is, rather, a result of multiple choices and decisions by professionals working in a structured environment with well-defined rules, incentives, and expectations.

Suggested Readings

C. Anthony Broh. 1987. *A Horse of a Different Color: Television's Treatment of Jesse Jackson's 1984 Presidential Campaign.* Washington, D.C.: Joint Center for Political Studies.

Peter Clarke and Susan Evans. 1983. *Covering Campaigns: Journalism in Congressional Elections.* Palo Alto: Stanford University Press.

Timothy Crouse. 1972. *The Boys on the Bus.* New York: Random House.

Edward Epstein. 1973. *News from Nowhere.* New York: Random House.

Mark Fishman. 1980. *Manufacturing the News.* Austin: University of Texas Press.

Herbert Gans. 1979. *Deciding What's News.* New York: Vintage Books.

Stephen Hess. 1984. *The Government/Press Connection: Press Officers and Their Offices.* Washington, D.C.: Brookings Institution.

S. Robert Lichter, Daniel Amundson, and Richard Noyes. 1988. *The Video Campaign.* Washington, D.C.: American Enterprise Institute.

Michael Robinson and Margaret Sheehan. 1983. *Over the Wire and on TV.* New York: Russell Sage Foundation.

Larry Sabato. 1991. *Feeding Frenzy: How Attack Journalism Has Transformed American Politics.* New York: Free Press.

Michael Schudson. 1978. *Discovering the News.* New York: Basic Books.

Leon Sigal. 1973. *Reporters and Officials.* New York: D.C. Heath.

Gaye Tuchman. 1978. *Making News: A Study in the Construction of Reality.* New York: The Free Press.

PART II

POLITICIANS

As Americans have become increasingly infatuated with television, the machinery of politics has also changed dramatically. Most importantly, the influence of the political party has steadily diminished. Instead of local party officials and activists, politicians now rely on media consultants, fund raisers, pollsters, and a coterie of political and administrative staffers who work for individual politicians rather than party organizations.

The diffusion of broadcast technology does not by itself account for the fundamental changes in American politics. In other industrialized societies, television is just as developed but exerts much less political clout. In Britain voters can watch their M.P.s in action just as easily as Americans can watch their elected representatives. Yet television is much less important to the careers of British politicians. Why the difference? In Britain political parties still provide the tie that binds voters to politicians; in the United States politicians have become free agents.

Political parties once played a much greater role in American politics. Throughout the nineteenth century and the first half of the twentieth, elected officials were recruited by the parties. Party leaders decided who would run for what office. At the turn of this century, though, a series of "progressive" reforms began to undermine party influence. The introduction of the secret ballot meant that

67

defections from the party could no longer be detected. Likewise, the elimination of party ballots meant that, instead of being limited to a choice between one party's slate of candidates and the other's, voters could choose a particular candidate for each office.

(2) The adoption of the "open" primary in the 1960s and 1970s virtually eliminated party leaders' control over nominations. All a candidate had to do to enter a race was to gather a qualifying number of signatures (usually minimal) on a petition. Judicial decisions requiring that legislative districts be redrawn according to population shifts further weakened the parties by reducing their ability (3) to create (or gerrymander) legislative districts that provided their candidates with electoral advantages. Finally, the adoption of campaign finance regulations further curtailed the parties' influence by (4) eliminating their major source of revenue—donations of more than $5,000.

All these reforms were adopted with the intention of making politics more democratic, less centralized, and more removed from the "smoke-filled room." In fact, political power was successfully transferred from party leaders to individual politicians. Individuals now decide on their own to seek elective office; they raise money, hire staffers, and formulate electoral strategies independently of their parties. Their campaign appeals are targeted at an electorate that is much less committed to party labels. Each candidate develops his or her own message, and electoral success is predicated upon the effectiveness with which the media can be harnessed to cover and transmit the individual candidacy—rather than a party platform—to the voters.

The internal workings of governmental institutions have also reflected these changes. As individual politicians have become more autonomous, they have gained influence within local, state, and national branches of government. The perquisites of holding office have improved; salaries, staff, and even the length of the legislative session have increased as politicians have become more professional and more independent of party organizations. Few legislators regularly vote along party lines. Most prefer to cast their votes in line with their constituents' interests so as to maximize their reelection prospects.

Concomitant with the demise of the political parties, candidates and elected officials have increasingly turned to the mass media to achieve their objectives. In this section we first describe the different media strategies candidates employ to seek electoral victory. We then show how elected officials use the media to bolster their ability to govern.

CAMPAIGNING ON TELEVISION

The importance of the mass media and the growth of television in particular have forced candidates to respond to the routines and incentives of news organizations. Candidates and their staffs devote a great deal of energy to influencing the decisions of reporters and editors. Successful candidates and campaigns also adjust their behavior to exploit the media environment in which they operate.

Many observers have condemned the new style of campaigning through the media as "bad for democracy and the American way." They have written wistfully of an earlier day when campaigns were dominated by strong party organizations.[1] But it is hardly self-evident that the historical emphasis on parties was desirable. For example, the nineteenth-century system of nominations placed a premium on the preferences of party bosses, and candidates had to cultivate relationships with a small number of elites. The system worked to the benefit of those candidates in a position to curry favor with these elites. The former emphasis on social position and political networking did not necessarily produce better statesmen than does today's emphasis on fund-raising and sound-bite skills. Moreover, contemporary alternatives—such as requiring the media to provide free coverage of political statements by candidates—would give the advantage to candidates with good speechwriters and excellent speaking skills. These abilities are neither essential to nor the measure of a good public servant. Thus, although the current system favors candidates who are skilled at fund-raising and "media

[1] Nelson Polsby, *The Consequences of Party Reform* (New York: Oxford University Press, 1983); American Political Science Association, *Toward a More Responsible Party System* (New York: Holt, Rinehart and Winston, 1950).

management," it is not clear that alternative systems would produce better candidates or better government, however defined. All methods of campaigning are biased in one way or another.

One thing is certain, however: Most politicians are rational. When they have to operate in a system that rewards the ability to generate news coverage and paid advertising, they will modify their behavior in ways designed to achieve maximum levels of both.

Of course, some of the most crucial interactions in campaigns are those between candidates and reporters. As we will show in this chapter, campaign organizations seek to "spoonfeed" the press in order to control the news coverage their candidate receives. Journalists react by striving to keep candidates off balance through independent reporting.

The Emergence of Media Campaigns

The widespread use of the mass media in campaigns is relatively new to American elections. Although elected officials have long recognized the power of radio and television as persuasive tools, the mass media had little presence in political campaigns during the first half of this century. Calvin Coolidge, for example, spoke frequently over radio as president, but used the medium on only two occasions during his 1924 presidential campaign.

Two developments led to today's system of media campaigns. First, television had penetrated nearly every household in the country by the beginning of the 1960s. Candidates could reach millions of voters at a time. Moreover, the development of precise audience-rating services allowed candidates to tailor their appeals to particular "target" audiences. Second, and most importantly, the decline of party organizations and the rise of primary elections forced candidates to communicate directly with the voters, making skilled use of the media absolutely essential.

Discovering Television

In 1948, the year that CBS began operating a national television network, it was the railroad and not the television that brought the candidate to the view of the public. President Truman's whistle-stop campaign across the country was credited with swinging the election to the Democrats. In 1952 and 1956 Dwight Eisenhower and Adlai Stevenson experimented with TV and radio advertising, but most of their campaign efforts were conducted through local party organizations.[2]

The presidential election of 1960 was a watershed in the conduct of campaigns. John F. Kennedy was the prototypical TV candidate. His defeat of Hubert Humphrey for the Democratic presidential nomination was an unexpected victory by a political outsider. His performance in a single nationally televised debate with Richard M. Nixon is widely regarded as having decided the general election.

When he declared his candidacy, Kennedy was just a freshman senator from Massachusetts, but the youthful and dynamic image that he projected on the television screen gave him a decided edge over more seasoned contenders for the Democratic presidential nomination. The party insider in 1960 was Senator Hubert H. Humphrey from Minnesota. Humphrey was widely perceived as a "shoo-in" for the Wisconsin primary election. But Kennedy's surprising victory in that state transformed the campaign overnight into a tight race. Later, in the West Virginia primary, Kennedy ran a successful media blitz throughout the entire state. Humphrey and Kennedy squared off in a televised debate. The press interpreted Humphrey's eventual defeat to the Roman Catholic Kennedy in this predominantly Protestant state as a sign of his general electoral weakness. Shortly thereafter, Humphrey bowed out of the race.[3]

The general election provided an even more dramatic display of the arrival of media politics. Late in September, the public was split evenly between Kennedy and the Republican nominee, Richard

---

[2] See Paul David, Malcolm Moos, and Ralph Goldman, *Presidential Nominating Politics in 1952: Volumes 1–5* (Baltimore: Johns Hopkins University Press, 1954); Kathleen Jamieson, *Packaging the Presidency: A History and Criticism of Presidential Campaign Advertising* (New York: Oxford University Press, 1988).

[3] See Harry Ernst, *The Primary That Made a President: West Virginia 1960* (New York: McGraw-Hill, 1962).

M. Nixon. Nixon and Kennedy agreed to square off in a nationally
broadcast debate. Most who heard the debate over the radio felt
that Nixon had, by a slight margin, done a better job. But because
Nixon's appearance was hindered by a lack of make-up and a recent
bout with illness, those who saw the debate on TV overwhelmingly
rated Kennedy the victor.[4]

   The lesson of the 1960 election was heeded, and politicians' use
of the mass media exploded during the coming decades. The portion of national candidates' budgets devoted to televised advertising
nearly doubled over the 1960s, from slightly less than 9 percent
to 16 percent. Televised debates came to be expected in presidential elections. And as state after state switched to primary elections
rather than state party conventions as the method of selecting delegates to the nominating conventions, candidates hired media experts
and campaign consultants to help them negotiate this minefield of
successive primaries. By the close of the decade, campaigns bore
only slight resemblance to those of the 1950s. One victorious consultant, Roger Ailes, declared following the 1970 midterm elections,
"This is the beginning of a whole new concept. This is it. This is
the way they'll be elected forevermore. The next guys will have to
be performers."[5]

Weakening the Parties

During the 1960s and 1970s the presidential nomination process
underwent fundamental changes. In particular, political party leaders lost control over the process through which candidates were
recruited and selected. Following the examples of Wisconsin and
West Virginia, state after state chose to let voters, rather than party
officials, select the parties' nominees through primary elections. In
1968, a full 40 percent of the delegates to the national conventions
were selected through primary elections. By 1976 this figure had
reached 75 percent. See Table 4.1.

---

[4]See Theodore White, *The Making of the President, 1960* (New York: Atheneum,
1961), especially Chapter 4.
[5]Quoted in "Broadcast Spending: No Election Guarantee," *Congressional Quarterly*
(July 30, 1971), p. 1622.

Table 4.1   The Rise of Presidential Primaries, 1912–1992

Year	Democratic Party		Republican Party	
	Number of Primaries	Percentage of Delegates Selected in Primaries	Number of Primaries	Percentage of Delegates Selected in Primaries
1912	12	32.9	13	41.7
1916	20	53.5	20	58.9
1920	16	44.6	20	57.8
1924	14	35.5	17	45.3
1928	16	42.2	15	44.9
1932	16	40.0	14	37.7
1936	14	36.5	12	37.5
1940	13	35.8	13	38.8
1944	14	36.7	13	38.7
1948	14	36.3	12	36.0
1952	16	38.7	13	39.0
1956	19	42.7	19	44.8
1960	16	38.3	15	38.6
1964	16	45.7	16	45.6
1968	15	40.2	15	38.1
1972	21	65.3	20	56.8
1976	27	76.0	26	71.0
1980	35	71.8	35	76.0
1984	30	52.4	25	71.0
1988	37	66.6	37	76.9
1992	37	79.4	39	81.8

Source: Compiled by authors from Congressional Quarterly, *Presidential Elections Since 1789,* 5th ed. (Washington, D.C.: Congressional Quarterly Press, 1991), pp. 12–76.

The primaries had the effect of not only democratizing the parties, but also emphasizing new sorts of political skills. When state conventions, rather than primary elections, were used to select candidates, nominations were the product of coalitions forged within each party. A candidate who got the nod from his party could rely on state and local party leaders to mobilize grass-roots support. Today's system of primary elections, by contrast, emphasizes mass appeal rather than coalition-building. To win the nomination, a candidate needs to construct a campaign organization that can reach and persuade large numbers of primary election voters. In the general elections, politicians can no longer count on party organizations to get out the vote. Most of the local party organizations have withered away, and individual candidates now rely on political "hired guns": pollsters, media consultants, advertising buyers, and professional fund-raisers.

Parallel to the changes that swept the nomination process, gradual reform of the Congress and state legislatures gave individual politicians greater autonomy and increased opportunities to attract news coverage. In the past, legislative proceedings were controlled by party leaders, which afforded junior legislators little opportunity to take positions on issues that drew media attention. But the decentralization of legislative power that has occurred in the U.S. House of Representatives and Senate over the last thirty years has given the typical member of Congress much more leverage. The increasing influence of congressional committees and the gradual professionalization of personal and committee staffs have combined to enhance individual legislators' expertise and authority over issues. When issues arise, the news media now turn to the relevant committee or subcommittee chairman to obtain his statement for the nightly news.

Finally, changes in campaign finance laws have also furthered the domination of individual candidates over party organizations. In the 1970s Congress and many state legislatures enacted comprehensive campaign finance regulations. These rules, which focus on the sources of campaign funds, require candidates to raise their own funds rather than rely on party financing. The Federal Elections Campaign Act (FECA) of 1971 and related amendments in 1974 and 1976 severely limited the parties' ability to tap into their traditional funding sources—wealthy individuals and organizations—and placed restrictions on the amount of money that party committees could donate to candidates. Individuals can give no more than $1000 to a candidate, and no more than $5000 to a political organization. Moreover, an individual's total political donations may not exceed $25,000. Interest groups (such as political action committees) and party organizations may give no more than $5000 to any House or

Senate candidate.[6] In the case of presidential campaigns, the legislation provided candidates matching funds in primary elections and full public financing in the general election if the candidates agreed to a cap on total spending.[7] Finally, the FECA required public disclosure of all campaign expenditures and contributions in excess of $200.

The responsibility for raising campaign cash now lies with the candidates, yet most politicians view fund-raising as the most distasteful part of the job. Campaign finance laws have compounded their difficulties. Imagine the work involved in locating 2,500 people who are willing to give $1000 for a Senate campaign, or 25,000 people who can spare $100 each. The system now rewards candidates who are willing and able to devote days to asking strangers for money. This means that they have little time for other important activities such as learning about issues, meeting with ordinary citizens, and formulating policy proposals. To put it simply, a candidate's schedule is driven largely by the pursuit of money and media.

Campaigning through the mass media has catapulted into prominence since the 1960s. With the diffusion of television, politicians could send their messages to virtually every voter. Changes in the rules of the game placed party leaders in a subservient position and elevated individual candidates into the role of autonomous decision makers. Through effective use of the mass media, these candidates could determine their own electoral fates.

Campaign Strategy $ EVENTS

Campaigns use the mass media to communicate with voters in two different ways: paid advertising and "free press" (news coverage). Campaigns for the most important elected offices in the United States—the House of Representatives, the Senate, the governors'

---

[6]The exceptions are the Democratic and Republican congressional and senatorial campaign committees, which can give up to $17,500 to any campaign, In addition, there is no limit on the total amount of money that political action committees may spend in a given year in support of several candidates.

[7]Candidates qualify for matching funds if they can raise $5000 in each of 22 states in contributions of $250 or less. Candidates who win the nomination of one of the major parties become automatically eligible for full public financing during the general election.

seats, and the presidency—are clearly driven by the quest for advertising and news coverage.[8] These goals determine how the candidate spends his or her time, how the campaign organization is structured, and what key strategic decisions are made by the campaign. The necessity of obtaining both paid and free media forces candidates to emphasize fund raising and the creation of newsworthy activities. The system rewards the candidates who have perfected these "media management" skills.

Paid Advertising vs. News Coverage

The importance of paid advertising and free news coverage varies relative to the circumstances of the particular electoral contest. Two factors are at work. Both are subject to limited influence by the candidates.

The first important factor involves how interested the media are in the race and, therefore, how much coverage they will accord it. When extensive coverage is given to a race, the candidate's press strategy is obviously important; on the other hand, not even the most ingenious press strategy is worth much when reporters decide not to cover the race.

The level of media interest in a particular race depends on some perception of the importance of the race relative to other issues and events competing for news coverage. A presidential campaign usually (though not always) generates considerable interest, both national and local. Most gubernatorial races are given substantial local coverage. A congressional race in a sparsely populated area might generate a great deal of media attention, although similar contests in metropolitan areas are frequently ignored. The relative lack of coverage of congressional elections in major metropolitan

---

[8] Local campaigns have a decidedly different flavor. One study of city council, county supervisor, and school board elections in California found that candidates spent at most 8 percent of their budgets on TV and radio. The handbill and the postal service are still the great communicators in local elections. This is not because candidates for these seats shun the mass media. Rather, it is not efficient for them to attract the attention of the local television news stations. See California Commission on Campaign Financing. *The New California Gold Rush* (Los Angeles: Center for Responsive Government, 1987).

areas is not surprising if one considers the number of congressional districts in major cities (e.g., 19 in New York City).

Clearly, each candidate has some ability to influence the amount of news coverage accorded his race. A "different" or "interesting" contender like former California governor Jerry Brown or Senator Paul Tsongas can attract considerable coverage. Creative press strategies can also be used to increase press attention, but only within limits. The Tsongas campaign was able to attract attention by emphasizing the candidate's lack of telegenic qualities. On the other hand, even the most telegenic and attractive candidate running for Congress in New York City will receive little coverage no matter what he does because congressional campaigns are not newsworthy in the New York media market.

The second variable affecting the relative importance of paid ads and free news coverage is the amount of money available to the candidates. Paid advertisements may not be important in a campaign whose candidate has little or no money to spend, but they can be determinative in well-funded campaigns.

Although candidates have some control over the size of their own coffers, the amount of money that can be raised generally depends on the nature of the race. Even the most productive fund-raisers in the House of Representatives rarely raise more than a moderately credible Senate candidate (see insert on the top fund-raisers in 1990). In presidential contests, federal law limits the amount that can be raised in the primary, and public funding provides equal levels of support for the major parties' nominees. In the general election, therefore, the ability to raise money has no bearing on the amount of TV advertising purchased by a presidential nominee.

In sum, news coverage (and as a result, a campaign's press strategy) tends to be most important when the newsworthiness of the election overshadows the candidates' ability to purchase TV time. Conversely, paid ads are more important in well-funded races that will attract little free coverage. Presidential campaigns (especially during the general election phase) are good examples of inherently newsworthy elections in which paid advertising plays a secondary role. Even though presidential candidates are given millions of dollars to spend, the money buys relatively little air time nationally. However, national and local news outlets provide incessant coverage of the race for several months. In contrast, paid advertising is abso-

Top Ten U.S. House and Senate Fund-Raisers: 1990

Senators	Amount Raised
Jesse Helms (R-NC)	$17,751,029
Phil Gramm (R-TX)	16,142,848
Bill Bradley (D-NC)	12,842,957
Paul Simon (D-IL)	9,504,734
John Kerry (D-MA)	8,016,051
Carl Levin (D-MI)	7,213,583
Tom Harkin (D-IA)	5,682,912
Mitch McConnel (R-KY)	5,419,669
J. Bennett Johnston (D-LA)	4,776,658
Daniel Coats (R-IN)	4,026,572

Representatives	Amount Raised
Richard Gephardt (D-MO)	1,647,415
Robert Dornan (R-CA)	1,615,282
Newt Gingrich (R-GA)	1,538,827
Mel Levine (D-CA)	1,496,790
Jolene Unsoeld (D-WA)	1,297,700
Tom Campbell (R-CA)	1,286,200
Richard Zimmer (D-NJ)	1,227,742
Nita Lowey (D-NY)	1,223,045
Stephen Solarz (D-NY)	1,218,914
Robert Matsui (D-CA)	1,207,843

Source: Federal Elections Commission, *Reports On Financial Activity, 1989–1990* (Washington, D.C.: FEC, 1991).

lutely crucial in contests such as U.S. Senate races in states where television time is relatively cheap. For example, in the 1986 Senate contest in South Dakota, each candidate was able to purchase enough time for the average viewer to see between 150 and 200 ads. Paid advertising is also important in regions where people and the media they rely on are relatively "removed" from the concerns of Washington D.C. (For example, in the 1988 Senate race in California, Los Angeles television stations ran, on average, fewer than five "free" stories on the contest.)

Attracting Media Coverage

Making the news and raising the money needed for advertising are separate but related skills. Successful candidates accomplish both through considerable planning and hard work. In this section we summarize the techniques employed by candidates to attract news coverage and influence the content and imagery of the news.

Pundits and experts like to pontificate about how candidates sell their "spins" and messages. These discussions, however, tend to ignore what is perhaps the most critical element of a successful press strategy: getting reporters to cover the candidate and his or her event.

Getting Reporters to Show Up

Every campaign press aide can tell a painful story about a diabolically clever press conference he conceived that, despite the effort, was not attended by a single reporter:

- A Republican candidate for lieutenant governor of California once assembled a bipartisan group of women leaders to testify to his support for a woman's right to choose, but the event was attended only by the facility's house photographer.
- A Democratic candidate for the U.S. Senate in California once presented his antidrug education program to a group of twenty doe-eyed, irresistible 10-year-old children who couldn't wait to climb in his lap—all for the benefit of one reporter from a small paper who was writing a story on why the press were ignoring the race.

With the possible exception of presidential nominees and primary front-runners, very few candidates are guaranteed a story every time they choose to open their mouths. So the first and most important element of a successful press strategy is getting the reporters to show up. Reporters are human beings, and a successful press strategy takes that into account. If a campaign wants to ensure that a particular issue is covered, the staff must make it easy. Thus candidates routinely hand out copies of their speeches to the press in advance of the appearance, and provide the ubiquitous press release detailing the candidate's schedule of activities and other newsworthy items.

In the task of facilitating coverage, the basics are critical. First, is it easy for the reporters to get there? Even the most picturesque, compelling press conference is doomed to failure if it is scheduled across town during rush hour. Conversely, the dullest, most routine event has a chance of success if it takes place in a generic hotel conference room five minutes from the reporters' desks.

Second, does the event concern a topic that's already in the news? Few things guarantee a successful press event like an ongoing story. Campaign strategists call this "riding the wave." Want to bring attention to the candidate's position on offshore oil drilling? Do it the day after the latest oil spill. Looking for a cheap and easy way to show off your patriotism? Hand out flags to veterans the week after the Supreme Court decides that a law banning flag burning is unconstitutional.

Third, does the would-be story contain an element that directly affects the lives of the media's viewers, listeners, or readers, and is there a local human interest angle? A sweeping antidrug plan is all well and good, but the candidate should make sure that reporters know that there will also be statistics available on the effects of the plan in their city. Better yet, let them know that there will be several people available to talk about how their lives have been ruined by drugs, and how the candidate's plan would benefit them.

Fourth, make sure the event is at a convenient time. Reporters, like the rest of us, have deadlines. Only the expectation of a particularly compelling story would induce coverage of a candidate talking about labor issues at a plant gate at 6:00 A.M. Nor is there much a reporter can do if an event takes place 15 minutes before the print deadline, or after the 5:00 P.M. news has started.

Fifth, given the nature of television news, it is imperative that television reporters are provided with an opportunity for good pictures (as long as this consideration doesn't conflict with the first rule, which relates to ease of access). Want to talk about protecting sea lions from pollution, but the beach is an hour away from the TV stations, and the event doesn't work in a hotel room? Solution: Go to the zoo, which is ten minutes from the TV stations. Zoo managers will appreciate the publicity, and will get the seals to applaud when the candidate has finished talking about protecting their ocean-dwelling kin.

Finally, reporters respond well to special treatment. Offering an exclusive interview with the candidate is a fairly obvious means of courting coverage. Experienced presidential campaign aides testify that merely providing creature comforts can also work wonders. A great deal of campaign time and energy is devoted to ensuring that reporters' hotel reservations are made properly, luggage arrives on time, and that telephone and fax access is available.

Conveying the Campaign's Message

Keeping in mind all of the things that a campaign must do to maximize the coverage of a proposed event, we now turn to the strategies employed to convey a winning message. Campaigns can and do seek to influence the content of news coverage, secure in the knowledge that news coverage will affect the outcome of elections.

There is a saying in some political circles that "any press is good press." Those circles, however, mostly comprise losing candidates and their unemployed former aides. One needn't be a genius to know that not all of Gary Hart's press was good press. Bad press is bad press.   *Focus on 1-2 issues/estab. a theme*

A successful press strategy recognizes that most voters are very removed from politics, cynical about politicians, and barely attentive to the news. In a perfect world, the candidate might wish to have his or her five-point plan to improve K–12 education evaluated on its merits; the successful press strategy, however, tries only to convey the message that the candidate cares about education and will try to do something about it.

Likewise, the active candidate might want voters to know that he or she cares about education, drugs, housing, transportation, senior citizens, the environment, and unemployment. However, the realistic campaign organization knows that if the candidate addresses each of these subjects, the message received by the voters may not be, "This candidate cares about a lot of important things," but rather, "Boy this candidate talks a lot; why doesn't he ever do anything?" So the successful press strategy relies on repetition of a few basic points.

Finally, although an intellectually vibrant candidate may be genuinely involved in the important problems of third world debt, global warming, and the societal consequences of new technologies, the successful candidate's press strategy translates these issues into the everyday concerns of ordinary voters, such as interest rates, unemployment, health care, crime, and bedrock American values. In the same way that the amount of coverage accorded a campaign is in part determined by the importance of the contest, so too is the ability of a candidate to influence the content of the coverage affected by his importance and viability. A candidate for city council may try mightily to call new issues to the public attention; for the most part, however, he will fail. At the other extreme, a major presidential candidate has virtual carte blanche to determine news content, especially in local media outlets. In the 1984 Connecticut primary, for example, the Hart presidential campaign sought to highlight the candidate's concern for the nation's crumbling infrastructure, an important issue in that state at the time. The campaign held its press conference underneath the Mianus River Bridge, which only a few months earlier had collapsed, killing three motorists. Not surprisingly, Hart succeeded in conveying his message in that evening's TV news and the next day's newspapers. (Of course, one can't expect miracles. Had he tried the same event four years later, the only form of transportation up for discussion would have been the good ship *Monkey Business*, on which he was photographed with Donna Rice.)

No campaign understood the basic principles of successful press strategy better than the 1988 Bush team. Their pictures conveyed a clear message: cheering policemen, for example, meant that Bush was tough on crime. The text of messages was kept simple; no new taxes, and my opponent likes criminals. Repetition drove home the points; images of Willie Horton (the Massachusetts criminal who committed a murder while on release through Dukakis's furlough program) and schoolchildren saluting the flag were raised every day. No time was wasted on highbrow esoterica. As the *Columbia Journalism Review* noted, television reporters proved no match for Roger Ailes and Michael Deaver, Bush's press strategists.

"Read my lips. No access. Daily visuals. Simple message." Adhering religiously to that credo, Bush's handlers kept reporters at such a distance that some resorted to binoculars and megaphones. At at least once a day they cast their bait—carefully staged visuals concocted to exploit TV's hunger for lively pictures. With the bait came the hook, the so-called message of the day, usually a barbed one-liner about Dukakis. With astonishing frequency, the networks bit, the hook was set, and TV was running with the Republican message.[9]

Debates

Beginning with the 1960 presidential campaign, debates between the candidates have taken on increasing importance in both primary and general election campaigns. Campaign organizations, with the cooperation of civic-minded interest groups such as the League of Women Voters, have been able to persuade the television networks to cover these confrontations between the candidates (see chronology of televised presidential debates, 1960 through 1988). Not surprisingly, campaign organizations invariably seek to control *every* aspect of the event from the subject matter of the questions to the panel of questioners.[10] As a result, instead of providing the public with an opportunity to witness a relatively spontaneous exchange between the candidates, debates tend to resemble staged press conferences.

From the candidate's perspective, the most important goal in a debate is to avoid the glaring misstatement or blunder. In 1976 President Ford answered a question about foreign policy by asserting that the countries of Eastern Europe were free of Soviet domination. This pronouncement and follow-up commentary earned headline news for days after the debate. As we will see in Chapter 8, this gaffe was damaging to the Ford campaign.

In addition to avoiding gaffes, candidates strive to convey information about their personal qualities. In the 1980 New Hampshire Republican primary, the Reagan and Bush campaigns were embroiled in a dispute over the format of a debate. Because Reagan trailed in the polls, his campaign agreed to pay for a one-on-one debate with Bush. Later, however, the Reagan staff invited all the other Republican candidates to participate (without informing

[9]William Boot, "Campaign '88: TV Overdoses on the Inside Dope," *Columbia Journalism Review* (January/Febraury 1989), p. 24.
[10]See Sidney Kraus, *Televised Presidential Debates and Public Policy*, (Hillsdale, N.J.: Lawrence Erlbaum Associates, 1989).

the Bush campaign). On the night of the debate, Bush discovered that he was not to debate Reagan alone, and refused to participate. When the moderator of the debate (the editor of the *Nashua Telegraph*) attempted to persuade the "uninvited" candidates to leave, Reagan began to argue for their presence. When the moderator instructed technicians to have Mr. Reagan's microphone disconnected, he grabbed the microphone and proclaimed "I paid for this microphone Mr. Green."[11] This incident not only provided Reagan an opportunity to demonstrate that he could be a dominant leader, but also damaged Bush's reputation.[12]

A similar clue about personality was provided voters during the 1988 presidential campaign when CNN anchorman Bernard Shaw (one of the questioners in a televised debate) asked Michael Dukakis:

> By agreement between the candidates, the first question goes to Governor Dukakis. You have two minutes to respond. Governor, if Kitty Dukakis were raped and murdered, would you favor an irrevocable death penalty for the killer?
> *Mr. Dukakis:* No, I don't, Bernard, and I think you know that I've opposed the death penalty during all of my life. I don't see any evidence that it's a deterrent, and I think there are better and more effective ways to deal with violent crime.[13]

The next day many leading commentators and analysts asserted that Dukakis's answer (which failed to refer to his wife) had only served to confirm his negative "iceman" stereotype.

Paid Advertising

In most campaigns for important offices, paid advertising constitutes either the first or second (after news coverage) means for conveying

---

[11] It turns out that Mr. Reagan's line was borrowed from Spencer Tracy in the movie *State of the Union*. Moreover, as Sam Popkin has noted, the moderator's name was Breen, not Green. Popkin, *The Reasoning Voter: Communication and Persuasion in Presidential Campaigns* (Chicago: University of Chicago Press).
[12] See Popkin, 1991, pp. 178–79.
[13] Transcript of debate reprinted in The Congressional Quarterly Almanac (Washington, D.C.: Congressional Quarterly Press, 1988).

a message. But unlike news coverage, paid advertising permits the candidate to communicate with voters without any screens or filters. If a candidate wants to address an issue of stupefying obscurity, he can. If another candidate wants to talk about theories of democracy, that is also possible.

The first political "spots" on television were broadcast during the 1952 presidential election by the Eisenhower campaign.[14] Designed by Rosser Reeves, the advertising campaign ("Eisenhower Answers America") consisted of several spots in which the candidate answered questions from ordinary citizens. To contemporary viewers, these early efforts seem unpolished and unappealing, especially when compared with the slick campaigns produced in the 1980s.

Between 1956 and 1964, the use of televised political advertising spread dramatically. Eisenhower's heart attack in 1956 prevented him from traveling across the country, and the Republican National Committee embarked on an ambitious television campaign designed by two Madison Avenue giants—BBDO and Young and Rubicam. Even though Eisenhower won reelection handily, the Republican advertising campaign had only limited effects on congressional races.

In 1964 the Johnson campaign aired the infamous "Daisy" commercial in which viewers were confronted with a young girl plucking the petals off a daisy while an adult voice counted down to a nuclear explosion. The picture of the girl dissolved to a mushroom cloud and President Johnson's words were heard: "These are the stakes. To make a world in which all of God's children can live, or go into the dark. We must either love each other or we must die."

This ad, which was only aired once, was intended to challenge the policies of opposition candidate Barry Goldwater. The ad captured the attention of the entire nation, and set the stage for the widespread use of "attack" advertising in the 1970s and 1980s.

[14]Of course, advertising has always been part of American campaigns. In many respects, today's television spots are more serious and substantive than the slogans, banners and images used in the pre-television era. For a discussion of the historical evolution of campaign advertising, see Kathleen Jamieson, *Packaging the Presidency: A History and Criticism of Presidential Campaign Advertising* (New York: Oxford University Press, 1984).

Campaign ads have become so important that they are now a common subject of news coverage in and of themselves. Roger Ailes's ad for the successful Republican challenger in the 1984 Kentucky Senate race (which featured a bloodhound attempting to find incumbent Senator Huddleston) was played on the "Today" show. According to the producer of the famous "Willie Horton" spot: "There is so much focus now by journalists on the ads that it is considered a major event of the campaign when you have a press conference to unveil your latest ads. I have known of campaigns that have made ads and only bought one spot but released them in major press conferences to get it into the news."[15] The significant amounts of press coverage devoted to ads today testifies to the importance of political advertising.

The press has come to understand that political advertising constitutes an attempt by the campaigns to circumvent the media and go directly to the voters. In recent years many campaigns have taken advantage of the fact that there are no checks on paid advertising, and have produced ads that were untruthful in essential respects. However, because the right to advertising is protected by the constitutional guarantees of free speech, the ads cannot be banned, no matter how untruthful they might be. Opposition candidates are left with the classic remedy of retaliatory free speech.

 In the most recent election cycles, however, some media groups have tried to reinsert themselves into the process by running analyses of new ads. In the 1990 Texas gubernatorial campaign between Democrat Ann Richards and Republican Clayton Williams, an Austin television station (KVUE) ran several news stories analyzing the ads aired by both candidates. The station's analyses pointed out the numerous distortions, errors, and exaggerations in both candidates' ads. Likewise, in the 1992 New Hampshire primary, the League of Women Voters, the Advertising Council, and the John and Mary R. Markle Foundation jointly sponsored a program in which any person who felt that a candidate's ad was misleading could call a toll-free number to report the ad. Monitoring efforts

---

[15] Randall Rothenberg, "Commercials Become News and the Air Time is Free," *New York Times*, January 8, 1990, p. D1.

such as these are likely to have a positive effect, because campaign organizations know that if they stray too far from the truth, they risk having to deal with headline stories asserting, for example, that "Candidate Smith's ads distort the truth." On the other hand, the new trend toward news coverage of paid advertising may actually increase the payoff from paid advertising by generating a "ripple effect" in the news media. (Voters not only receive the ad's message in the paid time slots, but also see it in the news). The ripple effect tends to reinforce the positions of the better-financed campaigns that are able to run more ads. And because of the importance of paid ads in many races, this guarantees that a greater and greater proportion of news coverage will focus on commercials. For example, in the 1990 California Democratic gubernatorial primary between Dianne Feinstein and John Van de Kamp, the *Los Angeles Times* printed more reports on the candidates' televised spots than on any other aspect of the campaign.

Notwithstanding these recent developments, paid advertising still provides the best means for candidates to deliver an unadulterated message directly to the voters. The only factor that limits a campaigns' ability to communicate via paid advertising is money. As a result, candidates are forced to raise huge sums of money—sometimes in ways suggesting that the political process is being compromised.

Paying for Ads

Expenditures for campaign advertising have grown exponentially over the three decades from 1960 to 1990. In 1990 an estimated $203,000,000 was spent by political campaigns for air time.[16] Today, candidates routinely invest hundreds of millions of dollars in advertising efforts. Most media consultants estimate that an ad must reach the equivalent of 500 GRPs (audience ratings points) to have an impact on the outcome of the election. This means that candidates must make repeated broadcasts, often during prime time. A study of the 1990 elections by the *Los Angeles Times* concluded that

---

[16]Chuck Alston, "Forcing Down the Cost of TV Ads Appeals to Both Parties," *Congressional Quarterly Weekly Report* (March 16, 1991), pp. 647–49.

television advertising "represents the biggest single expenditure for the average Senate campaign."[17] This study also found that more than one-third of the money spent by Senate candidates in 1990 was used for television and radio advertising. In strongly contested races and in larger states, expenditures of $3,000,000 were common.

Among candidates for the U.S. House of Representatives, the average amount spent for television was one-fourth of the total campaign budgets even though many candidates—especially those from large, multidistrict media markets like Los Angeles and New York—spent little. But the real cost of advertising is in fact even higher, because raising money costs money. Fund-raising is an expensive activity, involving staff, meals, entertainment, printing, mail, and phone charges. For example, according to the *Los Angeles Times*, Senator Jesse Helms, of North Carolina, who spent over $5,000,000 on paid advertising in 1990, spent another $10,900,000 on fund-raising—not including fund-raising staff. In total, the cost of advertising and the cost of raising money for the advertising constituted over 86 percent of Helms's campaign budget. This is not an atypical figure. The bottom line is that in order to advertise, candidates must raise money. That simple fact has consequences.

First, candidates are forced to devote most of their time to fund-raising. In an ideal world, one might wish that candidates would spend their time developing policy proposals, speaking with the people, traveling around to see how the voters live, and debating with each other. In the real world, they spend their time raising money.

More significant is the perception (sometimes accurate, sometimes not) that the quest for money forces politicians to engage in activities that are not in the public's best interest. In the 1990s this issue exploded into the public's consciousness with the investigation of the "Keating Five"—five United States senators who accepted campaign contributions from Charles Keating, owner of the bankrupt thrift institution, Lincoln Savings and Loan. Keating was eventually convicted of multiple counts of criminal fraud relating to the management of the institution's funds. The senators were accused of taking a wide range of actions on Keating's behalf. When Lincoln Savings finally collapsed—costing savers and taxpayers

---

[17] *Los Angeles Times*, March 18, 1991, p. A1.

billions of dollars—the senators came under heavy fire. In the case of Democrat Alan Cranston of California, the political heat proved so intense that he announced his retirement. (The official explanation of his decision not to seek reelection was that he was in poor health.)

Numerous other examples abound: It has become commonplace for congressmen to sponsor legislation that provides financial benefits for specific groups who have contributed to their campaigns; congressmen change their policy positions shortly after the receipt of campaign contributions from an interested donor; legislators intervene with government agencies on behalf of campaign contributors; and so on. As Senator Cranston stated in his apology to the Senate: "How many of you, after really thinking about it, could rise and declare you've never, ever helped—or agreed to help—a contributor close in time to the solicitation or acceptance of a contribution. I don't believe any of you could say 'never.' "[18]

Of course, in conflict-of-interest situations like this, legislators defend their actions as being in the public interest and assert that any temporal connection between the receipt of campaign money and their own actions is coincidental or has been misinterpreted. At the very least, a perception problem exists; this is a problem that contributes greatly to the widely held public perception that politicians are crooks, and that government and public policy are controlled largely by wealthy campaign contributors.

Campaign Advertising Strategy

Campaign advertising is an art form; it is difficult to characterize, constantly evolving to match the public's mood, and devoid of any agreement as to what constitutes good or bad, effective or ineffective tactics. There are, however, two basic strategies—both designed to create more votes for the candidate than his opponent(s): (1) delivering positive messages about the candidate and (2) delivering negative messages about the opposition.

At an absolute minimum, advertising efforts are intended to produce high levels of name recognition for the sponsoring candidate. Voting studies reveal that most people cannot *recall* the names of their representatives or the names of the candidates for whom they

[18] *New York Times*, November 21, 1991, p. C19.

voted. Rather, they typically *recognize* the names. The high degree of electoral security enjoyed by political incumbents has been attributed partly to their generally high levels of name recognition.[19] In politics, familiarity may or may not breed affection, but it is usually a necessary condition for support. Some simply refer to this principle as "better the devil you know than the devil you don't know."

Name recognition is especially important at the beginning of the campaign, when politicians must demonstrate their electoral viability if they are to attract financial backing. The fund-raising efforts of candidates who enter the campaign with relatively low levels of name recognition suffer precisely because their relative invisibility is considered an inauspicious omen of their electoral prospects.[20] To avoid this vicious cycle of low recognition and inadequate financial backing, lesser-known candidates tend to invest heavily in recognition spots at the outset of their campaigns—spots that repeat the name of the candidate even to the exclusion of other relevant information. In 1986, for example, Georgia Senate candidate Wyche Fowler, who was generally unknown outside of his congressional district, began his campaign with an ad picturing a schoolgirl who was asked by her teacher to name the Senate candidates: "Wyche Fowler. That's Wyche. Like in Church," she said helpfully.

The influx of huge sums of money into major campaigns has made name recognition a less difficult obstacle to electoral success. With the right amount of funding, even the most obscure challenger can count on high levels of recognition by election day. In 1986, for example, a little-known congressman from California named Ed Zschau began his campaign for the U.S. Senate with recognition levels in the single digits. His first ad simply explained how to pronounce his name. After spending almost $12,000,000, he was nearly as recognized as incumbent Senator Alan Cranston. (Zschau still lost.)

---

[19]See, for instance, Bruce Cain, John Ferejohn, and Morris Fiorina, *The Personal Vote* (Cambridge, Mass.: Harvard University Press, 1987); and Gary Jacobson, *The Politics of Congressional Elections*, 2nd ed. (Boston: Little, Brown, 1985).
[20]See Frank Sorauf, *Money in American Elections* (Boston: Little, Brown, 1988), pp. 197–205.

For many voters, recognition of a candidate's name or realization that he or she is the incumbent may be a sufficient basis for voting in favor of that candidate. (During times when the public is unhappy and yearning for change, though, familiarity and incumbency may be grounds for *not* voting for the incumbent.) The majority of the electorate, however, must be convinced. The goal of persuasion may be accomplished through either positive or negative appeals. Through *promotional* spots, candidates attempt to strengthen their personal image or associate themselves with popular policies and favorable outcomes. Through *attack* spots, candidates attempt to propagate a negative personal image of their opponents or to associate them with unpopular or failed policies.

Promotional and attack spots typically focus on candidates' positions on major issues, their personal characteristics, or their track record in public office. During the 1990 gubernatorial campaign in California, for example, both candidates (Republican Pete Wilson and Democrat Dianne Feinstein) aired ads on the issues of crime and the environment (both of which matter to Californians), attacked each other's integrity and sincerity, and extolled (or condemned) their performances as mayors of San Diego and San Francisco, respectively.

When advertising on political issues, it is generally accepted that candidates should play to their own strengths and their opponents' weaknesses. That is, advertising should capitalize on voters' stereotypes of the political parties. Democrats, for example, are better off advertising their support for jobs programs and equal opportunity because the public generally regards the Democratic position on these issues as preferable to the Republican position. Applying this logic, it made sense for George Bush to associate Dukakis with Willie Horton and prison furloughs because the Republicans "own" the issue of law and order (i.e., they are perceived as being tougher on criminals than Democrats). The same argument extends to personality or image advertising. A candidate who is generally regarded as competent should emphasize this trait. A candidate running against an opponent with significant liabilities in his personal background (such as Senator Ted Kennedy) should highlight his own commitment to "family values" and high ethical standards.

Typically, campaign organizations conduct extensive research to determine which appeal will be most effective. A small group of voters is recruited and shown alternative ads that have been developed on the candidate's behalf. The voters are then asked to respond to the ads, and are tested for changes in their attitudes toward the candidates. These "focus group" studies suggest that voters are particularly responsive to negative advertising. When shown a positive ad touting Candidate A's accomplishments, many subjects will say "if he really did that, why haven't I heard about it?" and dismiss the information. But when shown a credible negative ad about Candidate B's votes against senior citizens, the typical response will be: "Boy, I hate those negative ads. But I'm not surprised that Candidate B hates seniors, and I'll never vote for him because of it."

There are any number of ways of presenting positive and negative statements through advertising, but some methods are special favorites. Here are some examples of the positive and negative genres produced by two prominent Democratic media consultants.

Positive Ads

1. *Success story* (for Senator Quentin Burdick, North Dakota Senate race, 1986).

    ANNOUNCER: The Highway Bill was making its typical trip through the Senate this year, making stops at the usual places, but it had to make a little detour on its way to the big hoedown—right across Senator Burdick's desk. Burdick's the new chairman that wrote the bill; so on its way, the bill picked up $400 million and 7,000 new jobs for a little state by the name of North Dakota. And the Senator said, "Drive safely, but drive 65."

2. *One of us* (for Senator Dan Akaka, Hawaii Senate race, 1990).

    AKAKA: I'm not the world's fastest talker, but fast talk is no substitute for commitment. That I have for Hawaii's working men and women. I have a reputation as a nice man. But I won't back down when it comes to fighting for Hawaii. I love our state and our people too much. My opponent says she has the ear of the president. But I have the people of Hawaii in my heart.

3. *Testimonial* (for Senator Tom Daschle, South Dakota Senate race, 1986).

WOMAN: It's my home. It's my way of life. I don't want another way of life. I feel like somebody's trying to force me off of my place.

ANNOUNCER: Ronnie and Eve Melius, like many farmers, are fighting to hang on.

WOMAN: PCA called our loan, and wouldn't give us any living expenses. I got really upset, and I called Tom Daschle's office, and they intervened for me, and the next thing we knew, we had a check in the mail, to pay at least half of the electric bill, so we could keep our electricity on.

ANNOUNCER: They've been forced to sell livestock, equipment, and part of their land.

WOMAN: We're here to stay, and we're fighting any way we can. I just wish there were more like him. I wish there were more people that cared, like Tom Daschle does.

Negative Ads

1. *Bad record* (for Senator Carl Levin, against Bill Schuette, Michigan Senate race, 1990).

ANNOUNCER: Hazardous chemicals. On the job, in our air and water. Yet Congressman Bill Schuette has voted against forcing companies to warn workers about exposure to dangerous chemicals. Schuette even voted to allow corporations to hide the release of toxic emissions. Why would he vote this way? Could it be Schuette's million dollars in Dow Chemical stock, or maybe he just doesn't understand the problems of working men and women? Either way, Bill Schuette's record could be hazardous to your health.

2. *Flip-flop* (for Senator Frank Lautenberg, against Millicent Fenwick, New Jersey Senate race, 1982).

ANNOUNCER: Millicent Fenwick refused to debate Frank Lautenberg before the *New York Times*. That seems strange. That is, until you look at her record. Fenwick needs to debate herself. Immediate nuclear freeze—for and against. Social security—against cuts, and then for cuts. The list goes on. If Millicent Fenwick will not agree to debate Frank Lautenberg before the *New York Times*, maybe she will at least agree to the Fenwick-Fenwick debate. Frank Lautenberg. New Jersey first.

3. *He's the devil* (for Senator Frank Lautenberg, against Jim Courter, New Jersey Senate race, 1988).

ANNOUNCER: These toxic waste barrels are on land owned by Jim Courter. They pollute local drinking water, and Courter failed to clean them up. So the state had to order the cleanup. Jim Courter has the worst environmental record of any New Jersey congressman. The worst. Courter even votes against protecting our drinking water from toxic waste. Like his. Imagine. It's almost unbelievable. A candidate for governor with toxic waste barrels on his own property.

4. *Hoisted on his own petard* (for Ann Richards, against Clayton Williams, Texas gubernatorial race, 1990).

ANNOUNCER: Clayton Williams in his own words: He called himself, quote, an anti-environmentalist. On rape, "it's like the weather; if it's inevitable, relax and enjoy it." On his campaign strategy, "I'll head and hoof her and drag her through the dirt." On Ann Richards: "I hope she didn't go back to drinking again."

ANNOUNCER: Governor Williams?

In general, research by campaign consultants finds that the public holds politicians in low esteem, and that they are more willing to believe negative information about particular candidates than positive information. In addition, focus group research suggests that negative ads are more memorable than positive messages. For these and other reasons, campaign consultants consider attack spots more cost-effective than promotional spots, and their usage has intensified in recent years.

This hostile style of campaigning has intensified criticism of the political process. The critics suggest that negative advertising increases the likelihood of voter manipulation, and contributes to widespread voter disenchantment with the entire political process. But for obvious reasons, campaigns rely on whatever seems to be most effective.

When confronted with a negative ad, the candidate under attack has four options:

1. Defend against the charges. ("That wasn't a vote against senior citizens. It was a vote for taxpayers. My own mother is on Social Security, and I'd never do anything to hurt her. Or you.")
2. Counterattack on the same issue or on one that voters care about even more deeply. ("My opponent coddles criminals, especially ones who prey on the elderly.")
3. Attack the credibility of the opponent. ("You've probably seen those disgusting negative ads my opponent is running. Well, did you know that when he was in college, he lied about his high-school grades. So how do you trust *anything* he says?")
4. Ignore the attack. ("Here's my four-part plan for addressing the federal deficit.")

The conventional wisdom among campaign experts is that the first three options can work, if handled properly. But the final course is generally considered a prescription for failure. Michael Dukakis's 1988 presidential campaign illustrates the fallacy of taking the high road. Under attack from George Bush for releasing dangerous criminals, failing to clean up Boston Harbor, being ignorant about foreign policy, and vetoing a bill requiring Massachusetts school children to salute the flag, Dukakis responded by offering a variety of economic prescriptions. His 17-point lead in the polls disappeared, and he was trounced by Bush on election day. Now Michael Dukakis serves mainly as an example of what happens when a candidate fails to respond in kind to negative attacks.

Running the Campaign

It should come as no surprise that the rise of media-based campaigns has changed the nature of the campaign organization and produced a new breed of campaign managers who are adept at manipulating televised advertising, press relations, polling, and fund-raising. Although there is no universal system for organizing a campaign's advisors and staff, the typical campaign is directed by a relatively small circle of people: the candidate, the campaign manager, the pollster, the media consultant, the press secretary, and sometimes, an additional general consultant. Very often, most of the members of this group are relatively unfamiliar with the candidate, having been hired just for the current campaign. Usually, the majority of the group will also be working for several other candidates running for other offices. In other words, most campaigns are directed by people who have considerable professional experience in conducting campaigns but little or no long-term involvement with the candidate.

The result is sometimes a strategy that is at odds with the candidate's past. In 1992, for example, presidential hopeful Bob Kerrey hired a media consultant whom he had met only once or twice. The consultant prepared a TV ad featuring Kerrey in support of a "tough" trade policy that retaliated against countries who put up barriers to American exports. The consultant had successfully used a similar approach with a previous client in 1988. But in this case, the consultant did not research the issue sufficiently to discover that the message did not square with Kerrey's actual voting record in the

Senate. The ad was widely discredited, causing political embarrassment.

In the era of media politics, no serious campaign is without its consultant. Political consulting is lucrative, and consulting firms have proliferated in the last two decades. Most consultants who work on major races are headquartered in Washington and tend to specialize in either Democratic or Republican campaigns. Prominent Republican consultants in the 1980s were Roger Ailes (widely credited with perfecting the attack ad) and Robert Teeter (who is closely associated with George Bush). On the Democratic side, the list includes Robert Squier and Frank Greer.

Consulting is big (if sporadic) business. Media consultants command as much as 15 percent of the value of their candidates' TV "buys" as well as a fee of $20,000 to $75,000 for producing and placing the advertisements. (In a large state the TV buy for a major candidate can range from $1,000,000 to $5,000,000.) Fund-raising consultants often work on a commission, and may also draw large payments. But campaign work is seasonal—there are relatively few elections in odd-numbered years—and there are no guarantees of work. An attractive statewide race can attract bids from as many as a dozen of these entrepreneurs, most of whom will be turned away.

The prominent role played by campaign consultants has led to questions about whether they have become more important than the candidates. In one highly publicized instance, Democratic consultant Clint Reilly "fired" his candidate, California gubernatorial candidate Dianne Feinstein. It has also become common for consultants to criticize their clients in the press. Understandably, some observers have cited these examples as proof that candidates are nothing more than "products" to be shaped, managed, and directed by their consultants.

Although there is some truth to these observations, the role played by the consultants is more likely to be determined by the individual candidates. Some candidates cede substantial discretion and authority to their consultants, and willingly deliver any message created by them. Other candidates cede nothing, and insist on retaining authority on all issues. Most candidates, of course, fall somewhere in between.

Summary

The modern campaign has largely evolved into a hunt for "money and media." Candidates have developed sophisticated strategies for pursuing news coverage, aggressively using techniques that will draw reporters and encourage them to file flattering reports. Candidates spend much of their time pursuing either "free media" or soliciting money to raise funds to purchase paid media. The constant need to raise funds can lead to the appearance, if not the fact, of impropriety.

The battle over paid media is fought in 30-second increments. More often than not, the victor is the candidate who is best able to condense his or her message into something that the average voter—who is far removed from politics, and usually hates commercials—will remember and care about. Out of necessity, such circumstances force candidates to highlight easily absorbed negative messages about the opponent. The consequences of these trends for the state of governance and leadership in America will be explored in Chapter 9.

Suggested Readings

Herbert Alexander. 1984. *Financing Politics*. Washington, D.C.: Congressional Quarterly Press.

American Political Science Association. 1950. *Toward a More Responsible Party System*. New York: Holt, Rinehart and Winston.

Christopher Arterton. 1985. *Media Politics: The News Strategies of Presidential Campaigns*. Lexington, Mass.: D. C. Heath.

James Barber, ed. 1978. *Race for the Presidency: The Media and the Nominating Process*. Englewood Cliffs, N.J.: Prentice-Hall.

Susan Casey. 1986. *Hart and Soul: Gary Hart's New Hampshire Odyssey—and Beyond*, Concord, N.H.: NHI Press.

Edwin Diamond and Stephen Bates. 1988. *The Spot: The Rise of Political Advertising on Television*. Cambridge, Mass.: M.I.T. Press.

Jack Germond and Jules Witcover. 1989. *Whose Broad Stripes and Bright Stars?* New York: Warner Books.

Gary Jacobson. 1985. *The Politics of Congressional Elections*. Boston: Little, Brown.

Kathleen Jamieson. 1984. *Packaging the Presidency: A History and Criticism of Presidential Campaign Advertising*. New York: Oxford University Press.

Nelson Polsby. 1983. *The Consequences of Party Reform*. New York: Oxford University Press.

Larry Sabato. 1981. *The Rise of Political Consultants*. New York: Basic Books.

Frank Sorauf. 1988. *Money in American Elections*. Boston: Little, Brown.

Paul Taylor. 1990. *See How They Run*. New York: Alfred A. Knopf.

Theodore White. 1961. *The Making of the President, 1960*. New York: Atheneum.

New Styles of Governing

"GOING PUBLIC"

The emergence of television news as the major source of information about American public life has not only affected how candidates run for public office; it has also created new strategies of political leadership. In the pre-television era, politicians attempted to govern by accommodating broad coalitions of groups and interests within the rubric of the political party, and by engaging in personal negotiations and diplomacy with rival elites. An "insider" strategy of leadership prevailed.

But political leadership in the age of television places a much greater premium on the ability to mobilize and wield public opinion. When two political figures clash over policy direction, more often than not, the winner will be the one who has the public's backing. Ultimately, policy winners are those who are best able to use rhetoric, imagery, and appearance to cultivate public support for their positions. This is the strategy of "going public." As Theodore Lowi has described this new brand of leadership at the White House: "Presidents spend the first half of their terms trying sincerely to succeed according to their oath and their promises. They devote the second half of their terms trying to create the appearance of success."[1]

The reason that politicians rely on public support to reach policy goals is simple. The decentralization of the political process has meant that public opinion is the critical determinant of political influence. By appealing directly to the public, elected officials hope to enhance their ability to negotiate and bargain with political ri-

[1]Theodore Lowi, *The Personal President: Power Invested, Promise Unfulfilled* (Ithaca, N.Y. Cornell University Press, 1985), p.11.

vals or competitors. Though this tendency is most apparent in the conduct of the presidency, the new concept of leadership has also been adopted by senators, representatives, and governors. Popularity is tantamount to credibility. To be liked by the public is a critical indicator of a leader's political reputation and staying power. As a noted scholar of the presidency, Richard Neustadt, has pointed out, a president's prestige in Washington depends upon his standing with the public.[2] The president's main source of power, said Neustadt, is his ability to persuade. In the age of television, the ability to persuade is directly linked to the ability to mobilize public support. A popular president (such as Ronald Reagan in his first term) inspires fear and respect, and enjoys considerable leverage over senators, representatives, bureaucrats and other relevant political actors. An unpopular president (such as Jimmy Carter), by contrast, becomes little more than a convenient target for everyone else in the political arena.

The Reagan presidency provides ample evidence of the connection between popularity and presidential influence. Facing a House of Representatives controlled by Democrats, President Reagan proposed a 1981 budget containing massive cutbacks in social welfare programs and huge increases in defense spending. The administration's formula for winning over congressional Democrats was to mount a public relations campaign in which Reagan's immense popularity was used to exert strong political pressure on members of Congress to vote for the president's budget. President Reagan made numerous trips and speeches across the country promoting his budget. A favorite theme of his rhetoric was that his proposed cuts in social welfare spending would not affect the "truly needy." He also attacked the Democrats for attempting to interfere with his "mandate" from the people, and urged citizens of all political stripes to convey their support for the Reagan budget to their representatives. Quoting Teddy Roosevelt, President Reagan made the threat of electoral defeat quite explicit in one of his addresses: "The American people are slow to wrath, but when their wrath is kindled, it burns like a consuming flame."[3]

[2] Richard Neustadt, *Presidential Power: the Politics of Leadership* (New York: John Wiley & Sons, 1960).
[3] Samuel Kernell, *Going Public: New Strategies of Presidential Leadership*, (Washington, D.C.: Congressional Quarterly Press, 1986), p. 117.

The president's numerous appearances around the country invariably included catchy phrases and colorful imagery designed to be easily transferrable into sound bites for evening newscasts. Interest groups and citizens were mobilized to call their representatives, and the White House kept the press updated on the number of calls and telegrams in support of the president's budget. In one case, a wavering congressman received some one hundred calls from businessmen in his district within the span of 24 hours. As David Gergen, President Reagan's director of communications described the administration's methods:

> We learned about it [the impending congressional vote on the budget resolution] the next day. Reagan was flying off to Texas, I was back at the White House, and we worked it out by sending statements to the plane for Reagan to make a planeside statement in time to get it on the evening news. We wanted to give it hype, to elevate the issue on the evening news so that the nation was getting a message. We were calling the press and doing whatever we could to build the issue. At the same time, the political office went to work, notifying all their allies around the country, bringing the calls and pressure onto Congress as quickly as possible by telling them it's really important for Reagan.[4]

The strategy paid rich dividends; despite the political odds against the president—the large Democratic majority in the House, the radical shifts in government spending priorities contained within the budget, and shrewd legislative maneuvering by the House leadership designed to make it difficult for Democratic representatives to defect—Reagan's budget passed.

President Reagan's budget victory is by no means atypical. In general, the more popular the president, the more frequently he gets what he wants from Congress. Douglas Rivers and Nancy Rose have examined every incumbent president's success rate with Congress between 1954 and 1974.[5]

They found that, even after adjusting for factors such as the partisan composition of the Congress, more popular presidents were

[4]Mark Hertsgaard, *On Bended Knee: the Press and the Reagan Presidency* (New York: Farrar, Straus, Giroux, 1988), p. 120.

[5]Douglas Rivers and Nancy Rose, "Passing the President's Program: Public Opinion and Presidential Influence in Congress," *American Journal of Political Science*, 29 (1985), pp. 183–196.

able to get Congress to enact a higher proportion of their legislative proposals. On average, an increase of eight points in the president's approval rating boosted the success rate by 2 percent. The authors concluded that "public opinion is an important source of presidential influence."[6]

The Public Presidency

Contemporary presidents are at the center of national events and issues. The president is not only inherently newsworthy, but also equipped with a potent arsenal for managing the flow of news. His rhetorical weapons include presidential speeches and addresses. He can manufacture "instant news" by holding press conferences, news briefings, "photo opportunities," private interviews, and a variety of official ceremonies. Through careful allocation of these resources, the president can wield considerable influence over what Americans see and hear about the state of their country, and when this information will be covered.

When delivering a nationwide adddress on the environment, for example, the president knows that the topic of the environment will be particularly interesting to editors and reporters and that the public will be exposed to a steady stream of news reports on environmental problems. One study demonstrated that a presidential speech on a given issue can generate as many as 10 network news reports concerning that subject.[7] That coverage (as we will see in Chapter 7) serves to boost public concern about the issue in question.

Conversely, the administration can also arrange to shield the public from particular information. By requiring the Bureau of Labor Statistics to release the monthly unemployment statistics on Friday morning (the day on which the network newscasts have the smallest audience), the administration minimizes any adverse effects of this particular piece of "bad news."

[6]Rivers and Rose, 1985, p. 194.
[7]Roy Behr and Shanto Iyengar, "Television News, Real-World Cues, and Changes in the Public Agenda," *Public Opinion Quarterly*, 49 (1985), pp. 38–57.

Organizing the News

The new style of presidential leadership has brought about significant changes in political management and staffing at the White House. The president's many media and communication-related activities have to be organized and coordinated. In fact, a good index of the transformation of presidential leadership is the number of offices and personnel within the executive branch whose principal responsibilities concern the dispensing of publicity and information. Herbert Hoover's staff of 37 people included but one assistant for press relations. Since Hoover's time, the White House staff has expanded to 380 full-time employees.[8]

Located within the executive office of the president is the command center of the administration's media management activities—the White House Press Office. Headed by the press secretary, this office is responsible for coordinating the production of information from hundreds of executive agencies and offices. Given the vast quantities of information involved, the different forms in which information is released, and the large number of "spokespersons" for the federal government, coordination is often a herculean task. Despite the Press Office's efforts to make the administration speak with "one voice," the press secretary and his assistants are often called upon to explain and reconcile inconsistencies in statements or speeches by prominent members of the administration.

The Press Office prepares the president's daily news summary—a brief description of the newspaper headlines and network newscasts. This is designed to give the president a "pulse" of what reporters and editors are talking about. The summary is intended to be generally objective (rather than an exercise in "wishful thinking") and to give the president and his advisors ideas for responding to particular news items.

The Press Office is also the administration's immediate contact point with the army of reporters who cover the presidency. It issues reporters' credentials (without which they have no access to the White House), maintains facilities (telephones and fax machines for print reporters, sound booths and transmissions equipment for

---

[8]Gary King and Lyn Ragsdale, *The Elusive Executive* (Washington, D.C.: Congressional Quarterly Press, 1988), p. 205

television crews), and conducts a daily press briefing at which the press secretary answers questions. This briefing is often the major source of "hard" news for the press, especially during periods when the president sees fit to avoid public appearances and statements (as was the case with President Nixon during the Watergate investigation and President Reagan following the Iran-Contra disclosures).

On occasion, the administration may arrange for reporters to be given background briefings on a particular event or issue. On occasion these informal sessions between reporters and spokespersons for the administration are "off the record," meaning that the reporter cannot use the information at all. More typically, the information is considered "background only," meaning that it can be attributed to senior officials.

The press secretary's functions often make him (a woman has yet to be appointed) tread a fine line between "public relations" and "facts." As a member of the president's staff, he is expected to interpret events with the appropriate "spin" in order to make the administration look good. By doing so, however, he risks arousing the wrath of reporters who do not appreciate being misled. In some situations, political pressures result in serious damage to the Press Office's credibility. When the White House bypassed the Press Office in an effort to keep the impending invasion of Grenada secret, the daily briefings were necessarily inaccurate. Later, Les Janka, the foreign affairs assistant to Press Secretary Larry Speakes, saw fit to resign.[9]

In addition to the press secretary, the assistant to the president for communications is also a major participant in presidential communication. The person filling this position is usually a member of the president's "inner circle." Typically the job is given to someone who has worked on the president's campaign.

The press secretary is primarily a liaison with reporters and a dispensor of information. The assistant to the president, on the other hand, is more of a strategist whose role is to design the president's media schedule and stage the president's television appearances. Gerald Rafshoon, President Carter's adviser, for example, decided that when the president traveled he would be seen carrying his own bags. This was thought to project the image of "a man of the people." (According

[9]Cited in Mark Hertsgaard, 1988, p. 233.

to *New York Times* columnist William Safire, however, the president's bags were actually empty.) The assistant's other responsibilities include speechwriting, facilitating television coverage of the president's schedule, and providing advance publicity for daily presidential activities.

In summary, the management of information has become a crucial function of the White House bureaucracy. Through the actions of the White House Press Office and related organizations, the administration attempts to orchestrate the news so as to present the public with information that consistently depicts the president in a favorable light. In the rest of this chapter, we discuss two of the most effective methods of presidential media management—the presidential speech and the press conference—and show how both have evolved in response to changing styles of presidential leadership. We conclude by considering the political risks and benefits of "going public."

Presidential Speeches

For Americans who grew up in the latter stages of the twentieth century, the spectacle of the president making a public speech is routine. But the frequent use of public rhetoric by presidents is in fact a relatively recent phenomenon and represents a distinct break with traditional views of presidential leadership. The framers of the Constitution feared demagoguery and believed that the use of rhetoric by the president would weaken the legitimacy of the office by injecting undue passion into national affairs. Deliberation with members of the other branches of government—rather than direct rhetorical appeals to the masses—were intended to be the hallmarks of presidential leadership. Even that master of oratory, Abraham Lincoln, saw fit to make very few speeches while in office. On those occasions when presidents did engage in public rhetoric, their audience was primarily Congress and not the mass public.[10]

---

[10]Symptomatic of the political norms of the day, when Congress brought charges of impeachment against President Andrew Johnson, one of the charges was that Johnson "made and delivered with a loud certain intemperate, inflammatory and scandalous harangues ... [and was] unmindful of the high duties of his office and the dignities and proprieties thereof." Quoted in Jeffrey Tulis, *The Rhetorical Presidency* (Princeton, N.J.: Princeton University Press, 1987), p. 91.

Whereas only 7 percent of speeches by nineteenth-century presidents were addressed to the American people, twentieth-century
presidents have spoken to a national audience in 41 percent of their
speeches.[11] Moreover, presidential speech in the nineteenth century
was largely ceremonial as opposed to persuasive or partisan in objective.

The rise of rhetorical leadership can be traced to Teddy Roosevelt,
who used his considerable oratorical skills and strong personality to
galvanize public support for his policies. One of Roosevelt's major
successes with his "bully pulpit" approach was congressional passage
of the Hepburn Act—a bill establishing regulatory control over the
railroads. Woodrow Wilson continued Roosevelt's lead and initiated
the practice of delivering the annual State of the Union Address to
Congress in person. (Previously it had been read by a clerk.)

Technological advances provided a further impetus to the prominence of presidential communication. With the invention of radio,
presidents were able to speak to the entire nation on short notice,
as FDR did in his famous "fireside chats." With the advent of television, of course, the rhetorical reach of the presidency increased
still further. Today, when speaking to the nation during prime time,
the president has a potential audience of more than one hundred
million Americans.

The gradual increase in the level of presidential speech making
can be seen in Table 5.1, which traces the average number of national
speeches and press conferences made each month by presidents from
Harry Truman to George Bush. Eisenhower was the least locquacious
president, speaking on average once every three days. Ford was the
most voluble, making more than one speech every day. The trend is
clearly in the direction of more frequent speech making: whereas Truman, Eisenhower, Kennedy and Johnson averaged 18 speeches per
month, later-day presidents have averaged 28 speeches.

The fact that presidents make speeches frequently does not, in
and of itself, mean that they are heard or seen by the ordinary
citizen. The president who wishes to mobilize public opinion in
favor of his legislative proposals needs to get his message to as many
people as possible. A more meaningful indicator of the importance

[11]Tulis, 1987, p. 138.

Table 5.1 National Presidential Speeches and Press
Conferences from Truman to Bush

	Major Presidential Speeches	Press Conferences
Truman	15	160
Eisenhower I	21	99
Eisenhower II	20	94
Kennedy	15	65
Johnson	23	132
Nixon I	23	30
Nixon II	13	9
Ford	12	41
Carter	17	59
Reagan I	20	23
Reagan II	20	30
Bush	16	45

Source: Compiled by the authors from the *Congressional Quarterly Almanac*, years 1947 to 1991.

presidents attach to shaping public opinion, therefore, is the number of *nationally broadcast* (radio or television) presidential speeches. Presidents are increasingly aiming their speeches at the whole country. Ronald Reagan is the undisputed leader among recent presidents in this category. With his regular Saturday radio addresses, Reagan reached a national audience once a week. In contrast, Eisenhower was seen or heard nationwide less than once a month.

Which issues dominate the content of presidential rhetoric? Given the nature of the office, it is not surprising that foreign policy and the economy are the most frequently raised subjects. In fact, presidential speeches that address issues other than foreign policy or the economy usually indicate the onset of some major event or crisis. President Johnson addressed the nation on civil rights following the Detroit riot, and President Carter spoke on the energy crisis in the aftermath of the OPEC oil boycott of the United States in 1979.

Press Conferences

Like the presidential speech, the nature of the press conference has evolved in response to changes in technology and strategies of leadership. However, the political incentives to engage in nationally broadcast speeches have increased, whereas the reverse pattern applies to press conferences. Contemporary presidents have become much less willing to subject themselves to the rigors of regularly scheduled press conferences. The rate of presidential press conferences has declined steadily since the 1930s and 1940s. Presidents Nixon, Ford, Carter and Reagan held, on average, less than one press conference every month. However, President Bush has shown some signs of reversing this trend—Bush averages between one and two conferences per month.

Prior to the development of the press conference, presidents made news primarily by granting private interviews to individual reporters or editors. Teddy Roosevelt attempted to "collectivize" these interviews by increasing reporters' access to the White House while simultaneously insisting on full presidential control over what they could report. In particular, Roosevelt demanded that reporters not reveal the source of their information; those who failed to abide by the rule of confidentiality were subject to severe sanctions including exclusion from future meetings.

The practice of maintaining tight presidential control over the press was continued by Roosevelt's successors. President Harding imposed the additional requirement of written questions submitted in advance, while President Coolidge prohibited reporters from quoting the president. As a result, relations between the Washington press corps and the White House grew strained. Reporters increasingly began to complain about presidential censorship and their inability to get the news.

Presidential-press relations changed dramatically under Franklin Roosevelt. The president abolished most of the unpopular restrictions on reporters (including the written question rule and the prohibition on attributing comments to the president) and increased the frequency of the press conference to twice weekly. Under FDR's system, the press conference became the major source of news. The president used the press conference to announce major policy initiatives and to convey his views on current controversies. Moreover, the president's comments were generally presented and timed so as to maximize their newsworthiness, thus facilitating the reporters' task of "selling" their stories to their editors. The unparalleled significance of the press conference as a forum of presidential communication during FDR's tenure can be seen by the fact that Roosevelt conducted more press conferences than all his successors combined. The present system of prime-time televised press conferences was initiated by the Kennedy administration, which attempted to capitalize on the telegenic characteristics of John Kennedy. When Pierre Salinger (Kennedy's press secretary) first announced the plan, it was met by uniform derision by the press establishment (then dominated by newspaper reporters). James Reston of the *New York Times* declared that the proposal "was the goofiest idea since the hoola hoop."[12] Nevertheless, in January 1961 more than four hundred reporters attended the first televised press conference, and the president's remarks were watched by an audience of 65,000,000.[13]

Because of the transformation of the press conference into a television spectacle and the conflict between reporters' demands for hard news and the president's need to manage information, contemporary presidents are less attracted to the institution of the press conference. Theoretically, a televised press conference provides reporters with a rare opportunity to catch the president unrehearsed and off guard. It is this potential for spontaneity that presidents find threatening. As President Reagan demonstrated on more than one occasion, presidents often do not know the answers to important questions, and they occasionally commit major misstatements and gaffes.[14] To be revealed as ignorant or stupid on national television, of course, is an enormous political risk.

[12] Kernell, 1986, p. 70.
[13] Kernell, 1986, p. 70.
[14] President Reagan's fondness for the off-the-cuff remarks led the White House to implement what came to be known as the "Deaver Rule" (named for Michael Deaver, the President's media advisor) under the terms of which no reporter was permitted to ask Reagan questions during photo opportunities. The networks initially threatened to boycott these sessions if the rule was enforced, but NBC capitulated immediately and within the next two days the rule was in force (see Hertsgaard, 1988, pp. 141–143).

To counter the dangers of appearing inept and out of touch with events, presidents undertake extensive preparations for press conferences. Presidents Ford, Carter, and Reagan all staged elaborate "dress rehearsals" in which aides peppered them with questions anticipated to be "hot" to the press. According to President Reagan's press secretary Larry Speakes, "in press conferences, out of 30 questions and follow-ups the press would ask, we might fail to anticipate one. And often, we could even predict which reporters were going to ask which questions."[15] In general, administrations have ample evidence with which to anticipate questions, including the recurring themes in the news and the issues that appear frequently in the press secretary's daily briefings. Because Reagan was not at his best when unprepared, his press conferences

> evolved into elaborately choreographed exercises in damage control which...include a pair of dress rehearsals in the White House theater, seating charts and photographs of reporters in attendance, guaranteed questions to several reporters, and one senior Reagan advisor reluctantly admits, even an occasional planted question to a receptive journalist.[16]

Even with all this preparation, the real president sometimes shows his face. Perhaps the worst-case scenario of presidential blundering occurred during the press conference held in early 1987 after disclosure of the Iran-Contra scandal. President Reagan's answers to the questions were so confused and filled with factual errors (e.g., the president indicated that Israel had *not* been involved in the transaction) that the Press Office was forced to issue a news release immediately following the conference (even before the networks had concluded their coverage) "clarifying" the president's remarks.

Most presidents go even further than holding practice sessions in the effort to control the outcome of the press conference. Other steps taken to reduce the spontaneity of the event include the making of an opening statement in which the president addresses some particular issue or decision in the hope of setting the agenda for reporters' questions. In addition, a president may give the media little

[15] Larry Speakes (with Robert Pack), *Speaking Out: the Reagan Presidency from Inside the White House* (New York: Scribner, 1988).

[16] "Fine-Tuning the White House Press Conference," *Washington Journalism Review* (October 1982), p. 27.

advance notification. The most extreme case of this tactic was President Johnson's press conference given without notice to reporters who happened to be present in the White House press room at the time.[17]

The timing and setting of the event—determined by the White House, of course—also influences what questions are asked and which stories emerge. In the first two-and-a-half years of his presidency, George Bush held 103 press conferences. (As noted earlier, this figure represents a reversal of the post-FDR trend. However, very few of Bush's press conferences have been televised.) Of the 1,865 questions he was asked, 1,225 dealt with foreign policy. Moreover, all but a dozen of the questions he received were related to current events.[18] In short, President Bush was rarely put in the position of addressing tough issues like homelessness, job training, the budget deficit, or energy policy—issues that have much greater impact on Americans' daily lives than dramatic events such as the invasion of Panama.

Beyond setting the agenda, presidents also know which reporters tend to ask tough questions, and which tend to be more charitable. At each press conference, President Reagan was alerted to the location of reporters in the latter category. For a while, the White House even arranged for "friendly" reporters in this category to be seated together ("blackbirds sitting on a fence," they were once referred to) to make it easy for the president to find one when he got into trouble.

A more direct tactic for controlling the tone of press conferences is the use of planted questions. Although it is impossible to demonstrate the frequency of planted questions, it is generally accepted that administrations often induce reporters to ask a specific question. In return, the reporter may receive a variety of benefits ranging from an exclusive interview with the president to a better seat at the daily press briefings. The practice was widespread during the Eisenhower and Johnson administrations; press secretaries often boasted in public over their ability to control the flow of questions. President Johnson is said to have requested his staff to arrange a press

[17] Michael Grossman and Martha Kumar, *Portraying the President: the White House and the News Media* (Baltimore: Johns Hopkins University Press, 1981), p. 245.

[18] James Bennett, "The Flack Pack: How Press Conferences Turn Serious Journalists into Shills," *The Washington Monthly* (November 1991), p. 26.

conference in which all questions were planted.[19] In October of 1982, "several White House staffers confirm[ed] that questions have been planted at least twice" in the Reagan administration.[20] The most recent (and blatant) case of planting questions, though not in a national press conference, occurred during a telephone question-and-answer session between President Bush and newspaper reporters in Southern California. Not realizing that his microphone was live, the president complained aloud that one of the questions was not "in the right order." In general, however, recent administrations have been less able to insert their questions into press conferences.

Despite their ability to reduce the spontaneity of press conferences, presidents consider the political disadvantages of frequent press conferences to outnumber the advantages. As Table 5.1 showed, the overall trend is one of a reduction in the frequency of regularly scheduled conferences. Despite his reputation as the "great communicator," Reagan's monthly average of press conferences (less than one) was the lowest in history.

In short, the recent history of the presidential press conference illustrates the fundamental tension that governs the relationship between the national press and the president. Reporters crave information, particularly information that is objective and free of political spin or distortion. Presidents demand control over what gets reported. Ever since news conferences became prime-time events, the risks of losing control over the news have outweighed the benefits of television exposure, which has resulted in the gradual withering away of the institution.

Alternatives to the Press Conference

To take up the slack, presidents have turned to other methods of shaping the news, methods which are even more controllable by the White House. President Reagan managed to grant nearly two hundred private interviews to reporters during his first three years in office. Question-and-answer sessions with local reporters are partic-

[19]Grossman and Kumar, 1981, p. 249.
[20]"Fine-Tuning," 1982, p. 26.

ularly rewarding from the administration's perspective, because the president is typically depicted in the best light possible—handing out medals or awards to individuals, opening a federally-funded hospital and other such ceremonial actions. In addition, the local reporters are generally much less aggressive than their Washington counterparts.

What all these methods of presidential news making demonstrate is the extent to which reporters depend on the president for their stories, up to and including the subjects of these stories. Presidents are not so much *subjects* of news coverage as they are *sources* of news. One prominent national reporter found this to be the case with the Bush Press Office: "We don't find out anything they don't want us to know...But, of course, this president's giving us news a lot."[21] The president *gives* reporters news. He makes a speech; reporters, in turn, write stories about the speech and the issues it deals with. The president stages a photo opportunity with a visiting foreign dignitary, and the media reports what he has to say about U.S. relations with the visitor's country. In short, the White House enjoys enormous power to shape the news and, as a result, the public's perceptions of the president. An anecdote provided by former Reagan media adviser Mike Deaver shows just how effective this power can be:

> We saw in 1983 that education was one of the biggest negatives the president had.... We found that we had this task force on excellence in education that had been out there working this whole time that nobody knew anything about. And they'd come up with five recommendations, and when we tested them, we found that 80 percent of the public agreed with them. So Reagan began touring the country, visiting schools... The press dutifully tailed along...We took about six weeks and literally turned the whole thing around. He was 65 percent positive by the end of it. The policies stayed the same—the president hadn't launched an alternative certification program for teachers, hadn't funded a new lunch program for children, hadn't suggested a system for involving parents in their kids' education, hadn't created a national after-school literacy campaign. He'd just changed the news.[22]

[21]James Bennet, 1991, p. 21.
[22]James Bennet, 1991, p. 23.

The Public Congressperson

Television coverage of the president is a relatively simple phenomenon: All attention is focused on one individual. All his strengths and weaknesses are on display, and because of his power, prestige, and inherent newsworthiness, he has tremendous ability to influence his own news coverage.

Television coverage of Congress is much more complex, because Congress is an *institution*, and one which is composed of 535 prominent *individuals*. That makes it an extremely difficult entity for television to cover. One cannot put an institution on camera, and no single individual speaks for the whole body.

Members of Congress seek three objectives: their own reelection or advancement, achievement of policy goals, and movement up the leadership ladder. Before television, the key to all three objectives lay in the congressperson's ability to exploit relationships with other members, especially those in leadership positions. In most cases, one did best by working cooperatively with the party's leadership and committee chairs.

The emergence of television has made most (though not all) members of Congress far less dependent on their colleagues and party leaders to achieve their objectives. They can advance their own careers by aggressively courting local television coverage. They can help to further their policy goals by using television to mobilize public support behind them. In recent years, even internal votes to select party leaders have been influenced by assessments of who was best able to represent the party's position on television. In addition, television has become particularly important in the efforts to compete with the president or other elected officials for the public's support of a particular policy, and to enhance their chances for reelection or election to higher office.

Achieving Policy Goals

Like the president, the congressperson's ability to pursue policy objectives lives and dies with his or her ability to mobilize public support. However, unlike the president, who seeks television coverage as an individual, Congress is generally treated as an institution when policy matters are being covered. That puts Congress at a severe disadvantage vis-a-vis the president, and explains why presidents win their battles with Congress far more often than they lose.

Perhaps the main reason for Congress's disadvantageous position is the difficulty inherent in forging a single unified message when more than one individual is involved. When the president makes his case, he can easily marshall his facts and arguments into a cohesive, digestible message that the public will see repeatedly and absorb. But getting five or ten or more members of Congress to coordinate their message is far more difficult. Furthermore, Congress rarely speaks with one voice on any controversial issue. Even when all the members of one party are united, the other party will likely be united in opposition.

Perhaps no example demonstrates the president's public relations advantage over Congress better than President Bush's 1991 nomination of Clarence Thomas to the Supreme Court. Thomas's nomination was controversial because he had relatively little judicial experience, had an unknown position on abortion, and a much-criticized tenure as head of the Equal Employment Opportunity Commission (E.E.O.C.). Bush's pitch on behalf of Thomas was simple: Judge Thomas had emerged from a poverty-stricken, disadvantaged background, demonstrated admirable strength in his battles against hardship, and therefore had the personal character necessary to sit on the Supreme Court.

Thomas's opponents, however, were far from achieving unanimity in their message. Some focused on the abortion issue; others chose to zero in on his handling of age discrimination cases while at the E.E.O.C.; others criticized the credibility of his testimony in the Senate Judiciary hearing. Their message was further obscured by the fact that most Republicans supported Thomas. As a result, the president's message of:

> "Thomas pulled himself up by his bootstraps and has earned a spot on the Supreme Court,"

was placed in competition with Congress's messages of:

> "Some of us think he's not qualified. Some of us don't like him because he may not be pro-choice. Some of us think he lied to us. And some of us think he's just fine."

Ultimately, the nomination fight became much more personal when Thomas was accused of sexual harassment. But even then, Bush stuck to his message. And through it all, he built public support for Thomas. In the end, 11 Democrats, including 5 who were up for re-election the next year (primarily in Southern states where support for Thomas was strong) helped put Thomas's nomination over the top.

Another reason that Congress usually loses its fights with the President is that it has no single, well-known individual leader who personally commands the majority of press attention. For the last several decades, most congressional leaders have been untelegenic insiders (such as Tip O'Neil) with little or no ability to shape their press coverage. This is not surprising, given the personal skills and congressional seniority usually necessary to be elected to a leadership role in Congress. But as a result, national policy disputes generally develop into a fight between a president—whom the majority of voters once supported—and an institution that is perpetually unpopular.

Achieving Electoral Goals

Press coverage is a mighty weapon for members of Congress. Perhaps more than any other reason, members of Congress seek press coverage because it will help them get reelected. Or, in many cases, it will help them get elected to higher office, especially the U.S. Senate. Unlike in Chapter 4, where the focus was on press coverage of Congresspersons as *candidates*, here our focus is on coverage of them in their capacities as *elected officials* doing their jobs.

Although the key press players in the pursuit of policy goals are *national* reporters, the essential players in achieving electoral objectives are *local* reporters. Local reporters who cover Congress generally fall into one of two categories: They are either correspondents based in Washington for a national chain or wire service, or they are local reporters with little or no knowledge about Washington.

Few local television stations have their own Washington correspondents. Instead, they rely primarily on bureaus based in Washington that report news of local interest back to dozens of subscriber stations around the country. These bureaus are generally paid by the story. The more stories they sell, the more money they make. That means finding a local angle to national news. And that is where a member of Congress can find a niche.

Passage of a new national highway bill will be covered by the national networks, but a member of Congress can easily win local press coverage by holding a news conference to outline which local projects will be funded, and to assure grateful constituents that her district will get its share of the money. Another member of Congress might get local television coverage by inviting a well-known figure from her district to testify at a subcommittee hearing in the Capitol. In either case, the room will likely be filled with television cameras representing local stations. Afterwards, the reporters will trek outside to the area of the Capitol known as "the Triangle," where they narrate their stories with the Capitol Dome in the background. More often than not, the reporter will even hold a microphone bearing the insignia of the station for whom the story is being done. After she has finished taping one story, she will replace the microphone with one bearing a different insignia, and tape a new story. Only the local details will differ. A few hours later, the stories will be filed via satellite to the recipient stations.

The amount of press coverage received by a congressperson is far more dependent on how aggressively it is sought than on the congressperson's actual level of involvement in the issue. As was discussed in Chapter 4, the ability of elected officials to win press attention is also dependent on the size of the media market they represent. Few members of Congress from Los Angeles or New York are seen on local television no matter what they do, because those media markets cover the districts of literally dozens of representatives. In smaller media markets, however, a member of Congress carries enormous stature and has little competition for press. As a result, an aggressive press strategy can place the congressperson on television news once a week or more.

The congressperson or senator's formal role in the leadership structure (e.g., being an elected party leader or the chairperson of a standing committee) is a major determinant of the amount of news coverage he or she attracts. The majority and minority leaders of the Senate, for example, are frequently on network news and weekly interview programs, as are the counterpart leaders of the House of Representatives.

Among rank-and-file legislators, a key determinant of media visibility is motivation—the willingness of the congressperson or senator to pursue press coverage. Some members of Congress—especially the "inside operators" who can achieve their ends without being in the public spotlight—are relatively uninterested in press coverage. Others, such as presidential aspirants, aggressively court the press. And again, the critical factor determining success or failure with the press is not expertise with or personal involvement in a policy:

> When reporters are asked why some members consistently seem to receive better press than others, they often cite two basic attributes: accessibility and quotability. For a journalist on deadline, nothing beats being able to pick up the phone and get the quote that's needed to enliven, illustrate, or sometimes merely fill up a story.[23]

The Congressional Press Secretary

The congressional press secretary is a critical player in the congressperson or senator's bid for press attention. Press secretaries are on the staffs of 98 percent of U.S. Senators and 76 percent of House members. Typically, the press secretary has close ties to the congressperson, has some background in print journalism, and has worked his way up through the staff ranks.

Congressional press secretaries generally have different roles than their White House counterparts. Such differences are related to the fact that there is only one president, who is widely sought by the media. For press purposes, most members of Congress are replaceable, if not interchangeable. Presidential press secretaries needn't spend a great deal of time convincing reporters to quote their boss. They have prominent roles as spokesmen for the president, regularly appearing in the news themselves. In contrast, the role of House and Senate press secretaries often resembles that of a salesperson: They must make reporters aware that their "product" is available and suitable; they must be knowledgeable about the "product"; and they must be able to deliver it on time.

[23] Paul West, "Competing for Coverage in Congress," *Washington Journalism Review* (June 1986), p. 37.

"If they're [press secretaries] good traffic cops, they're good. If they're bad traffic cops, they're bad," says Leo Rennert, the Washington bureau chief of California's McClatchy Newspapers. Rennert just wants to be pointed in the right direction when he needs information.

Television has its own special requirements. "For the kind of access we're looking for in TV, a good press secretary can be enormously helpful," says ABC's (Brit) Hume. "We have to get to people and get to them quickly." ... The wire services have a similar need for a quick response. But meeting that need, says AP's Mike Shanahan, can pay dividends for members. "If a press secretary has easy access to senators and can get him on the phone quickly, then he gets the senator into print."[24]

The press release is an important weapon for a congressional press secretary in the search for news coverage. A typical Senate office produces ten releases each month, whereas the typical House output is between five and six.[25] Releases are written in the format of a news story and, not surprisingly, the great majority provide information about the congressperson's good deeds on behalf of his constituents. In one study, "advertising" and "credit taking" accounted for nearly three out of every four press releases.[26]

Going Overboard

For the most part, the methods used to seek press attention are perfectly benign: announcing local angles to national stories, serving the wishes of constituents, taking positions on critical issues, and so on. But occasionally, some congresspersons and senators develop reputations for going overboard. They exploit their official positions to attract news coverage. Arlen Specter, a Republican senator from Pennsylvania is one example. Senator Specter has often resorted to sensationalism in order to attract publicity. For example:

> In February Senator Arlen Specter wanted to hold hearings on Nazi war criminal Josef Mengele, and he wasn't going to be deterred by the

---

[24]Robert Timberg, "The Hill Handlers," *Washington Journalism Review* (June 1985), p. 40.

[25]Stephen Hess, *Live From Capitol Hill: Studies of Congress and the Media* (Washington, D.C.: Brookings Institution, 1991), p. 78.

[26]Stephen Hess, 1991, pp. 86–87.

fact that he is only Chairman of the Senate Subcommittee on Juvenile Justice. Strom Thurmond, Chairman of the Senate Judiciary Committee, failed to see the connection between the Nazi doctor and teenagers in trouble and had declined to authorize the hearings. But Specter persisted, and Thurmond finally relented. The first two hearings attracted so much media attention that Specter asked Thurmond to hold a third. When Thurmond adamantly refused, Specter took his show on the road, holding a meeting with Holocaust survivors in Philadelphia. Because Thurmond had refused authorization, the third hearing had no formal connection to the subcommittee, the Judiciary Committee, or the Senate. Nevertheless, Specter declared in his opening statement that the hearings were official subcommittee business, and the press duly reported them as such. A spokesman for Specter said the Juvenile Justice Subcommittee was involved with the search for Mengele, the Philadelphia Inquirer noted solemnly, "because of the experiments he conducted on children."[27]

Specter's media seeking has a clear logic to it. The senator's office attempts to keep him in the spotlight by specializing in issues they know will attract the television cameras—sex, children, drugs and violence. All these elements were present when Senator Specter presided over a subcommittee hearing on the effects of pornography on women and children. As described in the *New Republic*:

> The star witness was Linda Lovelace, first made famous for her role in *Deep Throat*, who told the committee that her boyfriend had forced her into pornography and prostitution with a semiautomatic M-16 machine gun. Specter invited two of the pornography industry's biggest stars, Veronica Vera and 'Seka,' to respond to Lovelace's charges...
>
> Vera read her statement from a prepared text. "I am the love toy, the object of your desires, exposed and vulnerable," Vera explained. "Picture yourself tying the ropes, keeping me as your prisoner, to be taken whenever you want, always open to—." She paused.
>
> "Should I go on?" she asked.
>
> Specter, who had a copy of her text in front of him replied, "You certainly may." The long and explicit description of intercourse, bondage, and sadomasochism that followed had little to do with juvenile justice. The television cameras recorded the scene in full.[28]

[27]Murray Waas, "Media Specter," *The New Republic*, September 30, 1985, p. 13.
[28]Murray Waas, 1985, p. 14.

Summary

Because they are members of a collective body, congresspersons do not enjoy the same access to the news media as the president. However, because they are newsworthy to media outlets in their home districts, congresspersons and senators can command considerable local coverage. At times, they may even use their special involvement with controversial and titillating issues to attract national publicity.

Summary

The politician's ability to govern is increasingly intertwined with his or her public image. A president's ability to exert control over information in general and the flow of television news in particular is crucial to his or her fate in office. By getting the television networks to focus on events, issues, or happenings generally considered "successes," the president hopes to maintain a high level of popularity. Conversely, when the news dwells on negative outcomes, the level of public approval is likely to fall, thus weakening the president's clout in Washington. The current treatment of a politician by the media has become the critical barometer of his or her political fortunes.

The preoccupation with public relations creates powerful incentives for politicians to ignore tough problems. Most politicians remember Walter Mondale's fate in 1984 when he publicly stated the need for a tax increase and lost 49 out of 50 states to Reagan. In 1988 Republican presidential candidate George Bush sought to divert the public's attention from the major issues of the day, preferring instead to campaign on such matters as the pledge of allegiance, prison furlough programs, and other matters more symbolic than substantive. In this sense, the new strategy of political leadership and the quality of public discourse are inversely related. As incumbent politicians become preoccupied with their image, so too do they shy away from addressing the fundamental problems of American life. The consequences of the "popularity game" on politicians' ability to govern are considered in Chapter 9.

Suggested Readings

David Broder. 1971. *The Party's Over*. New York: Harper & Row.

Timothy Cook. 1989. *Making Laws and Making News: Media Strategies in the U.S. House of Representatives*. Washington, D.C.: Brookings Institution.

Benjamin Ginsberg and Martin Shefter. 1990. *Politics By Other Means: The Declining Importance of Elections in America*. New York: Basic Books.

Michael Grossman and Martha Kumar. 1981. *Portraying the President: The White House and the News Media*. Baltimore: Johns Hopkins University Press.

Roderick Hart. 1987. *The Sound of Leadership: Presidential Communication in the Modern Age*. Chicago: University of Chicago Press.

Mark Hertsgaard. 1988. *On Bended Knee: the Press and the Reagan Presidency*. New York: Farrar, Straus & Giroux.

Stephen Hess. 1991. *Live From Capitol Hill: Studies of Congress and the Media*. Washington, D.C.: Brookings Institution.

———1988. *Organizing the Presidency*. Washington, D.C.: Brookings Institution.

Kathleen Jamieson. 1988. *Eloquence in an Electronic Age: the Transformation of Political Speechmaking*. New York: Oxford University Press.

Samuel Kernell. 1986. *Going Public: New Strategies of Presidential Leadership*. Washington, D.C.: Congressional Quarterly Press.

Burdett Loomis. 1988. *The New American Politician: Entrepreneurship, Ambition and the Changing Face of Political Life*. New York: Basic Books.

Theodore Lowi. 1985. *The Personal President: Power Invested, Promise Unfulfilled*. Ithaca, N.Y.: Cornell University Press.

Jeffrey Tulis. 1987. *The Rhetorical Presidency*. Princeton, N.J.: Princeton University Press.

PART III

Voters

In Part Two we discussed the incentives and risks facing politicians in the media age. We showed how the emergence of television has transformed the way in which they run for office, as well as the manner in which they govern.

Politicians, of course, are supposed to be the servants of the electorate. The widespread use of television advertising and "news management" during campaigns, and the increasing reliance on "going public" as a strategy of leadership both reflect the assumption that ordinary voters respond to information. We argued in Chapters 4 and 5 that politicians who are better able to control the flow of information enjoy longer and more successful careers. In Part Three we turn to the actual impact of the mass media on the beliefs, opinions, and actions of ordinary Americans. We begin (Chapter 6) by tracing the history of political communication research from the 1950s era of minimal campaign effects to today's media-dominated politics. Next, we develop a typology of the various effects of political communication on public opinion. In Chapters 7 and 8 we summarize the vast body of research bearing on different media presentations and their effects on the audience. Finally, we demonstrate how public opinion and the factors that shape it constrain what politicians can (and cannot) accomplish once they get elected.

THE EVOLUTION OF
MEDIA EFFECTS RESEARCH

The twentieth century has witnessed the election of dictators and demagogues in a number of democratic societies. The spectacle of ordinary men and women lending their fervent support to Adolf Hitler and Benito Mussolini demonstrated the power of political propaganda. The catastrophic consequences of the rise to power of the European dictators galvanized scholarly interest in the effects of mass communication on public opinion and voting. If the Nazis could fan the flames of anti-Semitism in Europe, someone like Huey Long, Joseph McCarthy, George Wallace, or David Duke might be able to similarly inflame extremist passions in America. Perhaps ordinary citizens are merely puppets whose political sentiments can be orchestrated by leaders endowed with commanding rhetorical skills or other forms of personal charisma.

The Era of Minimal Consequences

In the United States, initial research into the effects of mass communications explored the use of propaganda films during the Second World War. Although these films (most of which were produced by the Department of Defense) were found to be highly informative, they failed to either shift the audiences' attitudes toward the war in general or motivate young men to volunteer for military service in combat units.[1]

---

[1] Carl Hovland, Arthur Lumsdaine, and Fred Sheffield, *Experiments on Mass Communication* (Princeton, N.J.: Princeton University Press, 1949).

Presidential election campaigns were also a major testing ground for political communication research during this era. The sociologist Paul Lazarsfeld organized a series of studies into changes in voters' preferences over the course of a campaign. In 1940 residents of Erie County in Ohio were interviewed at the outset of the presidential campaign and again shortly before the election. The results of this survey showed that exposure to campaign events and information produced little alteration in the public's voting intentions. Only 5 percent of the Erie County residents who were surveyed changed their preference from one candidate to another. Instead, the principal effect of the 1940 campaign was to crystallize, reinforce, or activate otherwise latent preferences. For instance, newspaper readers who, because of their high socioeconomic status or professional occupation might be expected to vote Republican, became more entrenched in this predisposition over the course of the campaign.[2]

Following the Second World War, the presidential election of 1948 seemed to be the ideal setting in which to document the effects of campaign communication on voters. Early in the campaign, Republican Thomas Dewey build a considerable lead in the polls over Harry Truman, the Democratic incumbent president. Truman ran one of the most celebrated campaigns in American history, stopping and speaking in every town his campaign train took him through. In the end, even though pollsters and commentators predicted a Republican victory up to the very eve of the election, Truman defeated Dewey, 50 percent to 45 percent.

Notwithstanding Truman's furious whistle-stop campaign and his dramatic victory over Dewey, researchers were unable to detect evidence of last-minute shifts in voter preferences. In fact, several studies performed during the 1948 campaign indicated that voters who said they followed the campaign closely were the least likely to have changed their preferences.[3]

---

[2]Paul Lazarsfeld, Bernard Berelson, and Hazel Gaudet, *The People's Choice: How the Voter Makes up His Mind in a Presidential Campaign* (New York: Columbia University Press, 1948).

[3]Bernard Berelson, Paul Lazarsfeld, and William McPhee, *Voting: A Study of Opinion Formation in a Presidential Campaign* (Chicago: University of Chicago Press, 1954). As scholars were later to demonstrate, the relationship between political involvement and persuadability is crucial to understanding the dynamics of political persuasion.

Studies conducted in the 1950s continued to indicate that American voters were little swayed by campaign activities. Although control of the White House shifted from the Democrats to the Republicans in 1952, the change was attributable more to Eisenhower's status as a war hero rather than to the persuasive effects of his presidential campaign. This pattern of results led communication researchers to theorize that campaigns (and by inference, the media) exerted minimal influence over electoral outcomes. In the words of Joseph Klapper, "persuasive mass communication functions far more frequently as an agent of reinforcement than as an agent of change."[4]

Researchers attributed the pattern of minimal campaign effects to a variety of factors, most notably voters' strong sense of party identification. Following World War II, more than 80 percent of the electorate expressed a psychological affinity for either the Democratic or Republican party. Americans were found to acquire their partisan identities at a very early age (as early as six or seven). Once acquired, these attachments were remarkably immune to change over the entire life cycle. Because voting preferences during the 1940s and 1950s were dominated by party loyalty, campaign activities and events had little impact.

The centrality of party identification meant that campaign messages served chiefly to reinforce predispositions that voters already held. Indeed, voters often were attentive only to those messages that were consistent with these existing predispositions. Republicans would listen carefully to a speech by Dewey; Democrats would remember statements made by Truman. As the authors of *The People's Choice* put it:

> In recent years, there has been a good deal of talk by men of good will about the desirability and necessity of guaranteeing the free exchange of ideas in the market-place of public opinion . . . Now we find that the consumers of ideas, if they have made a decision on the issue, themselves erect high tariff walls against alien notions.[5]

In addition to the operation of consistency and selectivity biases in exposure to campaign messages, the persuasive effects of the cam-

[4]Joseph Klapper, *The Effects of Mass Communication* (New York: Free Press, 1960), p. 15.
[5]Lazarsfeld et al., 1948, pp. 89–90.

paign were thought to be further muted by the "two-step flow" of campaign communication. News about the campaign was frequently transmitted conversationally via politically attentive *opinion leaders*. These opinion leaders usually interpreted the news in a manner that was consistent with their group affiliations. A union shop steward, for example, would discuss campaign events with union members in a way that cast the Democratic candidate in a favorable light.

Revising Minimal Consequences

Beginning in the 1960s, the consensus that media effects were minimal began to crumble in the face of new evidence. Today, most scholars and commentators agree that the news media—especially television—play a crucial role in influencing the electoral choices of American voters. The increasing importance of the media has been attributed to several factors.

In the first place, party identification is no longer the dominant psychological force in political campaigns. Since 1952 fewer and fewer Americans have identified themselves as either Democrats or Republicans. The percentage of independents in the electorate has increased from 20 percent in 1952 to 30 percent in 1990. More importantly, the percentage of voters who say that they have voted for different parties in presidential elections has increased from 29 percent in 1952 to 57 percent in 1980.[6] In each presidential election since 1968, other than the 1976 election that was won by Jimmy Carter, the party that won the presidency was *not* the majority party (in the sense of having a plurality of voters who identify with it). In other words, Republican presidents have been elected and reelected even though more voters identify themselves as Democrats than as Republicans. Obviously, party affiliation is no longer the dominant determinant of voting in presidential elections.

Second, as we have already shown, the decades following World War II were marked by the emergence of television as the dominant medium of mass communication. Coinciding with this development was the implementation of fundamental alterations to the presiden-

---

[6]Martin Wattenberg, *The Decline of Political Parties, 1952–1980* (Cambridge, Mass.: Harvard University Press), p. 21.

tial nomination process. As described in Chapter 4, the emergence of direct primaries in the allocation of convention delegates made candidates increasingly independent of the political party organization. Decentralization of the nomination process meant that individual candidates could campaign as "free agents" for public attention and support. The news media and television in particular became critical intermediaries between presidential candidates and voters. Given the universal access to television, campaign messages were much more likely to get through to the public. This made public opinion more volatile.

Not only did campaigns become increasingly visible and audible to voters, but elections also became much more than opportunities for voters to express their party loyalty. In particular, voters increasingly used the occasion to either reward or punish incumbents for the state of the economy. "Am I better off today than four years ago?" became an important voting cue. Figure 6.1 plots the relationship between the percentage of the presidential vote received by the party controlling the presidency and the percent change in real disposable income during the year preceding the election. Clearly, changes in personal income are very good

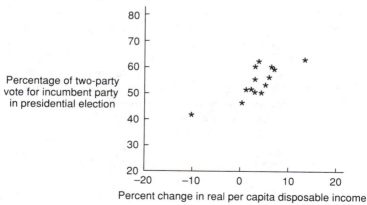

Figure 6.1 The Relationship Between Voting in Presidential Elections and Disposable Income.
Source: U.S. Department of Commerce, *Statistical Abstract of the United States, 1991* (Washington, D.C.: Government Printing Office, 1991).

predictors of voting; when voters do well economically, they reward incumbents (and vice-versa).

Some analysts have interpreted the robust connection between the state of the economy and electoral outcomes as further evidence of the law of minimal consequences. By these accounts, Harry Truman would have won without the famous whistle-stop campaign, and George Bush would have defeated Michael Dukakis without the "Boston Harbor" and "Revolving Door" ads. As we will show in Chapter 8, however, these purely deterministic explanations fail to account for the short-term fluctuations in voters' preferences (which turn out to be of considerable magnitude) that occur frequently during campaigns.

In addition to the state of the economy, salient issues (such as civil rights in 1964, law and order and the Vietnam War in 1968 and 1972, and the American hostages in Iran in 1980) are often injected into presidential campaigns. These issues create divisions among members of both parties. The personal qualities and images of the candidates also come into play, with voters often deserting the candidate of their party because he projects (or fails to project) particular traits. In short, since the 1940s the typical voter's portfolio of relevant cues has been significantly diversified.

To summarize, American presidential politics of the 1980s and 1990s bears little resemblance to the politics of the 1940s and 1950s. The bedrock of political party identification has gradually eroded, and political campaigns have taken on added meaning as a result. The upshot of these altered conditions is that the news media (television in particular) play an ever-increasing role in determining voters' attitudes and choices. As we will show in the next two chapters, politicians who are best able to use the news media are generally victorious in the battle for public opinion.

Appendix: Changes in Research Method

To complete this brief overview of the history of political communication research, we should now address the question of methodology. In the social sciences it is generally true that the answers derived from particular questions depend upon how these questions are tackled. In the particular case of political communication, the answers vary dramatically depending upon whether researchers rely on surveys or experiments.

Survey research rests on the fact that a relatively small sample can be studied to yield evidence about a much larger population. To know what Americans think about some issue, pollsters typically interview a thousand people, their results are, in general, highly accurate. How can the opinions of a thousand people be used to predict the opinions of over a hundred million? The answer lies in the laws of probability. The basic idea is that a random sample provides a true microcosm of the population from which it is drawn.

The key to survey research, therefore, is sampling. If the sample is not representative of the larger population, the results of the survey become meaningless. In 1936, for example, the editors of the *Literary Digest* decided to carry out a public opinion poll concerning the upcoming election between Franklin Roosevelt and Alf Landon. They used telephone directories and automobile registrations to draw their sample. Based on the opinions of their respondents, the magazine confidently predicted a big win for the Republican Landon. On election day, however, FDR carried all but two states. Despite the very large sample used by the *Digest* (some two million people), their forecast was wildly inaccurate. Why? In 1936, at the height of the depression, automobile and telephone ownership were both closely tied to wealth. By sampling automobile owners and people with phones, the magazine had, in effect, sampled Republicans. Among Republicans, not surprisingly, Landon was the preferred candidate.

The refinement of sampling techniques in the 1940s and 1950s and the increasing accuracy of surveys made the method especially attractive to researchers in the field of communications. Paul Lazarsfeld and his colleagues developed a special type of survey in which the same people were repeatedly interviewed. This "panel survey" became the cutting edge of political communication research; by observing the public's opinions during the early and later phases of the campaign, researchers could draw conclusions about the impact of the campaign.

The initial pattern of research showing limited campaign effects can be attributed, in part, to the exclusive use of surveys by political communication researchers. As the eminent psychologist Carl Hovland pointed out in his classic paper "Reconciling Conflicting Results from Experimental and Survey Studies of Attitude Change," the survey method is particularly insensitive to short-term shifts in political opinions or attitudes.[7] Because surveys can rarely be administered immediately following dramatic (and unplanned) events, the effects of the event are likely to decay before pollsters can take the public's pulse. Moreover, asking people whether they paid attention to a particular event may not be the most objective measure of their actual level of attention. Because of these and other inherent weaknesses, it is difficult to use a survey as a means of identifying cause and effect.

Laboratory experiments, unlike surveys, provide much stronger tests of communication effects. The logic of the experiment is disarmingly simple. The researcher physically manipulates some variable and then observes its effects, if any, on the phenomenon under investigation. In Iyengar and Kinder's experiments on agenda setting, the researchers manipulated the amount of television news coverage devoted to particular issues.[8] Typically, a group of experimental participants were exposed to one news story each day over the course of a week on some particular target issue (e.g., unemployment), whereas a second group was shown newscasts containing no news stories about this issue. At the end of the week, the former group was found to be significantly more concerned about the target issue. The random assignment of participants to the two conditions virtually ensures that this difference could have resulted only from the experimenters' manipulation, that is, the differing degree of news coverage accorded the target issue.

The ability to isolate causal factors is not the only requirement of scientific research. Researchers must also be able to generalize their findings with a high degree of confidence. Survey research, with its reliance on representative samples of the general population, affords

[7]Carl Hovland, "Reconciling Conflicting Results from Survey and Experimental Studies of Attitude Change," *American Psychologist*, 14 (1959), pp. 8–17.
[8]Shanto Iyengar and Donald Kinder, *News That Matters: Television and American Opinion* (Chicago: University of Chicago Press, 1987).

a strong basis for generalization. If more educated respondents in a national survey are found to be less likely to watch television news programs, the researcher knows that this relationship applies to all adult Americans. (This assumes, of course, that the survey was based on a probabilistic sample with an adequate number of respondents.) Experiments, on the other hand, suffer from limited generalizability. The Achilles heel of experimental research is the lack of representativeness of many experimental samples. Participants in experimental studies are generally drawn from a narrow strata of society: undergraduate psychology majors in the vast majority of experiments, and, in those experiments featuring "real people," housewives, the unemployed, and others who might be attracted by a small financial incentive.

Even if experimental participants are recruited to be representative of some broader population, the artificial properties of the experimental setting makes it difficult to extend the findings to "naturalistic" settings. Subjects in Iyengar and Kinder's experiments, for example, may have given the news their undivided attention because they knew they were participating in a university research project. Had they been watching the same reports in the privacy of their living room, they may have followed the news less carefully, thus reducing the possibility that their political agendas would change.

The complementary strengths and weaknesses of the survey and experimental methods led Hovland to conclude that the optimal strategy for communications research should be some combination of the two approaches: "I should like to stress the mutual importance of the two approaches to the problem of communication effectiveness. Neither is a royal road to wisdom, but each represents an important emphasis. The challenge of future work is one of fruitfully combining their virtues."[9]

The exclusive reliance on survey research has gradually given way to methodological diversity. Today, political communication researchers utilize a wide variety of methods including experiments, quasi-experiments, public opinion surveys of various kinds, content analysis and participant observation. This shift toward methodolog-

[9]Hovland, 1956, p. 17.

ical pluralism has enabled identification of a variety of media effects upon public opinion. In the following chapters we build a typology of these effects and summarize the evidence bearing on each type.

Suggested Readings

Bernard Berelson, Paul Lazarsfeld, and William McPhee. 1954. *Voting: A Study of Opinion Formation in a Presidential Campaign.* Chicago: University of Chicago Press.

Angus Campbell et al. 1960. *The American Voter.* New York: John Wiley & Sons.

Edward Carmines and James Stimson. 1991. *Issue Evolution: Race and the Transformation of American Politics.* Princeton, N.J.: Princeton University Press.

Fiorina, Morris. 1981. *Retrospective Voting in American National Elections,* New Haven, Conn.: Yale University Press.

Carl Hovland. 1959. "Reconciling Conflicting Results from Survey and Experimental Studies of Attitude Change," *American Psychologist,* 14.

Carl Hovland, Arthur Lumsdaine, and Fred Sheffield. 1949. *Experiments on Mass Communication.* Princeton, N.J.: Princeton University Press.

Joseph Klapper, 1960. *The Effects of Mass Communications.* New York: Free Press.

V. O. Key, Jr. 1967. *Public Opinion and American Democracy.* New York: Alfred A. Knopf.

Paul Lazarsfeld, Bernard Berelson, and Hazel Gaudet. 1948. *The People's Choice: How the Voter Makes up His Mind in a Presidential Campaign.* New York: Columbia University Press.

Norman Nie, Sidney Verba, and John Petrocik. 1977. *The Changing American Voter.* Cambridge, Mass.: Harvard University Press.

Martin Wattenberg. 1984. *The Decline of American Political Parties, 1952–1980.* Cambridge, Mass.: Harvard University Press.

CHAPTER 7

THE MULTIPLE EFFECTS OF TELEVISION ON PUBLIC OPINION

Since the classic studies of Paul Lazarsfeld and others described in the previous chapter, a considerable body of research has been accumulated concerning the effects of the mass media on American public opinion. This research demonstrates convincingly that, contrary to the law of minimal consequences, Americans' political thinking is profoundly influenced by the mass media, often in rather subtle ways. Television news reports and other media presentations exert a variety of effects on how people think about politics and what they think as well.

Researchers have identified at least four different avenues by which the media leaves its imprint on public opinion: enabling people to keep up with what is happening in the world (*learning*), defining the major political issues or problems of the day (*agenda setting*), influencing who gets blamed or rewarded for issues and events in the news (*framing responsibility*) and, finally, shaping people's political preferences and choices (*persuasion*).

These four categories of effects approximate a sequence. Dissemination of *information* is typically the initial effect of communication. Increases in awareness lead to *changes in the salience or prominence of particular issues or themes*. For example, during a recession, reading or watching the news makes people aware that thousands of Americans have lost their jobs. The information makes the audience more concerned about the state of the economy. Once people's attention has been directed at particular issues or events, they attempt to understand these issues by *assigning responsibility*. They seek explanations: Why is the economy in such bad shape, and who or what can turn it around? As we will see, differences in the way television news presentations frame political issues can lead viewers to make differing attributions of responsibility. Finally, the news can *persuade* individuals to alter their political preferences or electoral choices. After months of exposure to gloomy economic news, unemployment becomes the major issue in the eyes of the public; incumbent officials are blamed for the state of the economy; their approval ratings fall; and voters switch their support to challengers.

Learning

Learning corresponds to the general educational function of the news media. The dissemination of information is generally considered the most basic responsibility of the news media in democratic societies. Through the news, Americans might learn that American soldiers are being sent abroad, that the national unemployment rate has increased, or that charges of sexual harassment have been filed against a nominee for the United States Supreme Court. During political campaigns, voters find out who is running and what the candidates are saying about the issues.

Within the broad category of learning, we consider three different classes of effects. The most general type of learning effect concerns the impact of news presentations on the individual's knowledge about public affairs (*information gain*). Of particular importance to election campaigns, exposure to media presentations serves to boost candidates' *name recognition*. Finally, the acquisition of information also enables voters to express opinions about the candidates (*opinionation*). We focus in this chapter on general information gain, reserving the discussion of candidate recognition and opinionation for the next chapter, which deals with campaign effects.

Information Gain

Even by the most generous standards, most Americans are poorly informed about politics and the course of national affairs. This has occasioned a great debate among communications researchers concerning the causes of the public's ignorance. The conventional wisdom among political and media analysts alike has been that it is the public's reliance on television that is the primary cause of their low level of political information. With its emphasis on sound bites and good visuals, television news has been considered, at best, a source of trivial information.[1]

Research into the relative information value of print and broadcast news has yielded mixed results. During the 1972 presidential campaign, for instance, regular and irregular viewers of network newscasts did not differ in the extent to which they became more informed about the candidates' positions on major issues over the course of the campaign. In contrast, regular newspaper readers learned more than irregular readers by a margin of 2 to 1.[2] This pattern seems to suggest that newspapers are more informative than television news programs.

More recent work indicates that voters do receive and retain significant public affairs information from television sources, more so than they do from alternative print-based sources. One study investigated how much Americans learned from TV news and newspapers about a series of events that occurred during the summer and fall of 1989.[3] Whereas exposure to television news significantly boosted the level of information for *nine* of the sixteen events, exposure to newspapers proved to be a significant learning factor for only *one* (the trial of evangelist Jim Bakker) of the sixteen events. In a different study, researchers examined the relative contributions of newspaper reading and television news viewing to political information after controlling for socioeconomic differences between the users of the two mediums. (Regular newspaper readers tend to be more educated than regular viewers of television newscasts.) This study found that television news was just as informative as

---

[1] See John Robinson and Mark Levy, *The Main Source* (Beverly Hills, Calif.: Sage Publications, 1984).

[2] Thomas Patterson and Robert McClure, *The Unseeing Eye: The Myth of Television Power in National Elections* (New York: G.P. Putnams, 1976), pp. 50–52.

[3] The list of events included the resignation of the speaker of the U.S. House, former President Reagan's surgery, a major speech by President Bush, the crash of a United Airlines DC-10 in Iowa, and the Jim Bakker trial. See Vincent Price and John Zaller, "Who Gets the News?: The Measurement Problem in Media Research," Paper presented at the Annual Meeting of the American Political Science Association, San Francisco, 1990.

newspapers.[4] Overall, therefore, it is unclear whether television has contributed positively or negatively (by supplanting newspaper readership) to the dissemination of political information.

Agenda Setting   *LEARNING WHAT TO THINK ABOUT*

As we noted in Chapter 3, the devastating famine in Ethiopia attracted virtually no attention in the United States prior to October 1987, even though it had claimed thousands of victims. On October 23, 1987, NBC News aired a four-minute report (prepared by the British Broadcasting Corporation) called "The Faces of Death in Africa." The decision to air the report set in motion an avalanche of relief efforts and fund-raising activities by Americans. As Steve Friedman, executive producer of NBC's "Today" show explained: "This famine has been going on for a long time and nobody cared. Now its on TV and everybody cares. I guess a picture is worth many words."[5]

The idea of agenda setting is that the public's social or political priorities and concerns—their beliefs about what is a significant issue or event—are determined by the amount of news coverage accorded various issues and events.[6] The concept was initially proposed by analysts pursuing the connections between public opinion and the course of American foreign policy. In his book *The American Public and Foreign Policy*, Bernard Cohen outlined the agenda-setting hypothesis as follows.

> The press is significantly more than a purveyor of information and opinion. It may not be successful in telling its readers what to think, but it is stunningly successful in telling its readers what to think *ABOUT*

---

[4]Roy Behr, Pradeep Chibber, and Shanto Iyengar, "TV News as a Source of Public Affairs Information," Unpublished paper, Department of Political Science, UCLA, 1990.

[5]Quoted in Peter Boyer, "Famine in Africa: The TV Accident That Exploded," in Michael Emery and Ted Smythe (eds.), *Readings in Mass Communication* (Dubuque, Ia: William C. Brown, 1986) p. 293

[6]Antecedents of the agenda-setting argument can be found in the works of the great American journalist Walter Lippmann, who suggested that the press's job was to "signalize" events and who warned of the impossibility of the news and reality being one and the same.

about... The editor may believe he is only printing the things people want to read, but he is thereby putting a claim on their attention, powerfully determining what they will be thinking about, and talking about, until the next wave laps their shore.[7]

The most convincing evidence of agenda setting comes from carefully designed and realistic experiments that manipulated the level of news coverage accorded particular issues. These experiments reveal that the insertion of only a modest degree of news coverage into network newscasts can induce significant shifts in viewers' beliefs about the importance of issues. In one experiment conducted in 1982, for example, viewers were shown a series of newscasts containing either three, six, or no stories dealing with U.S. dependence on foreign sources of energy. When exposed to no news coverage on this subject, 24 percent of the participants cited energy as among the three most important problems facing the country. When participants watched three stories, 50 percent of them regarded energy as an important problem. Finally, when the participants watched six stories, energy was cited as an important national problem by 65 percent of the viewers.[8]

Researchers have discussed several antecedent factors that condition the media's ability to shape the public's priorities. These factors include the remoteness or immediacy of the issue, the demographic characteristics of the people who receive the news, and differences in the way the news is presented. Some research indicates that the more remote an issue or event is from the direct personal experience of the typical viewer, the stronger the agenda-setting effect of news coverage of the issue or event is likely to be. Perceptions of the importance of pervasive issues such as crime and inflation are less affected by news coverage because people have their own insights

---

[7] Bernard Cohen, *The Press and Foreign Policy* (Princeton, N.J.: Princeton University Press, 1963), p. 13.

[8] See Shanto Iyengar and Donald Kinder, *News That Matters: Television and American Opinion* (Chicago: University of Chicago Press, 1987), p. 24. Early agenda-setting studies were plagued by a number of methodological difficulties, most notably, confusion between cause and effect. Did the correlation between newspaper readers' political concerns and the content of the news mean that news coverage had set the audience agenda, or did it mean instead that newspaper editors had tailored their coverage of issues to suit the concerns and interests of their readers? Concerns such as these led the way to the use of experimental design in agenda-setting research.

into these problems. However, other studies show that people who are personally affected by issues in the news are particularly likely to have their agendas set by the media. After being exposed to news reports detailing the financial difficulties confronting the social security fund, elderly viewers of network newscasts were found to be much more likely than younger viewers to nominate social security as one of the most important problems facing the country. In addition, viewers who are more interested in politics and who participate more actively in the political process tend to be less susceptible to agenda-setting effects. As Iyengar and Kinder note, "The more removed the viewer is from the world of public affairs, the stronger the agenda-setting power of television news."[9]

Finally, the manner in which a news story is presented vastly affects its ability to set the public agenda. Stories that are more likely to catch the public's attention (such as front-page stories in the newspaper, newspaper stories accompanied by photographs, and lead stories in television newscasts) tend to be particularly influential. Although the finding is counterintuitive, it has been shown that episodic coverage of public affairs—news stories that deal with the vivid, human element of national issues—are *not* more effective in setting viewers' political agendas than more pallid stories featuring "talking heads."[10]

Framing Responsibility for Political Issues

People's attitudes and actions depend upon the manner in which they attribute responsibility. Psychological research shows that attribution of responsibility is a convenient method of simplifying and understanding complex issues. In fact, responsibility is such a compelling concept that people may even invent responsibility for purely chance or random events.

Politics is no exception to this rule. When issues and problems hit the public agenda, voters instinctively allocate responsiblity and blame (or credit, in the case of outcomes judged successes). This

[9]Iyengar and Kinder, 1987, p. 63.
[10]See Iyengar and Kinder, 1987, Chapter 4.

is why politicians rush to disassociate themselves from unfavorable outcomes and claim responsibility for favorable outcomes.

Television is one of several forces that influences the attribution of responsibility for political issues. In the case of network newscasts, the factor that most affects the attribution of responsibility is the manner in which the news is *framed* or presented. As we noted in Chapter 3, television can frame issues in either *episodic* or *thematic* terms. Episodic framing depicts issues in terms of concrete instances or specific events—a homeless person, an unemployed worker, a victim of racial discrimination, the bombing of an airliner, an attempted murder, and so on. The thematic news frame, on the other hand, places public issues in some general or abstract context. The thematic news frame typically takes the form of an in-depth, "backgrounder" report dealing with general outcomes or conditions. While episodic reports are often visually appealing, thematic reports, consist primarily of "talking heads."[11]

Given the nature of television news, it is to be expected that the networks rely extensively on episodic framing to report on public issues. Episodic framing is characterized by on-the- scene, live reports that are fairly brief. Thematic coverage, which requires interpretive analyses, would take more time and crowd out other news items. Moreover, producers regard extensive thematic coverage as simply too dull to keep viewers' interest.

As might be expected, television news coverage of political issues is more episodic than thematic. Eighty-nine percent of network news reports on crime broadcast between 1981 and 1986 focused on a specific perpetrator, victim, or criminal act. Of the nearly two thousand stories on terrorism broadcast between 1981 and 1986, 74 percent consisted of live reports of some specific terrorist act, group, victim, or event, while 26 percent discussed terrorism as a general political problem.[12]

---

[11]In practice, very few news reports are purely episodic or thematic. Even the most detailed, close-up look at a poor person, for instance, might include lead-in remarks by the anchorperson or reporter on the scope of poverty nationwide. Conversely, an account of the legislative struggle over budgetary cuts in social welfare might include a brief scene of children in a day care center scheduled to shut down as a result of the funding cuts.

[12]For details, see Shanto Iyengar, *Is Anyone Responsible? How Television Frames Political Issues* (Chicago: University of Chicago Press, 1991).

It is not true, however, that television always avoids the thematic frame. News reports on the economy tend to be heavily thematic, conveying information about the latest national economic indicators and presenting interviews with economists, businessmen, or public officials. Between 1981 and 1986, the networks' news coverage of unemployment was predominantly thematic (thematic reports outnumbered episodic reports by 2:1).[13]

The distinction between episodic and thematic framing of political and social issues has important consequences for the attribution of responsibility. Viewers who are exposed to news coverage that is thematically framed tend to assign responsibility for national issues to societal factors—cultural values; economic circumstances; or the motives, actions and inactions of government officials. For example, in the case of unemployment, viewers who are exposed to heavily thematic news coverage focus on politicians in assigning responsibility. However, when television news coverage is heavily episodic (as is usually the case for issues such as poverty, crime, and terrorism), viewers attribute responsibility not to societal forces, but to the private motives and actions of poor people, criminals, and terrorists, respectively. When confronted with news stories describing particular instances of national issues, viewers tend to focus on the individuals concerned rather than on public officials.

Overall, the manner in which television frames national problems has the effect of either shielding or exposing politicians to the public's attributions of responsibility. For those issues that are typically covered by thematically framed reports, public officials are more apt to be held responsible. Conversely, issues that are framed primarily in episodic terms tend to produce attributions of responsibility that do not focus on the behavior of politicans.

Persuasion

The concept of persuasion refers to instances in which individuals alter their preferences for a candidate, policy, or some other object or idea in response to a particular message. President Reagan,

[13] For details, see Iyengar, 1991.

for example, was a consistent opponent of gun control legislation. After leaving the presidency, however, he endorsed the Brady Bill (named for his former press secretary who was shot during John Hinckley's failed attempt to assassinate Reagan), which sought to impose strict registration requirements on handgun owners. As this case illustrates, people sometimes undergo a political rebirth of sorts (although not usually at such a late stage of their lives). A more typical example of persuasion might be found in the New Hampshire Republican who, in the aftermath of the war in the Persian Gulf, feels that George Bush is an outstanding president. One year later, amidst glaring signs of American economic decline, the same individual concludes that President Bush is not up to the task of economic recovery and decides to vote for Pat Buchanan in the New Hampshire Republican primary.

Persuasion via Priming

The case of the New Hampshire voter illustrates how persuasion—a change in political preference—can be the end product of learning, agenda setting, and attribution of responsibility. When the news was dominated by reports on the Persian Gulf War, this crisis was paramount in the minds of Americans. Because the outcome was so favorable, President Bush, as the commander in chief, was credited with the responsibility for the lopsided victory. One year later, when the flagging economy replaced the Gulf War as the paramount news story, President Bush appeared in a different light. What Americans saw was a president who initially claimed the recession was over, later showed up in a department store to suggest that Christmas shopping might help end the recession, and then traveled to Japan (ostensibly to open up the Japanese market for U.S. goods and services) in a highly publicized but disastrous policy initiative. Because of the salience of the economy and the apparent presidential impotence in matters of economic policy, President Bush's approval ratings dropped precipitously. On February 1, 1991, 83 percent of the public gave Bush a "good" or "very good" performance rating. One year later, the rating was down to 46 percent.

Clearly, the free-fall in President Bush's popularity during 1991 was brought about by changes in the public agenda and by the consequences of being held responsible for national issues. Communication researchers refer to this process as *priming*. While agenda setting reflects the impact of news coverage on the importance accorded issues, *priming* refers to the capacity of the media to isolate particular issues, events, or themes in the news as criteria for evaluating politicians.

The changes in President Bush's standing induced by priming occurred over a matter of months. In other instances priming works more rapidly, leaving its mark on the public's political preferences in a matter of days. In 1986 it was disclosed that the Reagan administration had been secretly channeling to the Nicaraguan Contras funds received from the sale of arms to Iran. The national media zeroed in on the issue. Because this issue dominated the news, the public's views on U.S. aid for the Contras (most people opposed such aid) became a major yardstick for evaluating Reagan, with the result that his popularity sagged to the lowest level of his second term.

Priming is really an extension of agenda setting, and addresses the impact of news coverage on the weight assigned to specific issues in making political judgments. In general, the more prominent an issue is in the national information stream, the greater is its weight in political evaluations. During the war in the Persian Gulf—while Americans were fascinated by images of smart bombs zooming in on Iraqi targets, Patriot missiles reliably intercepting Iraqi Scuds, and similar successes of the U.S. and allied forces—the news directed the public's attention to international affairs and defense (and simultaneously distracted them from domestic issues such as the savings and loan scandal). As a result, foreign policy and defense considerations became more important criteria for evaluating presidential performance. Americans surveyed during this period gave President Bush very high marks for his handling of foreign policy in general and the Gulf War in particular. At the same time, they gave him only average marks for his handling of the economy (see Figure 7.1). Yet his overall popularity reached record levels, suggesting that Americans gave precedence to the war and foreign affairs as bases for rating the president.

Priming by television news has been established in several experimental and survey-based studies, for ratings of both presidents and members of Congress. Such priming is found to take place across a

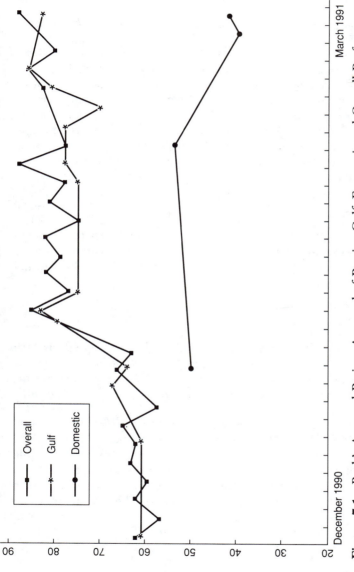

Figure 7.1 Bush's Approval Rating: Approval of Persian Gulf, Economic and Overall Performance (December 1990 to March 1991).

Source: Shanto Iyengar and Adam Simon, "News Coverage of the Gulf Crisis and Public Opinion: A Survey of Effects." Paper presented at the International Communication Association Meetings, Miami, 1992.

wide range of evaluations, including evaluations of job performance and assessments of political leaders' personal traits. In general, the priming effect is particularly strong when news stories explicitly suggest that incumbent politicians are responsible for the state of national affairs. For example, when television news stories suggested that "Reaganomics" was the principal cause of rising unemployment, evaluations of President Reagan's overall performance and competence were more strongly colored by assessments of his ability to manage the economy than were the evaluations of a control group who watched news stories that suggested alternative causes of unemployment.[14]

Finally, the priming effect is triggered by both news of political failures and news of political accomplishments. As the case of George Bush illustrates so vividly, priming can either help or harm incumbent officials. As we will see in Chapter 9, what this means is that public opinion is a double-edged sword; at times it boosts incumbents' ability to govern, but at other times it can shackle and paralyze them.

Direct Persuasion

Persuasion can also occur directly, without intervening effects such as agenda setting or priming. In such cases the central notion is that of diffusion—"who says what to whom?" The major determinants of direct persuasion, accordingly, are *source, message,* and *audience* characteristics.

A source can be evaluated with regard to how credible or trustworthy it is. One of the advantages enjoyed by people who work in broadcast journalism is that their product is seen as more credible than that of their competitors in the newspaper business.

Different properties of messages themselves have also been found to affect the likelihood of persuasion, but the relationship between message characteristics and attitude change is complicated by other factors such as the type of issue and the makeup of the audience. For example, *argument-based* messages tend to be more

[14]See Iyengar and Kinder, 1987, Chapter 9.

effective when the audience is relatively informed about the issue in question, but *image-based* appeals are more effective when the audience has no knowledge about the subject.[15]

Finally, two critically important aspects of the audience are the likelihood of exposure and acceptance of the message. Persuasion, according to McGuire's famous *two-factor theory*, depends upon people first getting the message (exposure) and then adopting it as their own (acceptance).[16] What is particularly interesting about McGuire's theory is that *the characteristics of the audience that increase the likelihood of exposure are the same characteristics that reduce the likelihood of acceptance.* More educated people, for example, are more likely to become exposed to information about current events. However, they are also more able to call upon alternative sources of information and a greater mass of stored information to question a particular item of new information. Thus, more educated people are better equipped to counterargue and hence less likely to accept or be persuaded by new information. Because exposure and acceptance work in opposite directions in determining the likelihood of persuasion, McGuire's two-factor model predicts a ∩–shaped relationship between characteristics of the audience such as education and the extent of attitude change. This pattern is shown in Figure 7.2.

Using McGuire's framework, the diffusion of preferences through the electorate can be predicted according to the intensity of particular news messages and the degree to which the message is consistent with the receiver's political values. When a pro-liberal message reaches a liberal audience, more-aware liberals—because they are more apt to get the message—will show more persuasion. When the same liberal message reaches a conservative audience, however, the more-aware conservatives—recognizing the message as liberal—will reject it and remain unpersuaded.

[15] For a review of message-related research, see Richard Petty and John Cacioppo, *Attitudes and Persuasion—Classic and Contemporary Approaches* (Dubuque, Iowa: William C. Brown, 1981).

[16] See William J. McGuire, "Personality and Susceptibility to Social Influence," in E. F. Borgatta and W. W. Lambert, eds., *Handbook of Personality Theory and Research* (New York: Rand-McNally, 1968).

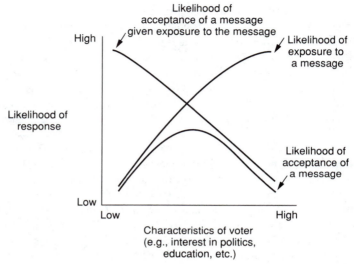

Figure 7.2   McGuire's Two-Factor Model.

McGuire's basic model can be extended to consider both one-sided and two-sided flows of information.[17] When information on a particular issue is one-sided, the more-aware receiver is more likely to accept the dominant perspective. However, when two sides of a story are presented (for example, a news story that includes both an official message and a countervailing oppositional message), the public's preferences on the issue are determined by a combination of their political awareness and partisan values. For instance, during the initial phases of the Vietnam War, news coverage conveyed a predominantly prowar message. During this period, less-aware liberals were more supportive of the war than more-aware liberals. The latter group, because of their attentiveness, were able to receive the less-audible antiwar signals. Over time, as the antiwar message in the media began to drown out the prowar message, less-aware liberals equaled their more attentive counterparts in opposition to the war.

---

[17] See John Zaller, *The Origins and Nature of Mass Opinion* (New York: Cambridge University Press, 1992).

Other researchers have searched for traces of diffusion at the collective or aggregate level of public opinion. Taken as a whole, the American public is relatively stable in its policy preferences. When public opinion does shift, it tends to follow the interpretations and "spin" conveyed by news reports. When the news suggests the desirability of a particular policy option, the American public increasingly prefers that option. Reports that emphasized the risks of American dependence on foreign sources of oil, for instance, had the effect of increasing public support for government subsidies to domestic energy producers.

In addition to the spin placed on particular policies, the public also responds to the preferences expressed by media analysts and commentators. When there is a preponderance of commentary suggesting that unemployment is a more pressing problem than inflation, public opinion will show a significant shift in this direction. [18]

Do the significant persuasive powers wielded by news commentators and anchors indicate that these individuals are particularly credible or trustworthy? Not necessarily. Research on news commentators shows that commentators tend to reflect the Washington "climate of opinion."[19] John Chancellor, Bill Moyers, and others who offer interpretation and analysis are, in this view, political chameleons whose interests are to reflect the dominant elite perspective in Washington. Even during the war in Vietnam, television coverage became critical of the war effort *only after key members of the Washington elite had come out in opposition to continued U.S. military involvement.*[20] In other words, elites develop preferences; because the media reflect these preferences, elite preferences shape the public's opinion. When newsmakers tilt in favor of a particular policy or ideology, the American public moves in that direction. The pattern of elite control over the flow of news, which is a recurring theme in this book, calls into question the idea of an independent or adversarial press. If reporters are unable to counter the official per-

[18]Benjamin Page and Robert Shapiro, *The Rational Public: Fifty Years of Trends in Americans' Policy Preferences* (Chicago: University of Chicago Press, 1992).
[19]See, for instance, Daniel Hallin, *The Uncensored War: The Media and Vietnam* (Berkeley, Calif.: University of California Press, 1986).
[20]See Hallin, 1987.

spective on events, the public's ability to evaluate issues independently is diminished. We will return to this issue in Part Four.

Summary

The study of media effects has come full circle since the 1940s and 1950s. The public's dependence upon television news and the ability of political elites to shape the course of news create significant potential for the media to shape opinion. As we have shown, news coverage affects public opinion in many ways. By providing voters with information, the media enable voters to develop relevant opinions. By emphasizing a particular issue, news coverage boosts the salience of that issue and encourages voters to use their opinions relating to the issue as the criteria for evaluating candidates. By presenting the news in episodic form, television directs viewers away from societal forces in attributing responsibility for political issues. Finally, depending upon their degree of political involvement and their initial predispositions, individuals may be persuaded by the news. The public is likely to adopt the views that are dominant in the news, and those views tend to be the views of the Washington policy-setting elites.

The multiple effects of the news may have contributed to the early conclusion that the media had minimal consequences in campaigns. Some of the effects we have just described can pull voters in opposite directions, and wash out in the aggregate. For example, a high-school graduate who encounters a news story on the shrinking job market for unskilled workers is likely to become highly concerned about this issue. Because his job prospects appear dim, the salience of the issue is likely to make him feel less positive about the performance of his incumbent representatives in Congress. However, if the news story is framed in episodic terms, he might absolve the incumbent of responsibility for the problem, instead blaming the Japanese for the loss of jobs. Thus, the combination of agenda setting and framing can result in no net change in the voter's political preference.

Analysis of the effects of the media on public opinion are complicated further because citizens can express their opinions in many ways. Of course, such expressions do not necessarily reveal the basis for the formation of the opinion. During elections, citizens may choose to vote for the candidate of one of the major parties, for a minor party candidate, or not to vote at all. Any of these choices may be motivated by different opinions about the state of the country and the qualities of the candidates. Those who vote for a Democrat may do so out of partisan loyalty, or because they were persuaded by television ads that attacked the Republican candidate. Those who do not vote may be either insufficiently informed about the issues and candidates or thoroughly alienated from the political process. In the next chapter we examine the effects of campaign communication on voting.

Suggested Readings

Larry Bartels. 1988. *Presidential Primaries and the Dynamics of Public Choice*. Princeton, N.J.: Princeton University Press.

Bernard Cohen. 1963. *The Press and Foreign Policy*. Princeton, N.J.: Princeton University Press.

Daniel Hallin. 1987. *The Uncensored War: The Media and Vietnam*. Berkeley, CA: University of California Press.

Shanto Iyengar and Donald Kinder. 1987. *News That Matters: Television and American Opinion*. Chicago: University of Chicago Press.

Shanto Iyengar. 1991. *Is Anyone Responsible?: How Television Frames Political Issues*. Chicago: University of Chicago Press.

Paul Lazarsfeld, Bernard Berelson, and Hazel Gaudet. 1948. *The People's Choice*, 2nd ed. New York: Columbia University Press.

Michael MacKuen and Stephen Coombs. 1981. *More Than News: Media Power in Public Affairs*. Beverly Hills, Calif.: Sage Publications.

Benjamin Page and Robert Shapiro. 1992. *The Rational Public: Fifty Years of Trends in Americans' Policy Preferences*. Chicago: University of Chicago Press.

Thomas Patterson. 1980. *The Mass Media Election: How Americans Choose Their President*. New York: Praeger.

Thomas Patterson and Robert McClure. 1976. *The Unseeing Eye: The Myth of Television Power in National Elections.* New York: G. P. Putnams.

Richard Petty and John Cacioppo. 1982. *Attitudes and Persuasion: Classic and Contemporary Approaches,* Dubuque, Iowa: William C. Brown.

John Zaller. 1992. *The Origins and Nature of Mass Opinion.* New York: Cambridge University Press.

THE CONSEQUENCES OF POLITICAL CAMPAIGNS

For candidates, winning is everything. But what it takes to win depends very much on the political setting. Campaigns do not occur in vacuums. As we noted in Chapter 6, the condition of the national economy has important consequences for the electoral fate of incumbents and challengers. More generally, the problems facing the state or nation determine the nature of the campaign—the caliber of the candidates, the issues that are emphasized, and the closeness of the race.

Often, campaigns are referenda on the state of the country and, by implication, on the performance of those in office. During periods of peace and prosperity, voters are generally content, and reelection comes easily for most incumbents. In anticipation of voters' response to "good times," the pool of qualified and electable challengers shrinks. During hard times, voters tend to hold the president's party responsible at the polls, and there is no shortage of challengers able and willing to take on incumbents.

For example, in February of 1991, immediately after the decisive and spectacular American military victory over the forces of Saddam Hussein, few Democrats dared to enter the presidential race against George Bush. Former senator Paul Tsongas (of Massachusetts) was the lone Democrat to declare his candidacy. President Bush's popularity was so high that a challenge for his party's nomination was inconceivable. However, the political realities of 1992 turned out to be quite different from those of 1991. Operation Desert Storm receded rapidly from the public view, and a continuous stream of news reports describing economic gloom and doom took over the limelight.

By September a large and eager slate of Democratic contenders had entered the race. Moreover, Patrick Buchanan, a conservative TV commentator who had never held elective office challenged President Bush in the Republican primaries and managed to obtain 36 percent of the vote in New Hampshire.[1]

The same logic applies to congressional elections. When the economy is strong, incumbents tend to face token opposition—candidates with little prior experience and weak track records. During hard times, however, incumbents are forced to face more seasoned challengers.

In addition to affecting the competitiveness of the campaign (by either attracting or deterring strong, well-financed challengers), the course of national events also affects the themes and issues that make up the flow of campaign communication. The presidential campaign of 1968 was dominated by the war in Vietnam and by issues of "law and order" associated with urban riots and antiwar protests. Similarly, the campaign of 1992 was dominated by economic and domestic issues because of the prolonged economic slump and because the venerable foreign policy problem (the threat posed by Soviet communism) had become essentially irrelevant.

Despite the importance of the historical context in which campaigns occur, the manner in which campaigns are waged—the candidates' skills at debating, their personal charm, the amount of money they raise, the quality of their advertising, or their ability to shape the news—does have a significant impact on the result. As we will show, statements made by candidates and their campaign organizations are the major source of information in elections. The campaign efforts are designed to inform the electorate who is running, clarify the important problems facing the country, and spell out what the candidates stand for. Campaigns also influence the extent to which people participate. When races are highly competitive and the candidates' messages are penetrating, more people are mobilized to vote.

[1] The decision by New York's Governor Mario Cuomo not to enter the 1992 presidential race is further evidence of the importance of economic conditions to campaign strategy. Because of the prolonged recession in New York, the state's budget was in shambles, and Cuomo had to raise taxes. Had he entered the race, his opponents could have used the economic difficulties of New York to attack his credentials and performance.

Similarly, campaigns that rely extensively on negative messages may leave the electorate disenchanted, not only with the candidates, but with the electoral process as well. Finally, by transmitting information, campaigns enable voters to choose one candidate over others.

The Dynamics of Campaigns

Political scientists and economists have become expert at predicting the outcome of presidential elections. Because the economy appears to be a dominant concern, the outcome of the presidential vote can be forecast (with considerable precision) on the basis of unemployment, inflation, and personal income statistics.[2]

These same forecasters, however, have been less successful at predicting the results of presidential primaries and elections for other offices. Moreover, they have been wholly unable to account for the sometimes dramatic shifts in the polls over the course of a general election campaign. In 1988, for example, Governor Michael Dukakis of Massachusetts registered a 17–point surge in the polls and then watched a 9–point lead in the polls in June evaporate to a 8–point loss on election day. These swings occurred in the face of stable economic and international conditions.

A closer look at the polls from 1952 through 1988 reveals that swings in voter loyalty exhibited in the Dukakis-Bush contest were unexceptional. Figure 8.1 shows the preelection polls in all presidential elections during these years. Each box in this figure shows the poll results for the period beginning 200 days before the election up to election day for each presidential election since 1952. The horizontal axis shows the numbers of days until the general election; the vertical axis shows the percentage of voters who said that they would support the Democratic candidate. A horizontal line is drawn in each graph at the 50 percent level to show which party had a majority of support among survey respondents.

The variability in the polls for each year is striking. Each box in the figure corresponds to a presidential election. There are three

---

[2] See Edward Tufte, *Political Control of the Economy* (Princeton: Princeton University Press, 1978); Steven Rosenstone, *Forecasting Presidential Elections* (New Haven: Yale University Press, 1985).

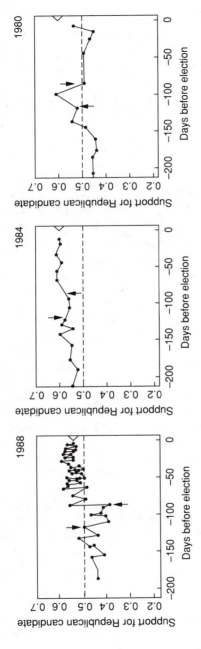
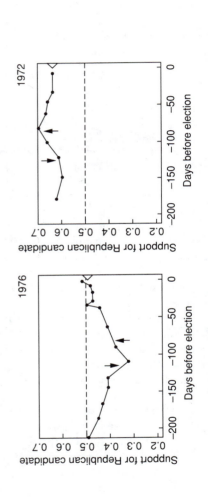

160

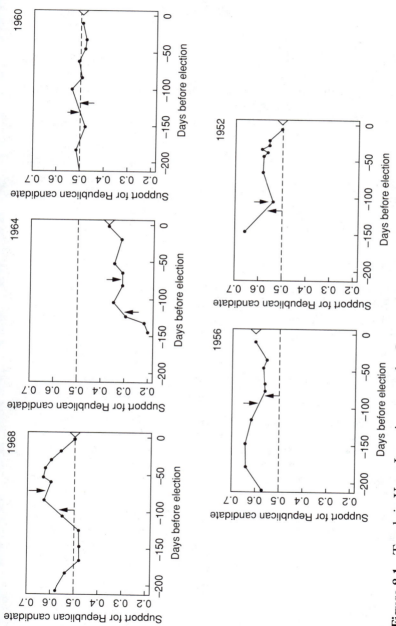

Figure 8.1 Trends in Voter Intentions over the Course of Presidential Campaigns.

Source: Andrew Gelman and Gary King, "Why Do Presidential Election Polls Vary So Much When the Vote Is So Predictable?" Paper presented at Midwest Political Science Association Meetings, Chicago, April 1992.

161

patterns. First, the variability in the polls declines over the course of the campaign. Second, there are large swings in mid-summer at the time of the nominating conventions. Third, there is little movement late in the campaign, when most voters have made up their minds. This pattern demonstrates that over the course of the election year, citizens become more certain about which candidate they support.

This general pattern can be appreciated more fully by examining the dynamics of public opinion during campaigns. To do so, we divide the campaign into three phases: the primaries, the conventions, and the two months prior to election day. In each period the fluctuations in the polls show distinct patterns that can be linked to the pattern of campaign communication.

Primary Elections: Media, Money, and Momentum

By all accounts the individual actions of the candidates have greatest influence during the primary election phase. Obviously, party is not a factor in primaries. Nor is the state of the economy important, unless an incumbent is being challenged. Rather, presidential primary campaigns are protracted struggles for momentum. The victors in the Iowa caucuses and the New Hampshire primary gain significantly in the national polls and strengthen their chances in the primaries to come. As Congressman Morris Udall complained:

> It's like a football game, in which you say to the first team that makes a first down with ten yards, 'Hereafter your team has a special rule. Your first downs are five yards. And if you make three of those you get a two-yard first down. And we're going to let your first touchdown count twenty-one points. Now the rest of you bastards play catch-up under the regular rules.'[3]

At the start of Senator Gary Hart's 1984 presidential campaign, Walter Mondale was easily the most popular Democratic candidate. In early February, before the New Hampshire primary, 54 percent of Democrats nationwide said they would vote for Mondale. Only

[3] Quoted in Sam Popkin, *The Reasoning Voter: Communication and Persuasion in Presidential Campaigns* (Chicago: University of Chicago Press, 1991), pp. 117–118.

2 percent indicated that they would vote for Hart, who was then relatively unknown. However, Hart's better than expected showings in the Iowa caucuses and the New Hampshire primary attracted extensive news coverage, and his level of name recognition spurted from 40 to 58 percent. In early March Hart was virtually a household name—85 percent of the electorate knew who he was. More importantly, Walter Mondale's huge lead in the polls evaporated: 40 percent of the Democrats said they would vote for Mondale; 33 percent said they supported Hart. In the span of less than a month, the Democratic race was transformed from total domination by Mondale into an extremely close contest between Mondale and Hart. Hart's meteoric rise almost enabled him to wrest the nomination from Mondale. As Hart himself acknowledged, "You can get awful famous in this country in seven days."[4]

Why do some candidates achieve such rapid outpourings of enthusiasm in the polls? Although we know it when we see it, momentum is something of a mystery. It is unclear, for example, why voters care about who is ahead in the polls or why momentum is rarely a factor in general elections.

One explanation is money. When a candidate surges ahead in the polls or makes a particularly strong showing in an early primary, his or her stock goes up, bringing with it an influx of campaign cash. The money is spent on even more campaign activity—precinct organizers, advertisements, and so on—giving the campaign an added boost.

In presidential primaries the role of money is especially dramatic. To qualify for federal matching funds, candidates need to demonstrate an ability to raise money from a broad spectrum of contributors. Specifically, candidates must raise $5,000 in each of 22 states in sums of less than $250 to begin to receive matching dollars. Continuing eligibility for matching funds, though, is tied to primary election performance. A candidate who fails to win a primary or receives less than 10 percent of the vote in successive primaries will lose matching funds. As a result, candidates who do

---

[4]Quoted in Larry Bartels, *Presidential Primaries and the Dynamics of Public Choice* (Princeton: Princeton University Press, 1988), p. 63.

poorly in the initial primaries will be financially handicapped, making it harder for them to advertise and maintain campaign organizations. In contrast, candidates who do well early on can use the additional boost from federal matching dollars to increase the level of their advertising and strengthen their campaign efforts in the upcoming primaries.

A further explanation of momentum is newspaper and television reporting. During primary campaigns, the media is especially likely to cover the campaign as a horse race. (Who's in the lead? Who's likely to place second? Who's the dark horse?) As we noted in Chapter 4, this pattern of coverage gives certain candidates disproportionate press and air time and increases their name recognition and thus their standing in the polls. This was certainly true of Gary Hart's 1984 bid for the presidency. Moreover, because of the prominence of horserace news coverage, the public tends to think about the candidates in terms of their electoral prospects rather than the issues.[5] For instance, in one 1976 survey virtually everything that the primary election voters recalled concerned the horse race.[6] Similarly, virtually all Democrats who were interviewed after the 1984 New Hampshire primary and who had heard of Gary Hart could offer an opinion on his prospects for gaining the nomination, but only three-quarters of them could offer an opinion concerning his position on the issues.[7]

Postconvention Euphoria

The primary election season culminates in the parties' nominating conventions. In recent years the nominations have been determined well in advance of the conventions, yet the parties continue to hold them. The reason is evident. Under normal circumstances, the media attention devoted to the convention provides the party's candidate a substantial boost in the polls. = BOUNCE

[5]Henry Brady and Richard Johnston, "What's the Primary Message: Horse Race or Issue Journalism?" in Garry Orren and Nelson Polsby (eds.), *Media and Momentum: The New Hampshire Primary and Nomination Politics* (Chatham, N.J.: Chatham House, 1987).
[6]Thomas Patterson, *The Mass Media Election: How Americans Choose Their President* (New York: Praeger, 1980).
[7]Bartels, 1988, p. 42.

The magnitude of these shifts is displayed in Figure 8.1. Two arrows denote the time of the parties' national conventions. The downward-pointing arrow corresponds to the Republican National Convention, and the upward-pointing arrow corresponds to the Democratic National Convention. Clearly, each convention benefits the party's standard bearers. Over the past 30 years, the average surge for the nominee in the polls has been seven points.

The reason for this sudden surge in public support is generally explained in terms of media coverage. For one thing, the conventions receive high television ratings, attracting nearly 80 percent of the households for some part of the proceedings.[8] With a large audience to play to, the parties are careful to stage an impressive event replete with patriotism, traditional values, and reminders of their past accomplishments. During the 1984 Republican convention, for instance, the Reagan campaign showed a videotape summarizing the president's accomplishments in office. The sight of cheering delegates and former opponents hailing the nominee contributed to an image of an effective and electable candidate.

Failure to create such an image can be costly, as the Democrats found out in 1968. The election had already been a rough one for the Democratic party. President Lyndon Johnson bowed out of the race after a poor showing against an antiwar candidate (Senator Eugene McCarthy of Minnesota) in the New Hampshire primary. Riots erupted in a number of major cities after Martin Luther King, Jr., was assassinated in Memphis in May. Robert F. Kennedy was assassinated in Los Angeles later that month after winning the California primary. By the time the party's convention met in Chicago in August, President Johnson was under siege from the right and the left within his own party as well as from the Republicans. During the convention, violent protests staged against the Vietnam War just outside the convention hall attracted as much coverage as the speeches within. The image conveyed by television was that of a party divided by domestic and foreign policies. As a result of the controversy, turmoil, and bloodshed, Hubert Humphrey, the Democratic nominee, did not enjoy a much-needed boost in the polls following the convention.

---

[8]These ratings have, however, declined in the 1980s, leading the networks to abandon the "gavel-to-gavel" coverage they provided in the 1960s and 1970s.

General Elections: Closing the Gap

August is typically the calm before the storm. On Labor Day general election campaigns begin in earnest. The next two months see the candidates squaring off against one another in televised debates, appearing at rallies and events across the country, and spending most of their campaign funds.

The intensification of the campaign during September and October produces surprisingly little movement in voters' preferences. In 1976, for instance, Jimmy Carter's support slipped from 54 percent of those intending to vote on September 1 to 50 percent on election day. In 1980 Carter and Reagan were deadlocked at the onset of the campaign, but Reagan was able to build a 9-point advantage by election day, winning 50 to 41 percent. In 1984 Reagan maintained his 10-point margin over Mondale. In 1988 George Bush gradually increased his lead from 5 percent to 7 percent. In fact, since 1948 the average shift in the polls between September 1 and election day has been only 6 percent. Sometimes this shift is enough to affect the outcome (as in 1980); at other times, it merely enables the losing candidate to narrow the gap (as in 1976).

The average impact of the general election campaign (6 percentage points) might seem insignificant, but in a close race this can make all the difference between winning and losing. The "winner-take-all" system of allocating electoral votes puts a premium on winning the big states—California, New York, Texas, Illinois, Ohio, Pennsylvania, and Florida—which together hold 38 percent of the electoral votes. In 1988, for instance, Michael Dukakis won New York's 36 electoral votes with only 51 percent of the vote. George Bush locked up Florida, Texas, and Ohio with better than 55 percent of the vote, but won by the smallest of margins (51 to 49 percent) in California, Illinois, and Pennsylvania. A small shift toward Dukakis in these three states would have given him 106 more delegates and called Bush's victory into question.

In summary, fluctuations in the polls over the course of the election are not necessarily predictable, but they do seem to correspond to the flow of campaign events and news coverage. The nature of the fluctuations in the polls, in fact, suggests that campaigns have an important informative role in elections. Each event brings new information, and the cumulation of campaign messages gradually brings the electorate to a decision on election day. In the next section we elaborate on the connections between campaign messages and the voting decisions of citizens.

The Multiple Effects of Campaign Messages

Electoral victory depends upon both the number of people who vote (turnout) and the number of voters who support particular candidates (preference). The analysis of the effects of campaign messages is complicated because the same messages that might help candidates on the dimension of turnout may harm them in the area of preference. For example, the airing of "attack" ads intended to keep the supporters of a candidate's opponent away from the polls may reduce interest in the campaign among all voters, including those likely to vote for the candidate airing the ads.

A further complication is that the messages and events generated by opposing campaigns interact with one another to inform and influence voters. People do not respond to each individual's campaign unilaterally with little regard for the messages of the competing campaign. As we will see shortly, the effects of George Bush's advertising in the 1988 presidential race sprang not only from his own advertisements, but also from the competing messages coming from the Dukakis campaign.

The dual objectives of maximizing the number of supporters who will vote (or minimizing the number of opponents who do so) and of projecting a favorable impression require a multiplicity of communication strategies. These include messages designed to make voters more familiar with the candidates and more able to form impressions about their personal traits, ability to perform in office, ideology, and electability. Campaigns also hope to shape voters' perceptions of the issues that are at stake in the campaign, thus affecting the standards by which candidates are evaluated and, ultimately, their level of electoral support.

In general, campaign messages affect viewers in two stages. First, news coverage and advertisements provide information about events, issues, and the candidates. Second, the messages influence voters' evaluations of the candidates.

Individuals come to campaigns with their own preferences about what government should be doing and what kind of person should represent them. Campaigns provide specific information about the various candidates, the activities of government, and the problems facing the country at the moment. Based on this information, voters begin to evaluate which of the candidates is best able to govern. The key to electoral choice is deciding which of the many issues, government policies, and candidate traits are important. Theoretically, a voter could compare two candidates with respect to 20 or 30 different characteristics—their party affiliation, prior experience, age, gender, liberal or conservative ideology, physical appearance, position on the death penalty, perceived honesty and competence, and so forth. In reality, however, most voters pay attention to relatively few criteria—those emphasized by the campaign.

Stage 1: Learning

A full year before a presidential election, most citizens have only their personal interests, partisanship, and ideologies to guide their decisions. They know little or nothing about most of the candidates or even who they are and, quite often, have thought little about public policies. In fact, many do not even know the dates of the primary and general elections, where they can vote, and how to register.[9] What and how much do American voters learn from campaigns? Beyond basic information about when and where to vote, the campaigns and the media inform the electorate about the candidates and the issues.

Name Recognition

Candidates enter campaigns with wide disparities in their public visibility. At one extreme are those universally recognized candi-

---

[9]Some political scientists have argued that the complexities of registration laws are one of the primary deterrents to electoral participation. Most unregistered voters do not know that they are not registered or how to register until the registration deadlines have passed. See Raymond Wolfinger and Steven Rosenstone, *Who Votes?* (New Haven: Yale University Press, 1980).

dates whose campaigns cannot reasonably be expected to make them more well known. Ronald Reagan, Gerald Ford, John Glenn, Ted Kennedy, and Walter Mondale (to name a few) entered their presidential campaigns with name recognition levels approaching 95 percent.[10] At the other extreme, some candidates enter the campaign virtually unknown. When Senator Lloyd Bentsen entered the 1976 presidential campaign, for instance, he was recognized by only 7 percent of the electorate.[11] There are two possible trajectories for those candidates who have little recognition at the outset. Most of the time, these candidates are unable to attract adequate news coverage, their visibility remains low, they are labeled hopeless causes, and they quickly withdraw from the race. In recent times the presidential campaigns of Joseph Biden, Birch Bayh, Bob Kerrey, Tom Harkin, Sargent Shriver, Jack Kemp, and John Connally have fit this "early exit" pattern. In other cases, however, (illustrated by Gary Hart) an initially unknown candidate attracts significant media attention early on by which he or she gathers momentum and is catapulted into national prominence. Jimmy ("Who?") Carter's level of name recognition went from 20 percent in early 1976 to 80 percent just before the Democratic convention.

The importance of visibility extends beyond mere familiarity. Candidates who attract early news coverage are also more likely to attract financial support. The amount of television news coverage directed at presidential candidates in January and February significantly boosts the amount of money these candidates raise.[12]

The final advantage of visibility is that in politics, familiarity breeds comfort. Although the voters' desire for a change of direction may occasionally reach such extraordinary levels that they will vote for candidates they've never heard of, in ordinary elections familiarity is an asset that contributes greatly to the electoral security

---

[10]Typically, name recognition is measured literally by presenting voters with a list of names. This is a relatively generous measure of recognition. An alternative (and more stringent) indicator is to ask survey respondents whether "they know anything" about the candidate in question.

[11]Bartels, 1988, p. 59.

[12]Diana Mutz, "Checkbook Public Opinion: The Influence of Horse Race Coverage on Campaign Contributors," Paper delivered at the Annual Meeting of the American Public Opinion Association, Phoenix, Ariz., 1991.

of incumbents. Name recognition, though, can only carry a bid for office so far. Voters also need to know what the candidates represent and what they intend to do if elected.

2. *Issues*

If the level of information concerning the specifics of the candidates' positions on major issues is a significant criterion for evaluating campaign messages, most campaigns are woefully inadequate. Americans tend to be poorly informed, and their ignorance persists through election day.

The Markle Foundation (a nonprofit organization concerned with elections) conducted a national survey during the 1988 campaign to compare the number of voters who became reasonably informed about issues that received extensive press coverage (such as taxes and capital punishment) and little coverage (such as the line-item veto and federal tax credits for day care). Between September and October, the public became (on average) more informed about where Bush and Dukakis stood on high-visibility issues by a margin of 10 percent. For low-visibility issues, the comparable average gain was only 3 percent. Two weeks before the 1988 election only 29 percent of the public knew about Bush's pledge to be the "education president." Similar levels of information applied to Michael Dukakis's positions. Although 58 percent of the public were aware of Dukakis's support for some form of universal health care, only 30 percent were familiar with the candidate's proposals to strengthen U.S. conventional forces.[13]

The timing of the Markle surveys (during the last six weeks of the campaign) makes these comparisons conservative estimates of the amount of campaign learning. Had the surveys spanned a longer period (e.g., between May and October), the degree of information gain might have been greater. More importantly, even though voters may know little about the specifics of the candidates' positions, they can differentiate fairly accurately between Democrats and Republicans on "traditional" issues such as welfare spending, tax cuts for the wealthy, or maintaining a strong defense. During the closing weeks of the 1976 campaign, for example, only 58 percent of Americans

[13]Bruce Buchanan, *Electing a President: The Markle Commission Research on Campaign '88* (Austin: University of Texas Press, 1991), chapt. 5.

could name the two vice-presidential candidates (Walter Mondale and Robert Dole). But 62 percent knew that President Ford was more concerned with inflation, and 72 percent knew that Carter was more concerned with unemployment.[14]

Thus, while knowing relatively little about the content of the candidates' policy proposals, voters appear fairly well informed about general differences between the candidates as long as the candidates' positions are consistent with those ascribed to their party. Similarly, voters also tend to be well informed about the groups and interests that stand to gain from Democratic or Republican policies (e.g., blue-collar workers and senior citizens in the case of Democrats, business in the case of Republicans). Overall, therefore, campaigns provide voters with "a surprising amount of information about the basic policy directions offered by opposing presidential candidates."[15]

3. *Characteristics of the Candidates*
Voters not only learn who the candidates are, but over the course of the campaign they also become more familiar with their respective backgrounds and qualities. The information generated by the campaigns enables voters to develop differentiated—though not necessarily accurate—images of the candidates, including impressions of their policy preferences, personal traits, and electoral prospects.[16] Voters figure out who is liberal or conservative. who favors or opposes the death penalty or affirmative action; whether the candidates are tough, sincere, smart, or compassionate; and, finally, whether they have a chance of winning. In short, the campaign serves to fill in voters' impressions of the candidates.

In one study of the development of policy-related images, researchers monitored changes in voter opinionation during the last week of the 1982 congressional campaign. One group of experimental participants received a news story (embedded into a local television newscast) each evening about the candidates.[17] Another

---

[14]Popkin, 1991, p. 41.
[15]Popkin, 1991, p. 41.
[16]See Popkin, 1991.
[17]The study was run in New Haven, Connecticut, and the candidates were Lawrence DeNardis (Republican) and Bruce Morrison (Democrat).

group was given no news at all about the congressional campaign. At the end of the study 44 percent of the participants in the "candidate" condition expressed an opinion on the candidates' positions on five different policy issues. Among participants in the control condition, the figure was 26 percent.[18]

Voters also learn about the candidates' personal characteristics. Relatively minor campaign incidents often form the basis for impressions of the candidates' personalities. In 1976 President Gerald Ford's unfamiliarity with Mexican cuisine (Ford neglected to remove the husk of a tamale before biting into it at a rally in San Antonio, an act that received extensive television coverage) was interpreted by Hispanic voters as indicating that Ford was not particularly sensitive to their needs. Ronald Reagan's insistence that the 1980 New Hampshire debate be open to all Republican candidates ("I paid for this mike . . . ") projected an image of assertiveness and conviction. In general, voters develop opinions about the candidates' qualities as human beings.

The traits of competence and integrity are particularly important components of voters' images of the candidates. In 1984, for example, over 90 percent of the public was able to rate Reagan, Mondale, Jackson, Hart, and Glenn on a series of traits relating to competence and integrity as early as January.[19] To be seen as intelligent, decisive, honest, and sincere is a prerequisite for electoral success. Senator Edward Kennedy has been unable to run successfully for the presidency because large numbers of the public question his integrity. In 1980 Jimmy Carter's candidacy was damaged by widespread perceptions that he was a weak person.

The prominence of character traits in the public mind seems to have been magnified by the trend toward media campaigns and sound-bite news coverage, which provides candidates with little opportunity to put forth their positions on the issues. In 1988 the public cited character traits as relevant qualifications for the pres-

---

[18] See Shanto Iyengar and Donald Kinder, *News That Matters: Television and American Opinion* (Chicago: University of Chicago Press, 1987), chapt. 11.
[19] Brady and Johnston, 1987, pp. 164–66.

idency far more frequently than issue positions.[20] Moreover, there is evidence that spontaneous references to personality and character as a basis for evaluating candidates are made most frequently by the most educated voters, who are most likely to tune in to the campaign.[21]

The impact of campaigns on opinionation is most apparent in the area of "viability." News stories detailing the candidates' electoral prospects dominate the flow of news. It is hardly surprising, therefore, that the American public thinks about the candidates in terms of their electability. Virtually all Democrats interviewed after the 1984 New Hampshire primary who had heard of Gary Hart offered an opinion on whether Hart could win the nomination. However, one out of every four of such Democrats failed to offer an opinion concerning Hart's position on the major domestic issue of the campaign—cuts in government social programs.[22]

Stage 2: Choice

Citizens must make two types of electoral choices. They must first choose whether or not to vote. If the answer is to vote, they must then settle on a candidate. In so doing, they must sift through the many facts they have learned about the issues and the opinions that they have developed about the candidates.

For some people the process through which the information is translated into votes is immediate and simple. For example, single-issue voters who are strongly prolabor might always favor the candidate endorsed by the AFL-CIO. This is the model of *direct persuasion* described in Chapter 7. It may be applied to many types of voters. Party Voters choose their party's nominees. Egocentric Economic Voters ask, "Am *I* better off today than I was four years ago?" Sociotropic Economic Voters ask, "Is the country's economy doing better today than it was four

---

[20] See Buchanan, 1991, Table 5.3.
[21] Arthur Miller, Martin Wattenberg, and Oksana Malanchuk, "Schematic Assessments of Presidential Candidates," *American Political Science Review* 80, (1986); 521–40.
[22] Bartels, 1988, p. 42.

years ago?" Interest Group Voters look for cues from group leaders. In all such cases the decision is straightforward: Acquire the relevant piece of information and choose accordingly.[23]

For most voters, however, electoral decisions are not so clear-cut. During primary elections, for example, party voting is not useful. Voters interested in the state of the economy may not know which of many primary candidates is a particularly good alternative to the incumbent candidate. They may also be in doubt over the state of the economy or the prospects for international conflict. In the face of uncertainty people must decide how to decide. They must determine which issues and characteristics of the candidates are important. This is the *indirect* or "persuasion-via-priming" model of persuasion discussed in Chapter 7. According to this view, people arrive at their electoral preferences gradually. They begin by identifying the most important issues in the election and the qualities most needed in political leaders. Next, they evaluate the candidates according to these criteria.

Setting the Campaign Agenda

Political campaigns constantly strive to focus the voters' attention on selected issues to reflect the public's most pressing concerns. Incumbents emphasize issues and policies for which they can claim success, while challengers point out policies that have failed. In 1992 the Bush campaign continually attempted to remind voters of the war in the Persian Gulf, while the Democrats worked hard to focus attention on the weaknesses in the economy.

How do candidates set the public's agenda? We have already documented the powerful agenda-setting effects of "free" media, for example, news coverage. During campaigns, paid media are even more important sources of political information. Research shows that voters' political priorities respond to the content of campaign advertising. The effect is most striking when both campaigns devote

---

[23] While different voters may employ different rules, the same voter may use a combination of rules at different stages of the campaign. Strong partisans, for example, use simple party voting in the general election, but their reasoning is more complicated in the primaries.

a considerable portion of their paid advertising to the same issue. In the Pennsylvania Senate race of 1991, for example, Democratic winner Harris Wofford made national health insurance the cornerstone of his campaign. When Wofford's standings in the polls surged, Republican opponent Richard Thornburgh decided to meet the issue head-on and ran several ads attacking Wofford's proposals and the entire concept of government-sponsored health care. Most accounts of this campaign suggest that health insurance became the central issue.[24] It was an issue that clearly benefited Wofford. Although he trailed by 47 percentage points in June, he actually won by 10 percent in November.

The selection of campaign issues is also affected by partisanship. Even though the importance of party identification as a basis for voting has diminished in the 1980s, traditional partisan positions on many issues are still widely held. The public knows where the parties stand on major issues and also differentiates between Democratic and Republican politicians in terms of their policy capabilities. Republicans, for example, are generally considered better able and more willing to maintain the nation's national security and tougher on the issue of crime than Democrats. Democrats are seen as having the edge on most economic issues and protecting the rights of minorities and the underprivileged. Candidates therefore seek to highlight the issues they "own" (based on their partisanship). Republican presidential candidates are likely to play to their strengths and dwell on foreign policy and defense; Democrats gain from campaigning on domestic issues such as education and the environment.

There is considerable evidence that candidates shape voters' perceptions most effectively when their campaigns resonate with these partisan stereotypes. For example, studies have shown that Democratic viewers of network newscasts that focused on civil rights and pollution were more likely to use these traditional Democratic issues as bases for evaluating the president than were Republican subjects who were exposed to the same sustained coverage. Similarly, Republicans were more responsive to news coverage of defense and inflation.

---

[24]Robin Toner, "The Restive Voters: Mixed Results at Polls Show Both Parties that Status Quo Won't Satisfy the Nation." *New York Times*, November 7, 1991, p. A1.

"Priming" Evaluations of Candidates

Priming refers to the power of the media to isolate particular issues, events, or themes in the news as criteria for evaluating politicians. In the context of campaigns, priming means that the issues that receive heavy news coverage or campaign advertising are likely to determine voters' evaluations of the candidates.

The effects of priming have been observed in a number of campaigns. For example, in a study of the 1982 election in the third congressional district of Connecticut, researchers found that voters who were more optimistic about national economic conditions tended to support the Republican incumbent, while those who were more pessimistic supported the Democratic challenger. However, after the subjects had been exposed to a week-long series of local newscasts that included a daily story on the state of the economy, the effect of economic outlooks on voting preferences had more than tripled! An even stronger priming effect emerged with respect to participants' perceptions of the personal traits of the candidates. Viewers generally intended to vote for the candidate in whom they saw more positive personal characteristics. But among voters who were exposed to a series of news reports about the candidates' personal backgrounds, the impact of these perceptions was increased nearly fivefold.[25]

An even more dramatic instance of priming took place during the closing stages of the 1980 presidential campaign. One week before the election every major poll showed President Jimmy Carter and his opponent Ronald Reagan running neck and neck. Three days before the election, the Iranian government issued a diplomatic overture regarding the American hostages who had been held captive in Teheran for more than a year. President Carter suspended his campaign and returned to Washington to oversee the negotiations. The national media became riveted on the issue. The consequences for President Carter were disastrous. Public opinion shifted convulsively toward Reagan as voters were reminded of the Carter administration's impotence in dealing with the issue. Thus, an extremely close race was transformed into a decisive victory for Ronald Reagan, largely as a result of the priming of the hostage issue. After

[25]Iyengar and Kinder, 1987, chapt. 11.

examining the results from his last preelection poll, Pat Caddell, the pollster for the Carter campaign, called Carter's chief of staff Hamilton Jordan with the news:

> The sky has fallen in. We are getting murdered. All the people that have been waiting and holding out for some reason to vote Democratic have left us. I've never seen anything like it in polling. Here we are neck and neck with Reagan and everything breaks against us. It's the hostage thing.[26]

By reminding voters of the hostage issue immediately before election day, the news elevated the importance of foreign policy as a criterion for choosing between the candidates. Since most voters judged Ronald Reagan to be tougher in the area of foreign policy, his candidacy was significantly strengthened, and on election day, he was elected by a landslide.[27]

Similar priming effects occur as a result of paid media. In presidential campaigns, for instance, the relative importance of voters' assessments of the candidates' competence and integrity has been found to vary in proportion to the degree of emphasis placed on these traits in televised advertisements.[28] In effect, candidates are able to invite voters to evaluate them on the basis of themes or traits that they choose to market.

Priming is especially important in primary election campaigns. Given the horse race focus of most news reports, primary voters are likely to be heavily primed with information about the candidates' electability. Voters thus come to favor the candidates that are viewed as electable.

The Special Importance of Debates and Advertising

In addition to attracting news coverage, candidates can also reach the voters by participating in televised debates and purchasing cam-

---

[26]Quoted in Hamilton Jordan, *The Last Year of the Carter Presidency* (New York: Putnams, 1982), p. 365.

[27]See Iyengar and Kinder, 1987.

[28]Darrell West, "Ads and Priming in Election Campaigns," Paper presented at the Annual Meeting of the American Political Science Association, Washington, D.C., 1991.

paign advertising. Debates are risky because a candidate's performance can leave a favorable or unfavorable impression. The role of advertising is quite complex: The increased use of "attack" or negative advertising can affect both turnout and voter preference.

Debates

Since 1976 televised debates have been regular campaign events. They are often broadcast during prime time and may be watched by millions of potential voters. How are these viewers affected? In 1976, in the midst of a debate with Jimmy Carter, President Gerald Ford answered a question about foreign policy by stating that the countries of Eastern Europe were free of Soviet domination. Stunned by the reply, the reporter repeated the question, and Ford repeated his answer.[29]

By all accounts, President Ford had committed a major gaffe. By demonstrating his own unfamiliarity with issues of foreign policy, the president effectively neutralized Georgia governor Jimmy Carter's major campaign liability—his complete lack of foreign policy experience. Notwithstanding Ford's blunder, polls conducted immediately after the debate showed that voters' support for the candidates had remained stable. By wide margins, Democrats responded that Carter had "won" the debate. By equally wide margins, Republicans gave the nod to Ford.

For the next few days the national press was saturated with stories about the gaffe and the impact of Ford's statement on the campaign. One week after the debate a new poll was conducted. This time there was a significant increase in the proportion of viewers who felt Carter had done a better job in the debate than Ford. Moreover, Carter began to increase his lead over Ford in the polls. Thus, while the debate by itself generated little change in voters' impressions of the candidates, the intense news coverage and analysis that ensued did produce a net gain in Carter's image.[30]

This example can be generalized to all televised debates. Typically, viewers evaluate the candidates' performance according to their partisan leanings. However, if a particular incident or response

[29]In 1991 Ford joked that he had merely been 15 years ahead of his time!
[30]Gallup Poll, *Gallup Opinion Index*, (Princeton, N. J.: Gallup Organization, 1976) p. 906.

generates considerable news coverage, and the coverage is one-sided in its impact, significant shifts in voters' evaluations of the candidates occur. Thus, it appears that debates fail to move voters on their own; when accompanied by news "spin," however, they can become significant persuasive cues.

Campaign Advertising

There have been innumerable studies of the effects of product advertising and political advertising. In general, this literature indicates that advertising can be a potent weapon. Candidates who are able to mount extensive advertising campaigns tend to do well at the polls. These studies also suggest that political advertising is an interactive process. What candidates can accomplish by advertising often depends upon their opponents' advertising.

In recent years consultants and campaign managers have increasingly turned to "attack" advertisements that attempt to discredit a candidate's opponents rather than promote the sponsoring candidate directly. The 1988 Bush campaign used this strategy extensively. Immediately after the Republican convention, the Bush campaign began an unrelenting attack on Dukakis's positions on major issues, his record as governor of Massachusetts, and his commitment to basic American values. Inexplicably, the Dukakis campaign failed to respond directly to these charges for over a month. Most postmortems of the 1988 presidential campaign emphasized the significant payoffs to Bush that resulted from the Dukakis campaign's inability or unwillingness to confront these ads. The Dukakis campaign violated Roger Ailes's first axiom of advertising strategy: "Once you get punched, you punch back."[31]

Although many studies of political advertising could be cited, we will limit our further discussion to two studies conducted during the California 1990 gubernatorial campaign.

Advertising and Turnout

According to several analysts, negative advertising is a significant deterrent to voting. By playing on voters' generally negative images

[31]Quoted in David Runkel, *Campaign for President: The Managers Look at 1988* (Dover, Mass.: Auburn House, 1989), p. 164.

of politicians, attack ads are thought to disillusion and alienate the electorate from the political process. This hypothesis was tested during the 1990 gubernatorial campaign in California. A cross-section of Los Angeles residents was shown a 15-minute clip from the local evening news, including the commercial breaks. Unknown to the viewers, the researchers had inserted one of four variants of a political advertisement they had created into the commercial break. All four political ads featured the identical visual track, but different voice-overs depending on which candidate was portrayed as having aired the ad and whether or not the ad attacked the opponent or promoted the sponsor. Thus, there were four versions of the ad in which Republican Pete Wilson either promoted himself or attacked Democrat Dianne Feinstein and Feinstein either promoted herself or attacked Wilson (see insert). Participants in the study were randomly assigned to one of the four treatment groups. After watching the news video, subjects were asked, among other things, whether and how they intended to vote.

This simple manipulation had a significant impact on intention to vote. Subjects who saw the attack versions of the ad were less likely to vote than those who viewed the self-promotion versions. The attack ads decreased expected turnout by almost 1 percent.[32] Although the 1 percent shift in voting turnout induced by this experiment might seem small, its stimulus was rather trivial—a single ad viewed once. Based on the results, it appears that a campaign strategy featuring extensive use of attack ads could substantially diminish turnout.

Advertising and Choice

The second study was designed to investigate the effects of attack advertising on voters' preferences. Specifically, the question was whether the use of attack ads had a stronger effect on voter preference than self-promotion ads. A further issue was the degree to which attack ads yielded similar payoffs for different candidates.

The results generally revealed that the effects of campaign ads are interdependent and that attack advertising works differently for

[32] Stephen Ansolabehere and Shanto Iyengar, "The Electoral Effects of Issues and Attacks," Presented at the Annual Meeting of the American Political Science Association, Washington, D.C., 1991.

Voice Tracks

Video Track	Pete Wilson Positive	Pete Wilson Negative
Scenes of the California coastline	"When Federal bureaucrats wanted permission to drill for oil off the coast of California, *Pete Wilson* said *No*."	"When Federal bureaucrats wanted permissions to drill for oil off the coast of California, *Dianne Feinstein* said *Yes*."
Scenes of trees and lakes	"When the auto-mobile industry wanted to weaken pollution controls, *Pete Wilson* said *No*."	"When the auto-mobile industry wanted to weaken pollution controls, *Dianne Feinstein* said *Yes*."
Scenes of waterfalls, rivers, forest, and lakes	"The Russian River, the Giant Sequoias, Yosemite Valley, Mono Lake — these are the treasures that make our state great."	"The Russian River, the Giant Sequoias, Yosemite Valley, Mono Lake — these are the treasures that make our state great."
Elk grazing	"*Pete Wilson* will *protect* these wonders."	"*Dianne Feinstein* will *destroy* these wonders."
Candidate logo	"California *needs a governor* like *Pete Wilson*."	"California *can't afford a politician* like *Dianne Feinstein*."

different candidates. What Feinstein could accomplish through her ads depended upon what Wilson's ads were saying and vice-versa. Overall, Feinstein's best strategy (in terms of the tactic that maximized the percentage of viewers who intended to vote for her) was to promote herself as an honest, compassionate, and ethical person.

In contrast, Wilson's most effective strategy was to attack Feinstein's honesty and moral standards.

These results suggest that attack ads cannot be used effectively by all candidates. Although Wilson clearly benefited by going on the attack, Feinstein clearly benefited by promoting herself. This asymmetry in the effects of advertising tactics (an exception to Roger Ailes's rule) we believe can be attributed to gender norms and stereotypes. Attack spots aired by women may violate cultural norms concerning gender-appropriate "feminine" behavior. In contrast, voters may expect male candidates to display more "aggressive" or dominance-oriented behavior.

In the real world, media consultants typically face more complex decisions than simply deciding whether to adopt a strategy of attack or promotion. They must also try to reach different demographic groups of voters with carefully tailored appeals. In California the 1990 gubernatorial race pitted a woman against a man. The Feinstein campaign attempted to capitalize on gender by mobilizing women voters. How did male and female voters respond to the candidates' ads? Among males, neither candidate had a clear-cut best strategy; whether they attacked or promoted did not have much impact on males' preferences. Among female voters, however, tactics mattered: Feinstein's best strategy was to promote herself, while Wilson's best strategy was to attack. The differences in the effects of particular advertising strategies for gender groups reveal the complexities posed by targeting. Feinstein's and Wilson's best tactics for males and females turned out to be quite different from one another and from their best tactics for the population at large.

Overall, the California studies indicate that televised political advertising can have powerful effects on electoral outcomes. Despite the modest scope of the experimental manipulations, the candidates' advertisements did significantly affect viewers' voting intentions and the candidate they preferred. It pays to advertise.

This section has described the multiple effects of campaign messages on individual voters. Campaign communication serves to educate and persuade voters. Information affects what people know about the election and what they regard as important. Based on the information they obtain, people decide whether to vote and which candidate to support. Debates and advertising are both important components of the stream of campaign information. The candidates' performance in debates, by generating considerable news coverage and analysis, can move voters' preferences. Finally, televised advertising affects both turnout and preference.

Campaign Finance and Electoral Competition

The research on advertising suggests that campaign messages can be powerful tools. Is it possible, then, to win an election simply by saturating the airwaves with advertisements? Perhaps. But in campaigns, as in the rest of politics, each action is met with a reaction from one's opponents. Unlike the laws of physics, the reactions in politics are not always equal nor are they necessarily opposite. One thing is certain, though: In the age of television they are expensive.

The best gauge of the cumulative effect of paid messages in the television era is obvious: How much do candidates spend? Candidates can send hundreds of campaign messages, but to do this is very expensive. In Chapters 2 and 4 we described the different ways in which media campaigns operate. Typically, advertising consumes a large and increasing share of the campaign organization's budget. A typical candidate for the U.S. Senate in 1990 spent approximately $2.5 million. Fully one-third of this budget goes to pay for televised advertisements. A typical House race in 1990 cost around $350,000. A quarter of this sum goes for television advertising. In addition, candidates invested heavily in consultants, travel, polling, and other expenses essential to media campaigns.[33]

Does money win elections? There is no simple answer to this question because there is very little accurate data on total media expenditures. It is true, however, that on average, winning candidates spend more money than losers. In fact, winners usually spend double the amount expended by their opponents. In 1990 the aver-

---

[33] In local elections the picture is quite different. Because media markets are much larger than city council, school board, and state legislative districts, candidates in these races often spend little on television and radio ads. Candidates for the California assembly, for instance, spent around 8 to 10 percent of their campaign budgets on radio and television throughout the 1980s. The biggest communications expenditures in such races are for handbills and direct mailings. See California Commission on Campaign Finance, *The New Gold Rush: Financing California's Legislative Campaigns* (Los Angeles: Committee for Responsive Government, 1987).

age winner in a House race spent $410,000 compared to just under $200,000 for the average loser. In the Senate the average winner spent $3.4 million, while the average loser spent $1.9 million. Past elections bear the same pattern. In the House, the ratio of winners' to losers' spending was 1.7 to 1 in 1978, 1.8 to 1 in 1982, 2.6 to 1 in 1986, and 2.2 to 1 in 1991.

In addition to this discrepancy in total spending, the margin by which winners outspend losers is correlated with their margin of victory. The average percentage of the vote received by winners in contested races in 1978 was 63, in 1982 it was 65, in 1986 it was 68, and in 1990 it was 65. This crude connection between spending and victory across years is born out within elections. Figure 8.2 shows the relationship between the share of votes received by incumbents in elections for the House of Representatives in 1990 and the incumbents' share of total spending. Clearly, the more a candidate spends, relative to his or her opponent, the more votes he or she receives. This is true of incumbents as well as challengers.

Of course, money is not everything. Other factors are involved as well. For example, Newt Gingrich barely won reelection in Georgia's 6th Congressional District despite spending five times as much as his opponent, Democrat David Worley. This close call can be attributed to the fact that Gingrich, who represents a marginally Republican district, is much more conservative than his constituency.

The most important determinant of congressional elections is incumbency. In contemporary elections knowing who is the incumbent is tantamount to knowing who will win. Incumbents who run for reelection to the House of Representatives win 95 percent of the time, and to the U. S. Senate 80 percent of the time.

Incumbents' electoral advantages, in fact, reflect their edge in media and money.[34] First, it takes less money for incumbents to win than it does for challengers. In 1978 incumbents who beat chal-

---

[34]There is some controversy over the extent of incumbents' campaign finance advantages. While the figures presented here are indisputable, early estimates found that the bang for the buck for incumbents was zero while the bang for the buck for challengers was positive. (See Gary Jacobson, "Money and Votes Reconsidered," *Public Choice* 47 (1985): 7–62.) Subsequent statistical work has corrected various problems and found that spending for both incumbents and challengers affects the vote and that the marginal effect of each is similar. The question is far from settled, however.

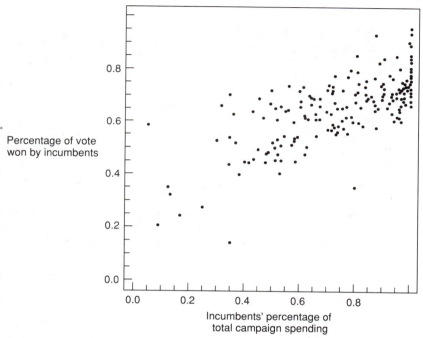

Figure 8.2   The Relationship Between Campaign Expenditures and Votes: Spending and Vote Shares in 1990 House Races.
Source: Compiled by authors from Federal Election Commission, *Reports on Financial Activity 1989–1990* (Washington, D.C.: F.E.C., 1991).

lengers spent $1.80 for every dollar spent by their challengers, and in 1986 they spent $2.80 for every dollar spent by their challengers. Challengers who beat incumbents, on the other hand, spent $4 for every dollar spent by the incumbents they faced in 1978, and $3.20 for every dollar spent by the incumbents they faced in 1986. The reason for this asymmetry is simple. Challengers start a campaign with a considerable deficit in name recognition that can be surmounted only with an enormous expenditure.

Second, almost all incumbents raise and spend more money than their opponents. Over the course of the 1980s House incumbents spent slightly more than $2 for every dollar spent by the challengers they faced. And only 5 to 10 percent of the challengers in any year managed to spend more than the incumbents they opposed.

The edge that incumbents have in monies spent is due largely to the ease with which they raise money. Elected officials begin their reelection campaign with a list of potential donors, those who gave to the last campaign, and a new set of sources, those organized interests that became familiar with the representatives' activities in office. Challengers rarely have such extensive and well-established connections for raising funds and instead have to rely more heavily on individual donors and their own resources. In 1990 House races, for example, incumbents raised 55 percent of their money from individual citizens, 34 percent of their money from political action committees (special interest groups), and 1 percent of their funds from political parties. Challengers, by contrast, raised 60 percent of their funds from individual citizens; 17 percent from political action committees; 1 percent from parties. The remaining 14 percent came from their personal wealth.[35]

In short, the growing importance of mass media in campaigns and the high cost of heavy television use have put a premium on campaign cash in contemporary elections. Not all candidates benefit equally. Heavy use of television can help challengers overcome the voters' ignorance of them. But incumbents, who start out relatively well known, have an easier time raising campaign money and broadcasting their campaign message.

Summary

What happens in campaigns depends greatly upon the political setting. Incumbents face either weak or strong challengers depending upon the state of economic conditions. Once campaigns get under way, the candidates' messages affect voters in several ways. First, people acquire information that affects what they know about the election. By spending money on advertising, by appearing in debates, and by attracting news coverage, the candidates become more

[35]Estimates of the marginal cost of raising money give incumbents a 3:1 advantage. See Stephen Ansolabehere, "Winning Is Easy, but It Sure Ain't Cheap" (Los Angeles: Center for American Politics and Public Policy, University of California, 1990).

visible, and voters become more able to express opinions on the candidates' personalities, policy preferences, and electability. Candidates who succeed in the early primaries benefit from favorable news coverage, which further strengthens their claims of electability and produces an upsurge in public support.

What voters learn during the campaign affects their evaluations of the candidates. By discussing some issues and ignoring others, candidates can shape the public agenda. The issues and themes raised by the candidates in their speeches and debates and the issues they highlight in their ads become the issues that voters think about. In general, Democrats and Republicans inject different issues into campaigns, issues on which they enjoy a reputational advantage. These efforts to shape the campaign agenda do have electoral payoffs. The candidate who makes his or her issue particularly salient to voters gains in support because voters' assessments of the candidates on that issue become the paramount criteria for choosing between the candidates.

Finally, advertising and televised debates play important roles in campaigns. In debates, it is important for candidates to perform well. Blunders guarantee unfavorable news coverage and commentary that can harm the candidate's image and strengthen the opponent's. Advertising clearly influences voters, but the effects of ads are interactive: What one candidate can accomplish through advertising depends upon what the other candidates do. Attack ads can be used to weaken the opponent's image, but they reduce voter turnout as well. Overall, the evidence clearly shows that campaigns affect votes: Candidates who raise and spend the most money on their campaigns are the candidates who win.

Suggested Readings

F. Christopher Arterton. 1984. *Media Politics: The News Strategies of Presidential Campaigns.* Toronto: Lexington Books.

Larry Bartels. 1988. *Presidential Primaries and the Dynamics of Public Choice.* Princeton: Princeton University Press.

Bruce Buchanan. 1991. *Electing a President: The Markle Commission Research on Campaign '88.* Austin: University of Texas Press.

Shanto Iyengar and Donald Kinder. 1987. *News That Matters: Television and American Opinion.* Chicago: University of Chicago Press.

Gary Jacobson. 1987. *The Politics of Congressional Elections.* Boston: Little-Brown.

Gary Jacobson and Samuel Kernell. 1983. *Strategy and Choice in Congressional Elections.* New Haven: Yale University Press.

Sidney Kraus. 1976. *The Great Debates: Carter vs. Ford, 1976.* Bloomington, Ind.: Indiana University Press.

Gary Orren and Nelson Polsby, eds. 1987. *Media and Momentum: The New Hampshire Primary and Nomination Politics.* Chatham, N.J.: Chatham House Publishers.

Samuel Popkin. 1991. *The Reasoning Voter: Communication and Persuasion in Presidential Campaigns.* Chicago: University of Chicago Press.

A. James Reichley, ed. 1987. *Elections American Style.* Washington, D.C.: Brookings Institution.

Frank Sorauf. 1992. *Inside Campaign Finance: Myths and Realities.* New Haven: Yale University Press.

Mark Westlye. 1991. *Senate Elections and Campaign Intensity.* Baltimore: Johns Hopkins University Press.

John Zaller. 1992. *The Origins and Nature of Mass Opinion.* New York: Cambridge University Press.

CHAPTER 9

PUBLIC OPINION AND THE POWER TO GOVERN

On November 5, 1991, New Jersey voters threw the bums out. They did so with a vengeance. Overnight, the party balance in the state legislature shifted from Democratic control to a substantial Republican majority. The traditional advantages of incumbency did not operate. What had aroused the anger of New Jersey voters? The answer was simple: Governor James Florio.

During his tenure, Florio, a Democrat who had been elected for a four-year term in 1988, dealt with the state's budget problems by increasing taxes rather than cutting services. He also initiated a plan to transfer resources from relatively affluent suburban school districts to needy inner-city districts. Because Florio was not on the ballot in 1991, his fellow Democrats in the state legislature bore the brunt of the voters' wrath.[1] In the ensuing two years, Florio was hamstrung by a Republican legislature that could override any veto. New Jersey's disenchantment with its governor was profound.

The 1991 elections in New Jersey demonstrate a more general rule: Elected officials need public support to govern. All successful politicians care first and foremost about their own electoral fates. They want to know, as Mayor Ed Koch of New York often asked, "How am I doing?" Information reflecting their public reputation and popular support provides politicians a simple and immediate gauge of how voters will react to their policies and decisions.

---

[1]Joseph Sullivan, "New Jersey Votes and Florio is Issue: Legislature's Control At Stake Today in Costly Election," *New York Times* (November 5, 1991), p. A1; Wayne King, "With Anti-Florio Voting Wave, Republicans Win the Legislature," *New York Times* (November 6, 1991), p. A1.

Public opinion, however, is more than a predictor of politicians' reelection chances. Chief executives such as governors and presidents must build coalitions with legislators and cultivate support with leaders of interest groups in order to implement their policy proposals. Legislators, in turn, must consider how their support or opposition to the chief executive's proposals will play with their constituents. If the governor is unpopular, a state legislator knows that he can vote against gubernatorial proposals without risking his own career prospects. On the other hand, if the governor is widely admired, a legislator will be more cautious about registering dissent. In short, personal popularity boosts the policy-making influence of governors (and presidents). POPUL₁ = POWER

In recent times several governors with low popularity ratings have experienced serious difficulties in running their states. Like Governor Florio, Governors Pete Wilson in California and Lowell Weicker in Connecticut have discovered that the task of balancing a state budget in the midst of a severe recession makes for few friends and can only antagonize important interest groups. When Wilson was elected governor of California in 1990, he was considered a rising star in the national Republican party and had serious presidential aspirations. In fact, he had resigned a seat in the U.S. Senate to run for the governorship, a position viewed by many as a stepping stone to the presidency. But in his first year as governor, California registered a budget shortfall of $14 billion. Wilson was forced to raise the state's already high sales tax, thus alienating the conservative wing of the Republican party. He also proposed deep cuts in popular social programs, a move that antagonized liberals and Democrats. One year after being elected with 52 percent of the vote, Wilson's approval level among Californians stood at 40 percent.[2] His poor public standing encouraged state legislators (both Democrats and Republicans) to criticize and amend his proposals. Negotiations over the state budget dragged on for months. A variety of interest groups—including gays infuriated by Wilson's refusal to sign a bill protecting homosexuals from employment discrimination, state employees angered by cuts in their benefits, and motorcycle riders opposed to a new mandatory helmet law—publicly demonstrated against him. When he was two years into his first term, many

[2]George Skelton, "Gay-Rights Bill Veto Narrowly Opposed In State" *Los Angeles Times* (October 6, 1991), p. A1.

political analysts began to speculate that he might not be able to win his party's nomination for a second term as governor, let alone make a serious bid for the presidency.

Rapid transformations in public reputation and influence have occurred even among U.S. presidents. Richard Nixon was reelected by a landslide in 1972. His first administration had undertaken several successful foreign policy initiatives, including the first-ever visit by an American president to the People's Republic of China. A few months later, as the revelations about the Watergate break-in and cover-up cascaded into a major congressional investigation, Nixon was effectively isolated in the White House and his administration was paralyzed. In 1974 the president was forced to resign.

Public opinion can also work in the opposite direction to empower chief executives. As we saw in Chapter 5, President Reagan enjoyed unusually high levels of popularity during his first year in office, and the Democratic Congress passed much of his legislative agenda. Southern Democrats and liberal Republicans, fearing that their constituents would punish them for not backing the Reagan revolution, refused to side with the northern Democrats who opposed his budget and tax proposals.[3]

Although popularity certainly affects political clout, it is not clear how much, if any, control politicians exercise over their poll ratings. In Chapter 5 we discussed the ways in which elected officials "go public" in the hope of maintaining a favorable public image. In the rest of this chapter we examine alternative views of the dynamics of presidential popularity.

The Ups and Downs of Presidential Popularity

Many observers of public opinon argue that the public relations efforts of presidents are futile and that, once elected, presidents become the captives of events and history. They cite the regularly observed cycle of presidential popularity, which begins with relatively high levels of popularity that fade, however, over time. Figure 9.1, which plots the course of presidential popularity over the last 40 years, illustrates this pattern.

[3] Samuel Kernell, *Going Public: New Strategies of Presidential Leadership* (Washington, D.C.: Congressional Quarterly Press, 1986); Alan Schick, *The Budget Reconciliation Act* (Washington, D.C.: Brookings Institution, 1983).

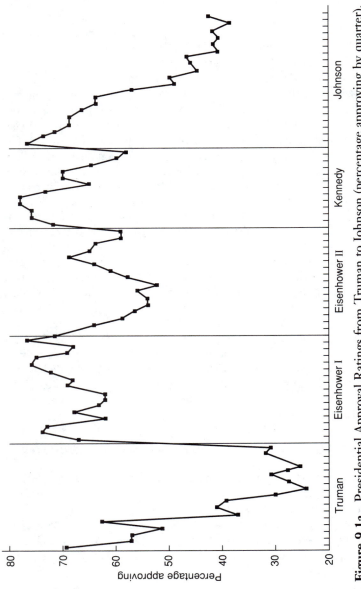

Figure 9.1a Presidential Approval Ratings from Truman to Johnson (percentage approving by quarter).
Source: Congressional Quarterly, *Guide to the Presidency*, Michael Nelson, ed. (Washington, D.C.: Congressional Quarterly Press, 1989).

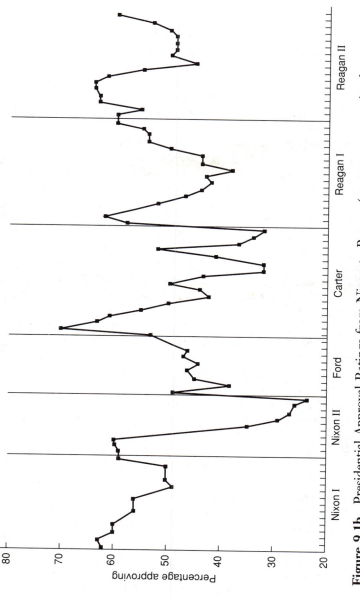

Figure 9.1b Presidential Approval Ratings from Nixon to Reagan (percentage approving by quarter).
Source: Congressional Quarterly, *Guide to the Presidency*, Michael Nelson, ed. (Washington, D.C.: Congressional Quarterly Press, 1989).

The graph reveals three phases in presidential popularity. First, all presidents begin with an initial "honeymoon" period of relatively high popularity. Presidents use this early phase to mobilize support for their major policy proposals. Following this honeymoon period, the president's popularity declines inexorably, in some cases significantly. Finally, presidents enjoy a rebound in their approval levels during their reelection campaigns.

The most plausible explanation of the fluctuations in popularity over the course of a president's term is that the changes are largely the result of the unfolding of events and issues. Peace and prosperity generally produce high ratings; recessions, military defeats, and policy debacles have the opposite effect.[4] When the United States is doing well (e.g., the unemployment rate drops, the Berlin Wall is dismantled, or the Iraqi army is routed in Kuwait), the president's approval rating surges. Conversely, when events indicate that U.S. interests are suffering, the approval rating drops.[5] The strong connection between events and presidential popularity suggests that voters assign blame or give credit to the president based on the state of national or international affairs.

The approval ratings of contemporary presidents, shown in Figure 9.1, seem to support the argument that the American public holds the president accountable for the state of national and world affairs. Jimmy Carter's approval ratings climbed dramatically (from 45 to 68 percent) in the aftermath of the 1978 Camp David peace accord between Israel and Egypt. However, when inflation reached double-digit levels in 1979 and 1980, his ratings dropped into a free-fall. Similarly, President Nixon's popularity dropped dramatically following the start of the Watergate investigations, and President Ford's ratings suffered after his controversial pardon of Nixon.

The importance of events in determining public opinion raises questions about the effectiveness of rhetorical leadership and public relations as methods of boosting popularity. Can a president's prowess as a communicator—including his ability to capitalize on

[4] See Richard Brody, *Assessing the President: The Media, Elite Opinion, and Public Support* (Palo Alto, Calif.: Stanford University Press, 1991.)
[5] See Charles Ostrom, Jr., and Dennis Simon, "The Man in the Teflon Suit?," *Public Opinion Quarterly*, 53 (Fall 1989), pp. 353–87.

the trappings of high office and his skill in distancing himself from negative outcomes—produce an illusion of effective leadership? Or, is the loss of popularity so frequently experienced over the course of a president's term symptomatic of a "throwaway" presidency?[6] Or, is popularity simply a matter of luck for those presidents who are fortunate enough to hold office during prolonged periods of approval-enhancing events?

Media Management Versus History

Although it often seems that a president's image is dependent on the course of events, there have been some rather dramatic instances where presidents have successfully defined the terms in which potentially damaging events would be discussed in the news media. In these cases the presidents were able to maintain or even increase their high popularity ratings in the face of policy failures.

Defining Events

The difficulty with the argument that presidential public relations and media management attempts make little difference to the president's popularity is that events rarely speak for themselves. Rather, they require classification, interpretation, and explanation. Because most people cannot experience "history" directly, and because public affairs are inherently ambiguous, the distinction between a positive (approval-enhancing) and negative (approval-diminishing) event is often blurred and dependent upon the terms in which the event is framed.

Consider the case of the U.S. invasion of Grenada, which turned out to be a significant approval-enhancing event for the Reagan administration. (The president's popularity increased by 4 percent following the invasion.) The administration effectively defined the event in its own terms by preventing the press from covering the invasion and then spoon-feeding reporters a steady diet of stories and images that portrayed the invasion in the most favorable light

[6]Theodore Lowi, *The Personal President: Power Invested, Promise Unfulfilled* (Ithaca, N.Y.: Cornell University Press, 1985), p. 11

possible. In the aftermath of the invasion, the news was filled with reports of an imminent communist takeover, of the airstrip being built by Cuban troops, and of the prospect that Grenada would become a Cuban colony and a haven for terrorists. There were also images of "rescued" American medical students kissing American soil. President Reagan delivered a formal statement on national television justifying the invasion in these terms. He was accompanied by the prime minister of one of the neighboring islands who enthusiastically commended the president for his actions.

As it turned out, there were several exaggerated or erroneous elements in the administration's portrayal of the conflict in Grenada.[7] The government of Grenada asserted that the airstrip was intended to benefit tourism. Funding for the project came from members of the European Economic Community and private American companies, as well as the Cubans. The number of Cuban troops based in Grenada was less than half of the administration's original claims, the warehouses of ammunition that had given rise to concerns were mainly empty, and the "urgent request" for U.S. intervention from Grenada's neighbors was less than spontaneous. Many of the American students did not even feel particularly threatened.

As this example makes clear, presidents have the power to interpret and define—or at least influence—the terms in which the media disseminates events to the public. Had the networks rejected the official interpretation, and instead described the American invasion as a public relations gimmick orchestrated by the president or as an instance of unjustified U.S. domination of a tiny nation, congressional and other leaders might have reacted less enthusiastically. Thus, by influencing the way in which events are depicted in the media, the president wields substantial influence over his popularity. In the case of Grenada, by restricting access and censoring news coverage of the event, the administration gained total control over the flow of information. By providing reporters an incomplete version of the facts, the administration succeeded in casting the invasion of Grenada as a policy success, rather than a fiasco. ABC's veteran Pentagon correspondent John McWethy explained the administration's effectiveness in shaping the news:

[7] See Mark Hertsgaard, *On Bended Knee: The Press and the Reagan Presidency* (New York: Farrar, Straus & Giroux, 1988).

When you are in a situation where your primary source of information is the United States government—and for three days basically your only source of information, except Radio Havana—you are totally at their mercy. And you have to make an assumption that the U.S. government is telling the truth... You report that Weinberger [then Secretary of Defense] **says** the fighting was heaviest here, or Weinberger **says** the barracks are under seige. Well, shit, he's the fucking Secretary of Defense. What are you going to do? You report what he says.[8]

By the time the several discrepancies between the administration's account and the actual facts were pointed out (some weeks after the invasion), the press had turned its attention to other matters, and no political harm was done to the president's image.

Dominating the News

A president's ability to shape his image depends upon the degree to which the administration's policies and decisions are challenged in Washington, and upon how the conflict is relayed around the country by the media. To some extent, policy conflict is built into our form of government. Powers are divided among the branches of government so that no one branch can dominate another. Increasingly, as the legislature has come to be dominated by one party and the executive office by another, the news has come to reflect interparty and intragovernmental disputes.[9] A Democrat-controlled Congress and a series of Republican presidents makes for considerable debate and disagreement in Washington as each institution attempts to gain the upper hand in some arena of public policy.

Despite the presence of divided government and the inherent tensions between the White House and Congress, the president's media weapons enable him to restrict competition in the news. From photo opportunities to Rose Garden ceremonies, virtually everything the president does is newsworthy. Presidential speeches are often broadcast live to a national audience during prime time.

[8]Quoted in Hertsgaard, 1988, pp. 233–34.
[9]For a thorough discussion of divided government see Morris Fiorina, *Divided Government* (New York: Macmillan, 1992).

During his first 18 months in office, President Nixon logged more hours of prime-time network attention than Presidents Eisenhower, Kennedy, and Johnson combined. All of Nixon's speeches were related to the Vietnam War, and were carried live on all the commercial networks, often reaching 60 percent of the prime-time audiences. Hoping to counter Nixon's media blitz, the Democratic National Committee eventually asked the networks for air time, under the Fairness Doctrine, to respond to Nixon's speeches. ABC offered 30 minutes of free time; CBS offered to sell them the time; NBC offered nothing. Nixon's dominance of the airwaves on the issue of the war in Southeast Asia continued.[10]

Presidential speeches also generate considerable news coverage. Each of President Carter's speeches on the issue of energy shortages, for example, produced an average increase of 10 network news reports on energy. Similarly, when President Reagan addressed the economy, there was a significant jump in the number of lead stories dealing with the economy.[11] In total, between the years 1953 and 1978, the *New York Times* printed an average of nine stories each day concerning the president, two of which were on the front page. On "CBS Evening News," the president attracted four stories each evening.[12]

Recent administrations have demonstrated considerable skill in adjusting the timing and format of the president's speeches to accommodate the needs of network television. In particular, because of the networks' limited ability to provide detailed coverage, speeches invariably include brief passages suitable for sound bites on the nightly news. In the words of Tom Griscom, a former speechwriter for President Reagan:

> You can take a Reagan speech...and I can point out to you the four or five sound bites we built in the speech. We wrote them that way. We wrote trying to give the lead to the media of what we hoped they

---

[10]See Fred Friendly, *The Good Guys, the Bad Guys, and the First Amendment* (New York: Random House, 1975), pp. 121–30.

[11]Roy Behr and Shanto Iyengar, "Television News, Real-World Cues, and Changes in the Public Agenda," *Public Opinion Quarterly*, 49 (Spring 1985), p. 38–57.

[12]Michael Grossman and Martha Kumar, *Portraying the President: The White House and the News Media* (Baltimore: Johns Hopkins University Press), Chapter 10.

would cover...But those speeches were written with four or five points in them that were short enough and that the President would say them short enough so they could probably fit into a newscast.[13]

Clearly, the president is *the* big story in Washington. It is not necessarily good public relations, though, to receive a lot of press. The real concern is the content and tone of reporting. When the White House faces concerted criticism, the presence of a scandal, or some other press crisis, it is the job of the chief of staff and the White House spokesman to use their rhetorical and political "fire extinguishers." These might include scheduling newsworthy events on alternative issues (e.g., scheduling an awards ceremony for servicemen injured in the Gulf War), and putting the best possible interpretation on controversial events (e.g., claiming that President Reagan was unaware of any of the illegal acts carried out by his subordinates). Speechwriter Tom Griscom has described the thinking in the White House during the Iran-Contra scandal: "When we were dealing with Iran-Contra, we were worrying about who was going to be seen on TV around this country every night...And if we could figure out how to shape the TV story up on Capitol Hill, which is part of what we did, we were satisfied we had done a good day's work."[14]

The administration's efforts to put a positive spin on the news yield rich payoffs. Of over 8000 stories in the *New York Times*, *Time*, and CBS News, positive stories outnumbered negative stories by a margin of 2:1. For both print sources, unequivocally negative stories were much less frequent than unequivocally positive stories. CBS was more balanced in tone presenting an equal number of positive and negative reports.[15]

[13] Quoted in "Press Secretaries Explore White House News Strategies," *Political Communication Report*, 2 (March 1991), p. 4.
[14] Quoted in "Press Secretaries Explore White House News Strategies," 1991, p. 1. *Political Communication Report*, 2 (1991), p. 1.
[15] See Grossman and Kumar, 1981, pp. 255–56. The discrepancy between CBS News and the two print sources in their study can be attributed to differences in the time period sampled. Whereas Grossman and Kumar examined *Time* and the *New York Times* between 1953 and 1978, CBS News was examined between 1968 and 1978. This later period included several policy debacles (such as the U.S. defeat in South Vietnam) as well as a major scandal involving the president (Watergate).

Silence of the Critics

The clearest evidence that debate and criticism of the president's actions, as reported in the media, adversely influences presidential popularity is the well-known rally effect. In the aftermath of major international events involving the United States, the president's popularity surges. Typically, the surge lasts for about six weeks, following which the president's ratings return to their normal range. This effect occurs even when the event represents a policy failure. Thus, President Kennedy's popularity increased 10 points following the Bay of Pigs incident (the unsuccessful attempt to "liberate" Cuba from Communism), despite the fact that the mission was a total fiasco; and President Carter's popularity virtually doubled (from 32 percent to 61 percent approval) when Iranian militants stormed the American embassy in Teheran, taking the occupants hostage.

Several explanations have been offered for the rally effect. Foreign policy events are said to evoke high levels of national pride and patriotism, and the public sees the president as the leader of the nation rather than a partisan politician. The most compelling explanation of the surge and decline in presidential popularity in the aftermath of foreign policy failures, however, concerns the behavior of the president's critics in Washington. When a foreign policy crisis occurs, congresspersons and senators from the opposing party typically remain silent or express support for the president. The administration's spin on events is thus unchallenged, and the public responds accordingly by supporting the president. If the crisis persists, opposition leaders begin to contest the president's interpretation. Their rhetoric attracts news coverage, and the president's ratings then suffer.

One recent instance of the rally effect—the Iraqi invasion of Kuwait in August 1991—fits this pattern precisely.[16] Following the Iraqi invasion, President Bush's popularity increased by 13 points. The key to this increase was the complete silence of congressional Democrats. By chance, Congress was not in session during the first month of the Iraqi occupation. The Bush administration's account

[16] See Richard Brody, "Crisis, War and Public Opinion: the Media and Public Support for the President in Two Phases of the Confrontation in the Persian Gulf," paper presented at the Social Science Research Council, Seattle 1991.

of the U.S. response to the invasion focused on the effectiveness with which the United States had created a worldwide coalition in opposition to Saddam Hussein, and the fact that Iraq had been deterred from further military expansion. With no dissenting opinion possible from Congress, these successes went unquestioned.

Even after Congress reconvened, prominent Democrats were generally supportive of President Bush and his actions. It was only toward the end of September that misgivings and criticism were voiced in the media. The *New York Times* noted that "Congressional criticism of the Bush Administration's position on the Persian Gulf, nonexistent in the first days after Iraq's invasion of Kuwait, then muted, is growing louder on both sides of the aisle as lawmakers openly attack the president on several major points."[17] At this point, President Bush's popularity began to fall. Later, when President Bush authorized the military liberation of Kuwait, all criticism of the administration ceased immediately and the president's popularity increased again (see Figure 7.1).

As the examples discussed above suggest, a president can maintain high popularity by limiting the debate over his policies and actions. In some circumstances (usually involving wars), the president can limit debate by cutting off the media's access to events. In other cases the president can use his considerable ability to command media attention to drown out the views of his critics. And in still other cases, competing politicians choose to remain silent.

To summarize, the public's evaluations of the incumbent president rise and fall in accordance with cues provided by the media: The more prominent the coverage accorded critics of the president, the lower the level of presidential popularity will be. Concerning the question of whether media management is no match for history, the answer is that the president's ability to manipulate his public image depends not only on the course of events, but also on the administration's ability to interpret events and reduce the visibility of alternative interpretations in the news. The more vocal the opponents of the president, the more competitive is the flow of news, and the less able the president is to divorce his image from the course of events. Popular presidents such as Ronald Reagan are more able to silence their critics and monopolize the news. In such cases, pop-

[17] Quoted in Brody, 1991, p. 11.

ularity feeds on popularity. But the real question, and one that is fundamental to the democratic process, concerns the presence or absence of competition in the flow of news. This is the focus of Part IV.

The Policy Costs of Popularity

Clearly, some presidents enjoy considerable leverage with the media, enabling them to successfully play the "popularity game" in Washington. However, media management and the continual quest for high approval ratings can, at times, weaken a president's ability to govern. In the first place, a great deal of the day-to-day discussions in the White House are taken up by concerns over public image. With the ever-growing significance accorded to popularity, presidents and their advisers are compelled to devote an ever-increasing share of their energies to rhetoric and public relations. This may impede the administration's ability to develop policy initiatives and programmatic responses to major national issues. The preoccupation with public image and the resulting opportunity costs was clear to Lloyd Cutler, special counsel to President Carter for domestic policy:

> I was surprised by how much the substantive decisions in the White House are affected by press deadlines, and, in particular by the evening television news. So that if something happened, let us say, on a Monday, or somebody strongly criticized the President or one of his programs, everything stopped! Whatever you'd been working on as the great priority of the next morning you had to put aside in order to reach a decision about how the President would respond in time for the evening television news.[18]

Second, by cultivating the image of effectiveness, the strategy of going public runs the risk of creating unrealistically high public expectations of public officials—expectations that few incumbents can hope to realize. The state of the American economy is increasingly tied to global forces beyond the reach of any president's influence.

---

[18]Colin Campbell, "27 Experts Give Prescriptions for Presidency's Ills," *New York Times*, November 2, 1981, B5.

GOING PUB, =

By constantly claiming credit for positive events, presidents, senators, and congresspersons run the risk of being blamed for negative
events. There was not much President Carter could do to prevent
the OPEC cartel from raising oil prices in the 1970s. Yet Carter was
widely blamed for the rampant inflation in the United States that
was produced by the sudden surge in energy costs. By constantly
drawing attention to the president, the strategy of going public produces an *attribution error*, in which politicians are held responsible
for outcomes even when their decisions and policies have no bearing whatsoever on the outcome. The strategy of image building thus
has both positive and negative consequences.

A more ominous by-product of the importance accorded to
popularity is that presidents are sometimes enticed to undertake
decisions or policies because of their anticipated contributions to
the president's image. In some situations, for instance, presidents
need to demonstrate their "toughness." Following the seizure of the
American embassy in Iran and the capture of the American diplo-
mats, the Carter administration faced intense pressures (including
a challenge for the party's presidential nomination from Senator
Edward Kennedy) to secure release of the hostages. In April 1980
a helicopter rescue mission was undertaken with disastrous consequences and significant loss of life. Despite the overwhelming odds
against the success of such a mission, it was approved.

> A peace-loving, religious man like Jimmy Carter did not take the risk
> of the Iranian rescue mission merely to give himself a convenient lever
> to move American public opinion. The leverage worked the other way:
> Public opinion had forced upon the president an act of the sheerest
> adventurism.[19]

The need for popularity may also deter presidents from making
decisions. In particular, because popularity is considered so essential to accomplish policy goals, presidents and other public officials
become less likely to tackle difficult problems or propose difficult
solutions. A catch-22 develops: Proposing tough answers to persis-
tent problems costs popular support, but without popular support,
there is no opportunity to address these problems. Politicians are
left to pursue and protect popularity for its own sake.

[19]Lowi, 1985, p. 173.

Finally, there is the possibility of governmental stalemate and paralysis produced by the rhetorical counterpart of the arms race. As the president increasingly turns to rhetorical leadership, his opponents in Congress and elsewhere have every reason to do the same. While President Bush attacks the Democrats in Congress for failing to eliminate wasteful social programs that enlarge the budget deficit, Democrats attack the administration for favoring the wealthy over the middle class and for ignoring domestic problems at the expense of foreign policy. In the words of Jeffrey Tulis, "We face the very real prospect of our two political branches talking past each other to a vast amorphous constituency."[20]

Suggested Readings

Richard Brody, *Assessing the President: The Media, Elite Opinion, and Public Support.* Palo Alto, Calif.: Stanford University Press, 1991.

Michael Grossman and Martha Kumar. 1981. *Portraying the President: The White House and the News Media* Baltimore: Johns Hopkins University Press.

Roderick Hart. 1987. *The Sound of Leadership.* Chicago: University of Chicago Press.

Mark Hertsgaard. 1988. *On Bended Knee: The Press and the Reagan Presidency.* New York: Farrar, Straus & Giroux.

Stephen Hess. 1991. *Live From Capitol Hill.* Washington, D.C.: Brookings Institution.

Samuel Kernell. 1986. *Going Public: New Strategies of Presidential Leadership.* Washington, D.C.: Congressional Quarterly Press.

Samuel Kernell and Samuel Popkin, eds. 1986. *Chief of Staff: Twenty-Five Years of Managing the Presidency.* Berkeley, Calif.: University of California Press.

Theodore Lowi. 1985. *The Personal President: Power Invested, Promise Unfulfilled.* Ithaca, N.Y.: Cornell University Press.

[20]Jeffrey Tulis, *The Rhetorical Presidency* (Princeton, N.J.: Princeton University Press, 1987), p. 178.

Kristie Monroe. 1984. *Presidential Popularity and the Economy.* New York: Agathon Press.

Richard Neustadt. 1980. *Presidential Power: The Politics of Leadership.* New York: John Wiley & Sons.

Charles Ostrom, Jr., and Dennis Simon. 1989. "The Man in the Teflon Suit?", *Public Opinion Quarterly.* 53, p. 353–87.

Fred Smoller. 1990. *The Six O'Clock Presidency: a Theory of Press Relations in the Age of Television.* New York: Praeger.

Jeffrey Tulis. 1987. *The Rhetorical Presidency.* Princeton, N.J.: Princeton University Press.

EVALUATING THE SYSTEM

This book has described the ways in which television affects the behavior of politicians and voters. As political parties have withered, the media have become the critical link between citizens and their elected representatives. Candidates and elected officials have altered their rhetoric and styles of governing in ways designed to attract the attention of the media. At the same time, reporters and broadcasters have become dependent upon official sources to write their news stories. This mutual dependence between journalists and politicians shapes the news and the manner in which it is presented.

This system of political communication has many critics. To many, the prominent role now played by the news media in the political process is fundamentally inconsistent with the practice of democratic government. The concern is that the reporters and editors who shape the news are answerable not to the public, but to the shareholders of their employer corporations. The need to maximize profits interferes with the ability of news organizations to provide citizens with adequate public affairs information. Moreover, critics contend that news programming is characterized by various distortions and biases, and that the media do not treat all politicians, issues, and points of view equally. Voters thus find it difficult to assign responsibility and to hold elected officials accountable. Politicians, for their part, have abandoned traditional methods of group appeals and coalition building in favor of public relations. This new style of leadership makes them less inclined to address deep-seated problems of American society, and more attentive to fine-tuning their public image. Meanwhile, major social and economic problems go unaddressed.

The views of John Chancellor, the long-time anchor for NBC News, are representative of these complaints:

> Journalism must give mankind a picture of the world on which it can act ... I wonder if we haven't missed that goal. We've gotten tied up in other perceptions of the world, and the readers and viewers don't think that we're trying to give them that picture of the world on which they can act ... We have failed in some way to get across to the public the essence of the craft, which is to enable people in a democracy to make decisions based on information.[1]

Chancellor's criticisms zero in on what is generally regarded as the journalist's most important role in the political process, namely, informing and educating the citizenry. In the next chapter we assess the media's performance in meeting this role of *educator*.

In addition to the task of informing the public, the media are also expected to perform a watchdog function: scrutinizing the policies and actions of public officials. Because the consequences of exposure and publicity can be fatal, media monitoring can deter public officials from violating their public trust. The ability of the American media to live up to this *monitoring* role is the subject of Chapter 11.

Ideally, then, the news media should provide voters with information about the issues and choices they face, and serve as an independent check on the behavior of public officials. Part Four addresses the ideal and the reality, and discusses the ways in which the system of media politics might be strengthened.

---

[1]Quoted in Lance Bennett, *News: The Politics of Illusion* (New York: Longman, 1988), pp. 12–13.

CHAPTER 10

The Media as Educator

One of the most important foundations of the American political system is the First Amendment, which states simply that "Congress shall make no law abridging the rights of Free Speech or Free Press." Over the years the courts have interpreted the First Amendment as essential to a vigorous and critical press. The provisions of the First Amendment not only protect the media from government control over the content of news, but also impose an obligation on the media to inform the public. As we saw in Chapter 2, this obligation is especially important in broadcasting where stations are licensed by the government to serve as public trustees. In this chapter we consider what the media's obligation to inform means and how well the media contributes to informed public opinion and choice.

The media relay information in both directions between public officials and ordinary citizens. For the public, the media are the prime sources of information about current events. For politicians, the media are effective and convenient means of communicating with the public. Whether the communicator is the president hoping to rally the nation behind his legislative proposals, a senator seeking reelection, or an interest group trying to mobilize public support—no political leader can speak to the public without the media, especially the electronic media.

On the surface, the media's informational role seems straightforward. All the media have to do is tell the public about the economic, social, and political circumstances in which they live and offer leaders frequent opportunities to speak to the public. But is the process really that simple?

Any effort to evaluate the news media's role as a conduit of information ultimately hinges on issues of (1) fairness or the absence of bias, and (2) the quantity and quality of information provided. Is the news free of systematic or deliberate efforts to distort or otherwise impede the free flow of political information? Do the media give people enough information to enable them to make the decisions a democracy requires of them? Given the complexity and ambiguity inherent in the world of public affairs, there is, not surprisingly, considerable disagreement over the extent to which news presentations are unbiased, fair, and informative. For instance, some critics see the American media as mere tools of multinational corporations, whereas others attack the same media for supposed opposition to capitalist values. Some say the media do not cover important issues; others say people do not care about important issues.

The notions of bias and informativeness are closely related: The failure to provide information is in fact a form of bias. Consider an incident of government wrongdoing brought to light by a whistle-blower: A newspaper story containing only the official governmental version of events and information discrediting the whistle-blower would obviously be biased. But the failure to print or broadcast the story at all is another—and equally serious—form of bias. So as we assess the media's performance as an informer, we must examine both forms of bias.

Alternative Perspectives on Fairness

A number of general criteria for gauging the fairness of the media have been proposed by scholars. We will consider three. The first asks whether the news faithfully reflects the issues and events of the day—that is, whether or not the news is a "mirror image" on happenings in the world. The second criterion asks whether news coverage is presented superficially or in depth. If news presentations are designed for their entertainment value rather than to promote critical reasoning, whose political values and interests stand to gain? The third and final criterion asks whether the news is tainted by the ideological or political preferences of those who gather and produce the news.

News as Mirror Image

Some people say the news should reflect reality. If an event occurs, the media should report it. Underlying this notion is the assumption that the news should reflect ongoing events and issues regardless of who stands to gain or lose from the transmission of information about these events. Accordingly, *fairness* is defined as the degree to which the content of news presentations converges with the actual course of public affairs. If unemployment is worsening, the news should focus on joblessness and its implications; if there is political turmoil in Eastern Europe, the news should alert people to these events; and so on. In short, the role of the national media is to reflect the state of the nation and the world.

In the narrower context of campaigns, this standard of fairness would also measure the extent to which the media enable all the candidates to communicate with voters. Are the proposals and speeches of all candidates equally newsworthy, or are serious contenders granted more attention? Similarly, are the president's economic proposals given more consideration than those of congressional leaders, some of whom may have just as much ability to shape economic policy?

There are several problems with the expectation that the news should be a mirror image of reality. First, as discussed in Chapter 3, the very practical reality is that not all events can be reported—some selection must be made. Second, and even more fundamental, the reality behind many events that all would agree are significant public issues is not or cannot be known. Consider the following examples:

1. Suppose that the earth's ozone layer is being depleted and that scientists issue reports from time to time discussing their findings on the extent and significance of the depletion. Clearly, the physical phenomenon is not likely to become news on its own—a scientific study is required to draw attention to the issue. When a story does surface, is "reality" the fact that the ozone layer is being depleted, or the fact that a new study has been released? If there is no study, or no new study, does that mean that the issue must remain obscure or fade from view?

2. Suppose that approximately 20 percent of all Americans lack health insurance and have no regular contact with doctors. The only source of medical care for the uninsured is the hospital emergency room, and they rarely have the money to pay for any care they receive. These patients' inability to obtain routine, nonemergency care generates enormous problems for hospitals, especially the emergency care system. Is this general situation news, or is there news only when somebody dies because he is refused admittance to an emergency room, and when a hospital closes a trauma care facility that it can no longer afford to maintain?

These examples illustrate that the media have an extremely difficult time covering "stories" when there are no concrete events. Ozone depletion is not news, but a study on ozone depletion is. The inadequacy of the health care system is not news, but a death that results from those inadequacies can become news. Moreover, issues like the state of the environment and the quality of the health care system are not easily amenable to precise measurement. Media coverage of these issues cannot be readily checked against observable indicators of "reality." In the absence of independent (i.e., nonmedia) indicators of the severity of social problems, we can never know if the media reflect reality.

On the other hand, other issues are both relatively concrete and subject to systematic recording by nonmedia organizations. For example, the government collects a great number of indicators relating to the economy, the FBI monitors criminal activity on a regular basis, public health authorities track AIDS and tuberculosis routinely, and the California Institute of Technology records seismic movement. For these issues, "reality" in the form of changes or trends in conditions is easier to assess. However, even with respect to these issues, the mirror image theory faces additional difficulties. For example, what is the appropriate (i.e., fair) rule for translating economic or public health indicators into news coverage and how should different indicators be weighed? Should there be a news story every month when the unemployment figures are released? Are decreases in unemployment equally as newsworthy as increases? In the case of public health issues, should news coverage respond to the number of people affected or the extent to which lives are threatened? Is skin cancer (which might potentially affect millions) more newsworthy than AIDS (which affects fewer people, but with more catastrophic consequences)?

Although the ideal of the "news as mirror image" provides a theoretical definition of media fairness, it is not a terribly useful standard. The limited availability of observable indicators of the scope and severity of political problems and disagreement over the interpretation of these indicators often makes it difficult to grade the media's fairness.[1]

Substantive News

Fairness can also be approached in terms of the informational content of news programming. Do news stories provide information concerning the complexities of public policies, the historical background of social problems, or the details of candidates' policy proposals? There is general agreement that news coverage—both print and broadcast—has become less serious and more entertaining in orientation over the past decade. Deregulation of broadcasting, the struggle for economic survival, and the intense competition for audiences have all exacted a toll on the amount and format of news programming. In the past, broadcasters were granted significant license protection in a particular locale. Now they must compete with 30, 60, or even 90 cable channels and a growing number of independent broadcast stations. The new stations have cut into each other's

---

[1]Because of these problems, few attempts have been made to test mirror image theory. The results of the studies reveal no clear pattern; for some issues, news coverage corresponds relatively well to objective indicators, but for other issues, the correspondence is weaker. In the case of the economy, for example, the actual state of inflation, energy dependence, and unemployment have been found to be significant predictors of the number of network news stories on these subjects (see Roy Behr and Shanto Iyengar, "Television News, Real-World Cues, and Changes in the Public Agenda," *Public Opinion Quarterly* (Spring 1985), 38–57). However, in the case of AIDS, there was virtually no news coverage of the disease until it had claimed its first celebrity victims (see James Dearing and Everett Rogers, "The Agenda-Setting Process for the Issue of AIDS," Paper presented at the Annual Meeting of the International Communication Association, New Orleans, 1988).

profits. In 1991 the combined losses for the three major television networks amounted to $86,000,000. The consequences of the red ink, as we noted in Chapter 2, have included the disappearance of the prime-time news documentary and of gavel-to-gavel coverage of the presidential nominating conventions. Newspapers have undergone parallel changes; the portion of the typical daily newspaper allocated to "hard" news has fallen off, while a variety of special features have been created to take the space formerly devoted to public affairs.[2]

Economic constraints also affect the form of news coverage. In the early days of television, the news divisions were protected from ratings pressures. When NBC first aired its award-winning "Huntley-Brinkley" report, the ratings were so dismal that the newscast attracted no advertisers. Yet NBC did not give up on the program, and it went on to become highly rated.[3] Today, however, the networks no longer exempt the news divisions from "bottom-line" considerations. Veteran correspondent Bill Moyers has described the new atmosphere: "the center of gravity has shifted from the standards and practices of the news business to show business. In meeting after meeting, 'Entertainment Tonight' was touted as the model..."[4] In the name of high ratings, news programs consist primarily of personalized, fast-paced stories. Instead of providing viewers with historical background and thematic context about the issues and events of the day, news stories typically present a series of unrelated happenings. "And now this," as Neil Postman has pointed out, is the trademark of television news.[5]

Given these characteristics of television news, it is hardly surprising that viewers have difficulty seeing beyond the particulars of news reports. Most observers would agree that poverty, racial inequality, crime, and drug use are closely interdependent political issues. However, television news regularly portrays these issues as isolated problems, and thus impedes viewers' ability to attribute

---

[2] See, for instance, Michael Emery, "An Engangered Species: the International Newshole," *Gannett Center Journal* (1989), p. 151–64.

[3] Cited in Jeffrey Abramson, "Four Criticisms of Press Ethics," in Judith Lichtenberg, ed., *Democracy and the Mass Media* (New York: Cambridge University Press, 1990), p. 260.

[4] Abramson, 1990, p. 260.

[5] Neil Postman, *Amusing Ourselves to Death: Public Discourse in the Age of Show Business* (New York: Viking, 1985).

a common cause. When exposed to episodic framing of poverty, crime or terrorism, viewers understand these events not in terms of some general process or set of societal conditions, but as isolated instances of personal failure. Poverty exists because of the character weaknesses of poor people; fanatics and power-seeking maniacs are responsible for terrorism; and so on. Episodic framing not only impedes viewers from perceiving systemic causes or cures for societal problems, but also encourages compartmentalization of issues — viewers may fail to draw connections between poverty and crime, or between unemployment and racial inequality. The public's limited ability to see political issues in broad terms may be in part a product of the fragmented and episodic nature of television news coverage.

The criticism that the news tends to be superficial most clearly applies to the area of election campaigns. The drama of the race, the hoopla and emotion, and the strategies of the winning and losing candidates achieve a prominence that far surpasses the substantive differences between the candidates. Although surface aspects must necessarily be taken into account by voters, democratic theory demands that the candidates' previous experience, their positions on the issues, and the groups supporting or opposing them must also become well publicized. Voters have to work much harder to acquire information about these substantive facets of the campaign.

In sum, economic pressures and the resulting demand-based programming have decreased the amount of time media organizations devote to news — especially national news — and lowered the quality of journalism. "Infotainment" is gradually replacing substance, depth, and analysis in public affairs reporting.

Ideological Neutrality

The preceding discussion has focused on impersonal and mechanistic factors (such as the "invisibility" of certain issues due to lack of concrete events, which diminishes the possibility that reality will be reflected). In addition, competition in the news business has eroded substantive fairness in the news.

The third criterion for judging fairness is ideological neutrality in the content of news presentations. Some critics of both the right and the left have contended that the people responsible for presenting the news are *ideologically motivated*—that news presentations are unfair and biased because the selection of events to be covered and the substance of the presentations are influenced by reporters' and editors' personal political values and preferences.

If the news is ideologically slanted, whose slants are represented and whose are ignored? Does the fact that the media largely ignore issues of declining personal morality establish that reporters subscribe to, or choose to promote, a liberal, hedonistic bias? If news coverage of corruption in the corporate boardroom is only sporadic, does that mean that the media are apologists for capitalism?

The framers of the Constitution realized that ideological bias in the flow of news would not be a problem if competing viewpoints were freely expressed. Accordingly, the First Amendment has long protected the "marketplace of ideas." Present-day media critics, however, suggest that the marketplace is no longer open to all and that media presentations are ideologically slanted.

One set of critics sees the media as proponents of conservative values. These critics suggest that business considerations frequently intervene to prevent objective coverage. The threat of lost advertising revenues, it is argued, discourages editors from pursuing particular subjects that might be damaging to the interests of advertisers. Although few reporters, editors, or owners will admit that the threat of withdrawn advertising affects public affairs programming, there have been several instances of broadcast stations and newspapers failing to report or provide adequate emphasis to stories that were in conflict with advertisers' interests.[6] The tobacco industry, for instance, spends billions of dollars on advertising in print sources. As Ben Bagdikian has suggested, it is not a coincidence that newspaper and magazine coverage of the public health consequences of smoking has been muted.[7] One study tabulated the editorial and advertising content of six major women's magazines to assess whether the amount of advertising purchased by the cigarette manufacturers was associated with reduced editorial interest in the

---

[6]In the case of entertainment programming, there is obviously a strong connection between the ability of the show to attract ratings and to bring in advertising revenue on the one hand, and the show's future prospects, on the other.

[7]Ben Bagdikian, *The Media Monopoly* (Boston: Beacon Press, 1983).

risks of smoking. The study found that the magazines devoted little space to the health hazards of tobacco use. One of the editors commented that the topic of smoking was "not very appealing" and "too controversial."[8]

In short, critics from the left contend that economic considerations often prevent fairness. Because the survival of the newspaper or network depends upon the profitability of the parent entity (typically a conglomerate), these critics suggest that the media are reluctant to attack business interests. In most cases, this tendency results in a tilt to the right of the political spectrum.

For every allegation of conservative bias in the news, there are counterallegations of liberal bias. The media's presumed hostility to conservative politicians, for instance, has been a hallmark of Republican commentators' explanations for periods of bad news. Throughout his career, President Nixon's stormy relations with the media were attributed to a predominance of liberals in the national press. Vice President Spiro Agnew suggested in a national speech that most broadcast journalists were the products of privileged childhoods, Ivy League educations, and the chic culture of New York City and Washington, D.C. The liberal views of these "nattering nabobs of negativism," he claimed, put broadcasters at odds with the "silent majority." During the early stages of the Watergate scandal, conservative critics accused the *Washington Post* and other media outlets pursuing the story as being motivated by anti-Nixon sentiment in the newsroom.[9]

The fact that the news media has been cast as simultaneously conservative and liberal suggests that ideological bias may exist largely in the eye of the beholder. Psychologists have identified a "hostile media" phenomenon in which people who call themselves conservative are more likely to view the media as anti-conservative, whereas liberals view the media as pro-conservative.

[8]Cited in Pamela Shoemaker and Stephen Reese, *Mediating the Message: Theories of Influence on Mass Media Content* (New York: Longman, 1991), p. 165.
[9]More recently, surveys of the national press corps show a predominance of Democrats over Republicans and self-identified liberals over conservatives [see Robert Lichter, Stanley Rothman, and Linda Richter, *The Media Elite* (Washington, D.C.: Adler and Adler, 1986)]. Of course, this does not mean that reporters' partisan preferences affect their writing.

For purposes of democratic functioning, the ultimate objective need not be that each station or newspaper present a perfectly balanced view of every issue. It is imperative, however, that divergent views gain visibility and meaningful public debate is fostered through the multiplicity of media outlets.

Most research into the actual content of public affairs reporting indicates that, in fact, the American media perform well according to the criterion of ideological balance. Reporters generally avoid one-sided reporting and analysis. Political issues and events are covered, for the most part, from a "point-counterpoint" framework in which the audience is provided at least two points of view (i.e., Democratic and Republican, conservative and liberal, pro and con, etc.). It is true, however, that the presentation of two points of view does not exhaust the range of perspectives on most issues. Moreover, the perspectives represented in the news are drawn primarily from the establishment. For example, social workers may be asked to react to new welfare proposals, but the views of poor people tend to be ignored.

Summary

The news is the product of a complicated set of interactions between the economic interests of the owners of the media; the professional interests of reporters, broadcasters and editors; and the political interests of candidates and elected officials. How may we assess the information that results from these interactions? This chapter has considered a number of criticisms of the media, each of which represents a distortion in the flow of public affairs information.

First, we have raised the possibility that news coverage may not reflect reality. The problem in evaluating this concern is that determining reality is not as easy as it may at first seem. There are no obvious ways to identify and treat appropriately those elements and aspects of reality that are not linked to concrete events. If one believes that "events" are news, but "nonevents" such as underlying social conditions are not, then identifying reality is not so complicated: A news program should consist entirely of wars, accidents, fires, and press conferences. But for those who believe that ongoing social, political, and economic conditions and trends are newsworthy, the current state of news reporting is probably inadequate.

A second serious criticism is that news organizations are increasingly adopting the format and logic of entertainment programs. It is certainly true that newspapers, television networks, and news stations have scaled back the scope of their news-gathering activities in response to economic pressures. These developments impede the development of informed public opinion because the public now receives less news programming and because current news programming is not as informative.

The media are frequently accused of engaging in political advocacy. There is, however, little evidence that news presentations are deliberately tailored to advance particular causes. Although the range and diversity of opinion that finds its way into the news is limited, the norms of journalism ensure that the audience is typically exposed to rival views on current issues.

What then is the bottom line? Any of the criticisms addressed in this chapter, if valid, would indicate a significant obstacle to the free and open discussion of political ideas. The criticism that the media form a defective mirror proves difficult to evaluate. The criticism that the news is, on the whole, superficial rather than substantive is true. Finally, the criticism that the news is ideologically biased seems to have little basis in fact.

Suggested Readings

Ben Bagdikian, 1987. *The Media Monopoly.* Boston: Beacon Press.

Roy Behr and Shanto Iyengar. 1985. "Television News, Real-World Cues, and Changes in the Public Agenda," *Public Opinion Quarterly,* 49, 38–57

James Dearing and Everett Rogers. 1988. "The Agenda-Setting Process for the Issue of AIDS." Paper presented at the Annual Meeting of the International Communication Association, New Orleans.

Michael Emery. 1989. "An Engangered Species: The International Newshole," *Gannett Center Journal,* 3, 151–64.

Judith Lichtenberg, ed. *Democracy and the Mass Media*. New York: Cambridge University Press.

Robert Lichter, Stanley Rothman, and Linda Richter. 1986. *The Media Elite*. Washington, D.C.: Adler and Adler.

Neil Postman. 1986. *Amusing Ourselves to Death: Public Discourse in the Age of Show Business*. New York: Viking.

Austin Ranney. 1983. *Channels of Power: The Impact of Television on American Politics*. New York: Basic Books.

Pamela Shoemaker and Stephen Reese. 1991. *Mediating the Message: Theories of Influence on Mass Media Content*. New York: Longman.

CHAPTER 11

THE MEDIA AS MONITOR

Many observers refer to the media as a "watchdog," a beacon of responsibility shining a light on wrongdoing, making sure that government does not exceed its bounds and exposing the truth. The media are expected to function as an independent "fourth branch" of government. How successfully do the media perform the watchdog function? What conditions make it difficult for the media to keep politicians in check? These are the subjects of this chapter.

The key premise underlying the watchdog role of the media is that reporters maintain an *adversarial* posture vis-a-vis those they cover. This premise assumes that the proper role of the press is to seek and reveal the truth about the people in the news — whether government officials, business leaders, or antiabortion protesters. Likewise, the premise assumes that such a role demands that reporters treat their subjects critically and, indeed, as adversaries. Accordingly, reporters are expected to seek confirmation of official and unofficial statements, make every effort to uncover hidden information, and referee factual disputes.

Adversarial journalism represents a cherished ideal, and there are ample rewards for reporters who succeed in the genre: Such reporters win awards and bring accolades to the media outlet. Bob Woodward and Carl Bernstein were obscure reporters and the *Washington Post* was considered a "company newspaper" until they broke many of the key stories of the Watergate scandal in the early 1970s. As a result of their work, the two reporters became household names and the subjects of a major movie (*All The President's Men*), while a generation of young reporters dreamed of breaking the big story.[1]

In routine journalism, on the other hand, rewards may be available to reporters who do not challenge the system. The chief reward is access to key governmental players. When a high-ranking government official wishes to give an exclusive story about a new policy proposal, he usually does not call a reporter known for his adversarial approach; rather, he chooses someone who has been "friendly." The chosen reporter will reap his reward when he publishes his "scoop."

Because it is convenient to rely on official sources and because the system actually rewards such reporting, institutional incentives are created that work against the media's fulfilling the "watchdog" function. In other words, there is a built-in tension between *adversarial* and *official* journalism.

As we have seen, it is relatively easy to engage in official journalism. In this chapter we will explore the impact of the institutional pressures toward official journalism on the media's performance of its classic monitoring role.

Adversarial Versus Official Journalism

We have already seen that, if the media is to play an unimpeded and objective informational role, no person or institution should be able to restrain, impede, or censor the free flow of news. Under the Constitution, government cannot, except in unusual and very rare circumstances, prevent the media from disseminating information.

Unfortunately, the enormous legal protections afforded the media may be somewhat diluted for practical purposes if the media cannot (or does not) maintain its independence from public officials. In practice, officials are powerless to *prevent* the media from covering a particular subject or story, but they are very powerful

---

[1]The ideal of succeeding at investigative reporting has even led to notorious excesses, as in the case of Janet Cooke, a reporter for the *Washington Post*. Ms. Cooke wrote a story about drug usage by children for which she was awarded a Pulitzer Prize. Later, she admitted to having fabricated the report.

(and skilled) in *getting* the media to cover a story. Public officials strongly influence the subjects that are reported and the contents of the reports. Clearly, the media have the freedom to challenge versions of events offered by government officials and the ability to ensure that alternative voices are heard. But the question remains as to what extent these rights are exercised in practice.

The prominence of the adversarial stance toward political leaders has varied somewhat during different periods of the development of American journalism. This style of reporting peaked during the late 1960s and early 1970s when the national media was filled with exposés of political corruption and wrongdoing in high places. Ralph Nader's indictment of General Motors (*Unsafe at Any Speed*), Seymour Hersh's disclosure that American soldiers had massacred Vietnamese civilians at My Lai, and the *Washington Post*'s aggressive investigation of the Watergate break-in and cover-up (which ultimately led to the resignation of President Nixon) typified this brand of independent and investigative reporting that subjected public officials to intense scrutiny. Public officials' accounts of their own actions were balanced by spokespersons advocating contrary positions. Reporters were seen as a permanent political opposition that somehow managed to expose the inner workings of government.

Although adversarial journalism may have been the norm during this particular period, the phase was rather short-lived. As the historian James Boylan proposed, "If an adversary journalism was to exist in America, if only for a moment, this had been the moment."[2] Conditions changed dramatically in the later 1970s and 1980s. Economic pressures dramatically reduced the ability of reporters and editors to carry out careful investigative reports. Although famous anchormen and reporters of the past such as Edward R. Murrow and Walter Cronkite did much more than simply read the news, the days when newscasters could make key editorial decisions free of "bottom-line" considerations had disappeared.

Experienced journalists are no longer central to the operation of the major networks. Cost cutting in the newsroom has altered

[2]James Boylan, "Declarations of Independence," *Columbia Journalism Review* (1986), p. 41.

career paths. Reporters with expertise in a considerable amount of subject matter now find themselves replaced by photogenic "stars" who are capable of commanding wider audiences, but incapable of carrying out in-depth, investigative reporting. National news shows have been converted into local programs, and cheaper "reality" programming has taken the place of more costly investigative specials such as "CBS Reports."

Professional journalistic norms have been further weakened by the closure of news bureaus across the globe and the resulting major reductions in the number of reporters. The networks have increasingly turned to free-lance reporters who have no ties to any particular station and whose major career goal is to sell a story. For these reporters, getting ahead in the journalistic profession means having access to the sources of the news, because they typically lack the financial backing to pursue tedious investigative work that may not "pay off" in the end. In the world of public affairs reporting, the clear incentive is to cultivate contacts and maintain good relations with public officials and candidates.

In addition to the myriad of economic and structural pressures facing news organizations, the transformation of the electoral process in the 1970s further contributed to the demise of adversarial journalism. A new breed of politician emerged, adept at attracting news coverage and manipulating news organizations. Foreign policy and national security issues took on a more prominent position on the national agenda. Public officials were able to exert much tighter control over the flow of information on these issues. When the United States intervened militarily in Granada, Panama, and Kuwait, journalists were—for all practical purposes—prohibited from carrying out "on-the-scene" reporting. (Some have suggested that the memory of Vietnam, still fresh in the memory of government officials, prompted the imposition of these controls.) Virtually all the daily news about these conflicts was provided by spokespersons for the U.S. military.

The upshot of these developments is that the relationship between news organizations and public officials has changed profoundly. Journalists have become less independent and less capable of questioning public officials' versions of events. News coverage is increasingly a vehicle used by elites to articulate their preferences and perspectives. In many ways, contemporary news resembles a transcript of official rhetoric. As Leon Sigal demonstrated in his study of the *Washington Post* and *New York Times* (papers renowned for their in-depth reporting), government sources accounted for more than 70 percent of all news stories. Only 17 percent of news stories in the newspapers could be traced to nongovernmental sources. As Sigal noted, "Imbedded in the words **news medium** is a connotation that aptly defines the function of the press: it mediates between officialdom and the citizenry of the U.S."[3]

The Iran-Contra scandal provides a vivid illustration of the system of official reporting. For months, the Reagan administration secretly funneled arms and supplies to the Iranian regime led by Ayatollah Khomeini. In clear violation of the law, the proceeds from these transactions were used to finance the military campaign being waged by Contra guerillas against the elected communist government of Nicaragua. An elaborate series of lies, distortions, and criminal activities involved numerous high officials and several government agencies. The television networks, the *Washington Post*, the *New York Times*, and other news organizations failed to uncover these events. The story was finally broken by *Al Shiraa*, a tiny Lebanese news weekly.

The media's dependence upon official sources means that when high-ranking opposition forces remain silent, news coverage will almost by default reflect the incumbent administration's policies and preferences. In 1982, for example, the Reagan administration was able to persuade congressional leaders to go along with its policy of arming the "democratic" regime of El Salvador. Such assistance had the effect of intensifying the civil war in that country. Surprisingly, there was little news coverage of developments in El Salvador. Liberal columnist Alexander Cockburn wrote: "How is it that over the past two years the United States has been organizing, supplying, overseeing and in many cases actually executing the heaviest bombing and most ferocious aerial war ever seen in the Americas and not one coherent report of the extent, viciousness or consequences of this campaign has appeared in any major U.S. newspaper or maga-

---

[3]Leon Sigal, *Reporters and Officials* (Lexington, Mass.: D. C. Heath, 1973), p. 130.

zine?"[4] NBC anchorman Tom Brokaw was asked why the networks were ignoring this bloody conflict in El Salvador. His reply was: "Congress is supposed to represent the people, and when there is no opposition in Congress, there isn't much that we can report."[5]

Under the present system of reporting, then, the biases and perspectives of government elites dominate the news. When there is consensus among elites, entire subject areas may be invisible (or inaudible). On the other hand, when the administration is challenged, news coverage becomes more competitive.

Monitoring the Candidates

The media have the ability to play two critical roles during political campaigns. If they choose to, they can be arbiters of truth, evaluating competing claims between candidates. And, through the use of sanctions and incentives, they can nudge candidates to behave more responsibly. As we shall see, though, many of the same forces that work against adversarial journalism in general also work against the media's assuming an activist role in political campaigns.

The Media as Seeker of the Truth

Commentators and analysts have many criticisms about the modern election process and those who participate in it. One of the most prominent criticisms is that the candidates regularly contradict each other's assertions of fact, leaving the public with no way of discerning the truth.

Consider the following example. Two candidates are involved in a debate. One says he supported a bill to toughen the sentences for certain crimes. The other disagrees, and calls the opponent soft on crime. Should the media report that the candidates disagree over their positions on crime, or should they investigate the issue and report that one or the other was telling the truth?

---

[4]Quoted in Lance Bennett, *News: The Politics of Illusion* (New York: Longman, 1988), p. 171.
[5]Quoted in Bennett, 1988, p. 138.

More likely than not, the media will report the exchange as two conflicting claims, leaving the public with little ability to sort out the matter. This hypothetical scenario illustrates one of the many ways in which the media could play the role of referee: in this case, simply sorting out and presenting conflicting claims. Other examples might include digging into a candidate's past or investigating his personal life.

Almost everyone agrees that the media should seek the truth. But few people agree on what that means. Sometimes, finding the truth should be a relatively simple matter. In a 1982 Connecticut congressional primary, both of the candidates claimed the support of certain numbers of delegates to the state convention. Both released a list of their supporters' names. Some names appeared on both lists. A spokesperson for one of the candidates asked a reporter writing a story on delegate support to call the people whose support was in dispute. "Ask them who they support," he said. "That's not my job," the reporter responded. "My job is to report what each of the candidates says." The news story eventually reported that both of the candidates claimed support from some of the same delegates. The reader was not informed as to which candidate was justified in his claims. Because the reporter failed to ascertain the numbers on his own, the public was left in the dark.

At other times, finding the truth is necessarily more complicated. In the 1992 Democratic presidential primaries, Senator Tom Harkin of Iowa aired an ad attacking several of his opponents for supporting "trickle-down Reaganomics" because each had supported cuts in the tax rate applicable to capital gains, ostensibly to provide businesses with incentives to create jobs. His opponents immediately cried foul, saying that their specific proposals were quite different from the tax reduction policies of Reagan and Bush. Who was telling the truth, and how could a reporter reach a conclusion without exhibiting a personal bias about the merits of different economic theories?

Sometimes issues of truth and falsehood become even more complex because of questions of relevance. Suppose a candidate for Congress is gay. Should the media report on his sexual preference, because people have a right to know about it; or should they ignore it, because it has no direct bearing on a candidate's ability to do the job?

Similarly, what if another candidate bills himself as a candidate of "traditional" values, and opposes legislation to eliminate discrimination against gays? What if the candidate goes even further and calls homosexuality "immoral?" If expressed by a heterosexual candidate, is this view more relevant than the personal sexual orientation of the aforementioned gay candidate? On the other hand, if this view is expressed by a gay candidate, is it relevant as reflecting on his basic truthfulness or sincerity?

Few people agree on the proper role the media should play in the dissemination of the "truth." Virtually every action or inaction by the media is open to criticism. It is easy to attack reporters for failing to report "objective" facts, such as the actual supporters of a given candidate. It is just as easy to criticize the press for not reporting whether Senator Harkin was being fair, or for reporting that he *was* being fair, or that he *was not* being fair. When it comes to matters of politicians' personal lives, there is very little agreement about how such news should be reported.

The key to understanding how reporters deal with these questions lies not with the reporters themselves, but with the requirements and incentives they face. As we indicated throughout this book, reporters are deadline driven, cautious, and concerned about what will interest their readers or viewers. Thus, if a political debate occurs in the evening, and the reporter has to write the story or miss a publication deadline, can he really be expected to carry out the research necessary to find out which candidate was telling the truth? And if a television reporter knows that a story about a candidate's marital infidelities will attract national attention, can he really be blamed for pushing ahead?

When criticized for investigating the personal lives of candidates, reporters typically counter with two arguments: that knowledge of personal conduct is relevant to making judgments about character, and that their readers or viewers are interested in these matters. The problem with the first rationale is that it is virtually impossible to reach a consensus on what information is or is not relevant. Is an extramarital affair that occurred over 10 years ago relevant to the candidate's attitudes toward women, his honesty in public matters, or any other item of conceivable public concern? Is it more important if it occurred within the past year? Does the date actually matter? Most people would agree that it would be relevant to know whether a candidate was affiliated with the Nazi party 30 years ago. Can objective standards be set for deciding which issues are relevant only when current, and which issues become irrelevant with the passage of time? Further complicating the discussion is the fact that some of the most distinguished public officials in U.S. history— for example, FDR, Eisenhower, and JFK—engaged in activities that would have probably made them unelectable if those activities had been subjected to the media spotlight.

The rationale that the public is interested in stories about the personal side of the candidates is equally difficult to evaluate. Certainly the media should respond, in some sense, to the interests of readers and viewers. But, of course, there may be topics that are of no legitimate public concern. Most people would agree that it would be inappropriate for an ordinary citizen to approach a presidential candidate to ask about his sexual habits. Why should it be different if a reporter does the asking?

The Media as Promoter of Responsible Behavior

A second common complaint of voters is that political candidates rarely address serious but difficult issues such as the budget deficit, health care, and crime. Instead, candidates tend to employ symbolism rather than substance—posing before flags, touring schools, shaking hands with law enforcement officers, and kissing babies. By virtue of their vast audience, the media—and only the media—have the ability to shape candidates' behavior. Because the electoral consequences of vigorous media scrutiny can be disastrous, reporters can deter candidates from distorting the truth and misleading the electorate. Similarly, through sanctions and incentives, the media can encourage candidates and elected officials to address serious problems. And if a front-running candidate refuses to debate his challenger, the press can keep the issue alive long enough to make the electoral costs of ducking a debate untenable. In short, the media have the power to force candidates to behave "more responsibly." Should they do so?

Although reporters will occasionally criticize candidates for their lack of substance, only rarely do they take full advantage of their own ability by refusing to give attention to empty gestures. Such selective journalism works to limit the effectiveness of candidates' symbolic activities. For example, it seems obvious that campaign news coverage should not be determined by the candidates and their handlers. A newspaper or television station would be well within its rights to determine that rallies, press conferences, and other events staged for the sole purpose of getting on the news are, in fact, simply *not* newsworthy. Such a determination would not impinge on the ability of a candidate to communicate with voters via the media; it would only mean that candidates would be required to communicate on matters of substance if they wished to receive coverage.

Such a policy would, of course, raise questions about what criteria should be applied in determining whether a candidate's actions or statements are sufficiently substantive to warrant news coverage. Policy positions and governmental experience are obviously important criteria. Is the character of a candidate equally important? Similarly, is the ability to get along well with individuals (as demonstrated by the ease with which a candidate greets workers while on a factory tour) relevant to performance in office?

These difficult questions notwithstanding, this is clearly an area where the media have the ability to exercise influence by rewarding substantive speech and ignoring grandstanding tactics and posturing. If a newspaper decides that there is too much negative campaigning, it could refuse to cover any attacks leveled by one candidate against another. Or it could develop a mechanism for assessing the accuracy of the attacks and covering only those that pass review.

A further criticism of media campaigns is that some candidates are shielded from public scrutiny and placed only in situations where they do not have to think on their feet. The public thus sees some candidates only in controlled settings, reading scripts written by others and advocating policies they did not develop personally. In some extreme cases the media never talk to the candidates at all. Reporters' questions are fielded by staff, requests for interviews are refused, debates are avoided, and the only time the candidate comes into the public view is through paid advertising or staged events.

Clearly, this type of behavior is related to job performance. If a Senate candidate can't debate his opponent, how can he debate on the floor of the Senate? If a presidential candidate isn't sufficiently informed about his own policies to explain them to reporters, how can he represent the United States when negotiating directly with the heads of foreign governments?

Just as clearly, the media have the ability to change the behavior of candidates who shirk public access. For example, the press could refuse to quote the staffs of candidates who remain inaccessible. They could cover candidates' policy proposals only when the candidates explain them in a setting where they are forced to demonstrate their own mastery of the subject matter. They could even refuse to provide any coverage to candidates who evade debates.

These kinds of moves would no doubt engender criticism, but they would be important statements of media autonomy that would almost certainly affect the behavior of candidates. If, for example, a network announced that it would give news coverage only to negative advertisements in which the attacks were made directly by the candidate, there would likely be two outcomes: the airing of fewer attack ads, and a greater willingness of candidates to speak for themselves rather than rely on surrogates.

In our judgment, the adoption of policies along the lines set forth above would enhance the quality of campaigns. By more aggressively seeking out information from non-campaign sources, the media would lessen candidates' control over the terms of political debate and would force politicians to document more fully their claims or attacks. By refusing to allocate coverage to symbolic events and statements, the media would force politicians to confront the important issues facing the nation. Such measures would make voters feel better about the political process, and more willing to participate in it.

Suggested Readings

Ben Bagdikian, 1987. *The Media Monopoly*. Boston: Beacon Press.

Lance Bennett. 1988. *News: The Politics of Illusion*. New York: Longman.

James Boylan. 1986. "Declarations of Independence," *Columbia Journalism Review*, 29–46.

Carl Bernstein and Bob Woodward. 1974. *All the President's Men.* New York: Simon and Schuster.

Todd Gitlin. 1980. *The Whole World is Watching: Mass Media in the Making and Unmaking of the New Left.* Berkeley, Calif.: University of California Press.

Graduate School of Journalism, University of California, Berkeley. 1991. *The Media and the Gulf: A Closer Look.* Proceedings of a conference held on May 3 and 4.

Daniel Hallin. 1986. *The Uncensored War: The Media and Vietnam.* Berkeley, Calif.: University of California Press.

Ralph Nader. 1965. *Unsafe at Any Speed: the Designed-In Dangers of the American Automobile.* New York: Grossman.

Larry Sabato. 1991. *Feeding Frenzy: How Attack Journalism Has Transformed American Politics.* New York: Free Press.

Leon Sigal. 1973. *Reporters and Officials.* Lexington, Mass.: D. C. Heath.

Conclusion

We have seen that, more often than not, news reflects the preferences and positions of governmental officials. We have also seen that, during elections, the content of campaign coverage is substantially determined by the candidates rather than by the independent investigatory efforts of reporters. Although the news is admirably free of overt ideological or partisan bias, the routines of news gathering and the economic incentives facing news organizations create enormous opportunities for elected officials and candidates to shape the news.

In situations where the administration's voice dominates, the news can be highly slanted. Major international events such as the wars in El Salvador, Grenada, and Kuwait were covered primarily from the perspective of official reports. Pressures toward episodic framing solidify governmental influence over such news. On the other hand, when there is dissent within government, the media provide much more varied coverage simply because there are conflicting official accounts on which a news story can be constructed.

The same pattern prevails in campaigns. Reporters seek most of their stories directly from the candidates, and the vast majority of campaign stories originate in campaign organizations. When reporters cover campaign activities such as press conferences and rallies, they allow the candidates and their staffs to set the news agenda. Only infrequently do reporters take the initiative in determining whether or not a particular issue or question is worthy of attention. In situations where a strong incumbent runs against a little-known challenger, the incumbent is able to determine the tone and content of news reports on the campaign. On the other hand, when an incumbent faces a strong challenger, coverage is more diverse.

In recent years, government officials and campaign managers have learned how to manipulate news coverage. Generally, the officials and candidates operate much faster than reporters. Moreover, the media have, for the most part, failed to understand how readers and viewers react to news.

The Changing Relationship Between the Media and Politicians

In a sense, the relationship between reporters and government officials or candidates is akin to a chess game in which each side vies for control. As conditions change, both sides must adapt. Politicians must learn to "game" the system for their own benefit, while reporters must respond in ways that prevent the government officials and campaigns from dominating the process.

The relationship between political figures and the media has changed dramatically since the advent of television. Politicians have been much quicker to adjust to these changes than the media. Elected officials, candidates, and their consultants have developed intricate strategies for using or evading the media to their advantage. The media, on the other hand, have only just begun to develop counterstrategies for protecting their independence and monitoring the candidates. Elected officials are adept at inducing reporters to cover their activities in the best possible light. Reporters don't always know how they're being manipulated, and if they do, they don't always know how to stop it. Candidates know they won't be hurt for refusing to debate, refusing to talk about important issues, or refusing to answer tough questions; the media have yet to figure out how to change that situation. Campaigns have learned how to ignore the press when it suits them; reporters have yet to insist on their rightful role in the democratic process in the modern media age.

Through the use of paid advertising, the candidates largely bypass the press. Candidates with enough money to purchase large amounts of advertising can ignore the press completely. They can evade debates or press interviews because they know that reporters will not—and in many cases, cannot—punish them for this behavior.

One of the most flagrant examples of this strategy was revealed in a 1988 memorandum written by two Los Angeles political consultants to Los Angeles city councilman Zev Yaroslavsky, who was then considering running for mayor. They urged him to stop attending council meetings so that he could devote more time to raising money for TV ads.

> "Three days a week tied down to City Hall and the Council is a waste," they said. "We believe that it should stop immediately. One Tuesday a week is enough to waste. You will definitely get a bad story or two for not showing up for votes. It is a small price to pay for the extra million or two you will be able to raise with the extra time."[1]

Embarrassed by the memo (which was apparently leaked), Yaroslavsky eventually dropped out of the race. But in 1991, a member of Congress from Los Angeles, running for the U.S. Senate and using the same two political consultants, was absent for 40 percent of the roll call votes in the House of Representatives, while amassing more campaign funds than any other nonincumbent Senate candidate in the country. It was the second worst attendance record in the country. This record produced only one negative news story.

Reporters are only now beginning to understand that they have been cut out of the campaign process. As the above example indicates, their responses have been weak and uncertain. If they chose to, reporters could have made an issue out of every instance where the congressman missed a vote because he was attending a fund-raiser. But they did not do so even once.

This is not to say that reporters have utterly failed to adapt. Realizing that voters get most of their campaign information from ads, reporters have recently turned their attention to—what else—advertising. In 1990 and 1992 some of the major newspapers and one television network (CNN) began to run detailed reports on candidates' advertising efforts and the strategies underlying the ads. In

---

[1] Bill Boyarsky, "Blunt Memo by Advisors Prods Yaroslavsky Camp," *Los Angeles Times*, August 9, 1988, p. A10.

these so-called "truth boxes," reporters attempt to apply journalistic objectivity to rate the accuracy of the ads.

Some reporters are going even further. Because the impact of a truth box—stashed on an inside page, in small type—is dwarfed by the onslaught of televised advertising, these reporters have begun insisting that especially misleading or inaccurate advertising be subjected to critical front-page news coverage. However, for every ad that is dissected by reporters, many go unanswered. Thus, some would argue that it will not be until the local television stations and the networks systematically screen ads for their truthfulness and editorialize against offending ads that the balance of power will truly shift away from the candidates.

None of this is meant as an argument that the media should focus on minor or tangential problems, or attack candidates for insignificant behavior, or act as censors, or otherwise behave irresponsibly. In fact, reporters have an additional duty to understand *how* the public absorbs the information they provide.

The Changing Relationship
Between the Media and Voters

One of the most serious criticisms of contemporary political reporting is that reporters generally fail to understand how ordinary citizens process information about public officials and the political process. Reporters do not realize that the public frequently cannot evaluate the quality or veracity of competing claims. Journalists fail to consider that most readers and viewers do not listen to every word that is uttered or printed. Moreover, they fail to understand that a story based on rumors or allegations may leave a longer-lasting impression than a story based on cold facts, or that the effects of false information will persist well after the rebuttal has been forgotten. And they do not realize that in the case of TV news, the impact of the pictures may sometimes be far more powerful than the impact of the words.

The bottom line is that most reporters fail to consider how their stories will be interpreted and understood by the average viewer or reader. Consider the following hypothetical example:

SEN. SMITH ACCUSED OF DRUG USE

Senator Joe Smith was accused today of using illegal drugs while a college student.

The accusation was aired in "Scandal Weekly," a political tabloid magazine. The magazine quoted two anonymous sources as saying "everybody knew Smith was a druggie."

An investigation by this newspaper concluded there was no evidence that Smith had ever used drugs. In fact, his college newspaper once wrote a profile about his volunteer efforts to help children stay off drugs.

In response, Smith pointed out that "Scandal Weekly" is owned by the father of City Councilman Tom Brown, who is opposing Smith in his bid for reelection.

Is this story unfair?

The reporter would in all likelihood defend it, saying that he reported that his investigation had found Smith to be innocent, and had established a motive for Smith's being framed in a tabloid.

However, if one factors in how the average voter would likely read this story, it is extremely unfair. Most people would see only the headline. Of those who began to read the story, few would make it past the first or second paragraph. And even those few who made it all the way through the story and read all the facts might assume that there is some truth to the story or the newspaper would not have printed it.

The concern is not merely hypothetical; there are many real-world examples. For instance, in the 1988 presidential campaign, Republican activists began circulating the rumor that the Democratic nominee had a history of mental illness. The story burst onto the front pages when Ronald Reagan made an off-the-cuff joke about it.[2] Reporters defended their decision to print the story— they argued they had refused to write about the rumor, but that once the president had commented on the issue, it was news. The rumor was immediately discredited; Dukakis had no history of mental illness whatsoever. The air was cleared; the truth was reported. But several months later, in a focus group of California voters, several

---

[2] Reagan was asked by a reporter whether he felt Governor Dukakis should make his medical records public. He answered, "Look, I'm not going to pick on an invalid."

participants volunteered that they were concerned about voting for Dukakis because of his history of mental illness. Whether they had forgotten the evidence that the story was false, or believed the story even in the face of the clarifications wasn't clear. All that mattered was that these readers had absorbed the attack and nothing else.

Similarly, in 1992, even prestigious newspapers including the *New York Times*, *Washington Post*, and *Wall Street Journal* saw fit to take their news lead from a tabloid (*The Star*), and gave front-page coverage to a woman's unsubstantiated allegations that she had been Governor Clinton's lover. At the time, this was the first damaging story to come out about Clinton. Even though the newspapers reported that there was no evidence to support the charges, within a matter of days, most summary stories on Clinton contained references to allegations of marital infidelity, and Clinton's sex life became grist for late-night talk show jokes.

Not only do voters seem to have a selective memory favoring sensationalized allegations over factual rebuttals, they may also be especially susceptible to the influence of visuals. People may absorb more information from pictures than words. As a result, the effects of a news story are complex and sometimes can be at odds with what the reporter intended. In 1984 and 1988 a number of TV correspondents aired critical stories on the Reagan and Bush campaigns, complaining that the candidates refused to discuss serious issues, preferring instead to appear before happy, cheering crowds with balloons and flags. The text of these stories was hard-hitting. But the visuals featured footage of happy, cheering crowds. Republican campaign officials were elated with the stories because they felt that the power of the pictures would outweigh the power of the reporter's words, and that most people would retain the positive images rather than the negative text. In at least one case, polling confirmed these suspicions.

In 1988 ABC correspondent Richard Threlkeld aired a story that criticized one of George Bush's campaign ads. This particular ad attacked Michael Dukakis for being "soft on defense." At the time, Threlkeld's story was hailed as a breakthrough example of a television reporter dissecting and discrediting a political ad. But the story included the ad itself, which contained much-ridiculed footage of Dukakis riding in a tank. A study later showed that the story actually benefited Bush, because the dominant impression left with viewers was that of a silly-looking Dukakis sticking his helmeted head out of the tank. "What he (Threlkeld) had managed to do, with the best of intentions, was magnify the very power of the ad he was trying to correct," said Kathleen Jamieson, the study's author.[3]

We as a society have unintentionally delegated many responsibilities to the media. Newspapers and television are to function as educators, monitors, and watchdogs; they must duel with elected officials and candidates; they must assert their rightful role in the political process; they must give the public what it wants, yet not indulge in the lurid excesses which the public often seems to enjoy; and, on top of everything, they must be cognitive psychologists, tailoring their products to meet the limitations of a disinterested and cynical public. Sometimes, one set of expectations we have for the media conflicts with another.

Do our expectations place unreasonable demands on mere mortals—men and women who, with the exception of a few stars, must work long and irregular hours for mediocre pay, dealing with uncooperative politicians and an unappreciative public? Is the idea that media organizations (which are, after all, businesses) can disregard the wishes of advertisers (i.e., customers) or viewers fanciful? Possibly.

The media, like public officials and voters, has a critical role to play in the political process. Although it is popular to condemn the media, the possibility must be considered that many of the political problems and dysfunctional behavior discussed in this book are attributable to the other two parties not holding up their ends. If the candidates met their obligation to tackle important issues and make themselves available for public questioning, reporters would not have to develop strategies for punishing those who don't. If voters met their obligation to pay attention to public affairs—dismissing unsubstantiated allegations and rewarding candidates who treat the process seriously instead of habitually reelecting incumbents—reporters would not have to worry about whether their readers and viewers were paying more attention to pictures and headlines than to substance.

[3]Ed Bark, "Care Advised in TV Reporting on Political Ads" *The Daily News* (San Fernando Valley, CA), February 27, 1992, page 15.

All three parties are failing to meet their obligations, and each is blaming the others for it. "We write about the personal lives of the candidates because it's what our readers want," say the reporters. "We focus on style over substance because the media don't cover us when we offer serious proposals, and the public will only punish us if we dared to raise taxes in order to address the many problems we face" say the candidates. "We don't pay attention to politics because politicians don't care about real problems and only want to be reelected," say the voters.

All three groups have legitimate complaints. So how do we find our way out of the morass? There is no simple answer. Like any complex relationship, the interactions between the media, elected officials, and the public are tainted by past history, failed expectations, and human frailty. Perfection is not a realistic goal, but improvement is a reasonable objective.

In this book we have focused primarily on the limitations of the media and have sought to identify the precise mechanisms that account for observed media effects, both good and bad, on the behavior of politicians and voters. The present limitations of the media as an effective educator and monitor can be addressed by making changes along many of the dimensions summarized here—making the news mirror events more closely, more substantive in content, or more independent from government officials. However, attempts to reform the media will have only limited success unless voters and candidates also participate in a renewed commitment to the democratic process.

INDEX